SIMMONS COLLEGE
DEPARTMENT OF EDUCATION
AND HUMAN SERVICES
MATESL PROGRAM
300 THE FENWAY
BOSTON, MA 02115

VISIONS

Language ◆ Literature ◆ Content

Mary Lou McCloskey

Lydia Stack

THOMSON

™

HEINLE

Australia ◆ Canada ◆ Mexico ◆ Singapore ◆ United Kingdom ◆ United States

SIMMONS COLLEGE LIBRARY

VISIONS STUDENT BOOK C
Mary Lou McCloskey and Lydia Stack

Publisher: *Phyllis Dobbins*
Director of Development: *Anita Raducanu*
Director, ELL Training and Development: *Evelyn Nelson*
Developmental Editor: *Tania Maundrell-Brown*
Associate Developmental Editor: *Yeny Kim*
Associate Developmental Editor: *Kasia Zagorski*
Editorial Assistant: *Audra Longert*
Production Supervisor: *Mike Burggren*
Marketing Manager: *Jim McDonough*
Manufacturing Manager: *Marcia Locke*
Photography Manager: *Sheri Blaney*
Development: *Proof Positive/Farrowlyne Associates, Inc.; Quest Language Systems*
Design and Production: *Proof Positive/Farrowlyne Associates, Inc.*
Cover Designer: *Studio Montage*
Printer: *R.R. Donnelley and Sons Company, Willard*

Cover Image: © *George Grady Grossman/Index Stock Imagery, Inc.*

Copyright © 2004 by Heinle, a part of the Thomson Corporation.
Heinle, Thomson, and the Thomson logo are trademarks used herein under license.

All rights reserved. No part of this work covered by the copyright hereon may be reproduced or used in any form or by any means—graphic, electronic, or mechanical, including photocopying, recording, taping, Web distribution or information storage and retrieval systems—without the written permission of the publisher.

Printed in the United States of America.
7 8 9 10   08 07 06 05

For more information, contact Heinle, 25 Thomson Place, Boston, Massachusetts 02210 USA, or you can visit our Internet site at http://www.heinle.com

For permission to use material from this text or product contact us:
Tel   1-800-730-2214
Fax   1-800-730-2215
Web   www.thomsonrights.com

ISBN: 0-8384-5249-3

SIMMONS COLLEGE LIBRARY

Reviewers and Consultants

We gratefully acknowledge the contribution of the following educators, consultants, and librarians who reviewed materials at various stages of development. Their input and insight provided us with valuable perspective and ensured the integrity of the entire program.

Program Advisor
Evelyn Nelson

Consultants

Deborah Barker
Nimitz High School
Houston, Texas

Sharon Bippus
Labay Middle School
Houston, Texas

Sheralee Connors
Portland, Oregon

Kathleen Fischer
Norwalk LaMirada Unified
School District
Norwalk, California

Willa Jean Harner
Tiffin-Seneca Public Library
Tiffin, Ohio

Nancy King
Bleyl Middle School
Houston, Texas

Dell Perry
Woodland Middle School
East Point, Georgia

Julie Rines
The Thomas Crane Library
Quincy, Massachusetts

Lynn Silbernagel
The Catlin Gabel School
Portland, Oregon

Cherylyn Smith
Fresno Unified School District
Fresno, California

Jennifer Trujillo
Fort Lewis College
Teacher Education Department
Durango, Colorado

Teresa Walter
Chollas Elementary School
San Diego, California

Reviewers

Jennifer Alexander
Houston Independent School District
Houston, Texas

Susan Alexandre
Trimble Technical High School
Fort Worth, Texas

Deborah Almonte
Franklin Middle School
Tampa, Florida

Donna Altes
Silverado Middle School
Napa, California

Ruben Alvarado
Webb Middle School
Austin, Texas

Sheila Alvarez
Robinson Middle School
Plano, Texas

Cally Androtis-Williams
Newcomers High School
Long Island City, New York

Minerva Anzaldua
Martin Middle School
Corpus Christi, Texas

Alicia Arroyos
Eastwood Middle School
El Paso, Texas

Douglas Black
Montwood High School
El Paso, Texas

Jessica Briggeman
International Newcomer Academy
Fort Worth, Texas

Diane Buffett
East Side High School
Newark, New Jersey

Eva Chapman
San Jose Unified School
District Office
San Jose, California

Elia Corona
Memorial Middle School
Pharr, Texas

Alicia Cron
Alamo Middle School
Alamo, Texas

Florence Decker
El Paso Independent School District
(retired)
El Paso, Texas

Janeece Docal
Bell Multicultural Senior High School
Washington, DC

Addea Dontino
Miami-Dade County School District
Miami, Florida

Kathy Dwyer
Tomlin Middle School
Plant City, Florida

Olga Figol
Barringer High School
Newark, New Jersey

Claire Forrester
Molina High School
Dallas, Texas

Connie Guerra
Regional Service Center 1
Edinburg, Texas

James Harris
DeLeon Middle School
McAllen, Texas

Audrey Heining-Boynton
University of North Carolina-
Chapel Hill
School of Education
Chapel Hill, North Carolina

Carolyn Ho
North Harris Community College
Houston, Texas

Donald Hoyt
Cooper Middle School
Fresno, California

Nancy A. Humbach
Miami University
Department of Teacher Education
Oxford, Ohio

Marie Irwin
University of Texas at Arlington Libraries
Arlington, Texas

Mark Irwin
Cary Middle School
Dallas, Texas

Erik Johansen
Oxnard High School
Oxnard, California

Marguerite Joralemon
East Side High School
Newark, New Jersey

Karen Poling Kapeluck
Lacey Instructional Center
Annandale, Virginia

Lorraine Kleinschuster
Intermediate School 10 Q
Long Island City, New York

Fran Lacas
NYC Board of Education (retired)
New York, New York

OCT 1 2 2007

Robert Lamont
Newcomer Center
Arlington, Texas

Mao-ju Catherine Lee
Alief Middle School
Houston, Texas

Leonila Luera
Pharr-San Juan-Alamo ISD
Pharr/San Juan, Texas

Gail Lulek
Safety Harbor Middle School
Safety Harbor, Florida

Natalie Mangini
Serrano International School
Lake Forest, California

Linda Martínez
Dallas Independent School District
Dallas, Texas

Berta Medrano
Pharr-San Juan-Alamo ISD
Pharr/San Juan, Texas

Graciela Morales
Austin Independent School District
Austin, Texas

Karen Morante
School District of Philadelphia
Philadelphia, Pennsylvania

Jacel Morgan
Houston ISD
Houston, Texas

Lorraine Morgan
Hanshaw Middle School
Modesto, California

Dianne Mortensen
Pershing Intermediate School 220
Brooklyn, New York

Denis O'Leary
Rio del Valle Junior High School
Oxnard, California

Jeanette Page
School District of Philadelphia (retired)
Philadelphia, Pennsylvania

Claudia Peréz
Hosler Middle School
Lynwood, California

Yvonne Perez
Alief Middle School
Houston, Texas

Penny Phariss
Plano Independent School District
Plano, Texas

Bari Ramírez
L.V. Stockard Middle School
Dallas, Texas

Jacqueline Ray
Samuel High School
Dallas, Texas

Howard Riddles
Oak Grove Middle School
Clearwater, Florida

R.C. Rodriguez
Northside Independent School District
San Antonio, Texas

Randy Soderman
Community School District Six
New York, New York

Rita LaNell Stahl
Sinagua High School
Flagstaff, Arizona

Dean Stecker
School District of Palm Beach County
West Palm Beach, Florida

Mary Sterling-Cruz
Jackson Middle School
Friendswood, Texas

Rosemary Tejada
Carlsbad High School
Carlsbad, California

Camille Sloan Telthorster
Bleye Middle School
Houston, Texas

Vickie Thomas
Robinson Middle School
Plano, Texas

Claudio Toledo
Lynwood Middle School
Lynwood, California

Christopher Tracy
Garnet-Patterson Middle School
Washington, DC

Lydia Villescas
Pharr-San Juan-Alamo ISD
Pharr/San Juan, Texas

Stephanie Vreeland
T.A. Howard Middle School
Arlington, Texas

Jennifer Zelenitz
Long Island City High School
Long Island City, New York

We wish to thank the students at the following schools who helped us select high-interest readings at an appropriate language level. Their feedback was invaluable.

Student reviewers

Cooper Middle School
Fresno, California

De Leon Middle School
McAllen, Texas

Garnet-Patterson Middle School
Washington, D.C.

Hanshaw Middle School
Modesto, California

Intermediate School 10 Q
Long Island City, New York

Jackson Middle School
Friendswood, Texas

L.V. Stockard Middle School
Dallas, Texas

Liberty Middle School
Pharr, Texas

Martin Middle School
Corpus Christi, Texas

Memorial Middle School
Pharr, Texas

Newcomer Center
Arlington, Texas

Nimitz High School
Houston, Texas

Oak Grove Middle School
Clearwater, Florida

Oxnard High School
Oxnard, California

Pershing Intermediate School 220
Brooklyn, New York

Samuel High School
Dallas, Texas

Serrano International School
Lake Forest, California

Silverado Middle School
Napa, California

T.A. Howard Middle School
Arlington, Texas

Trimble Technical High School
Fort Worth, Texas

Contents

UNIT 2 Survival — 70

To the Student

We hope you like *Visions*
We wrote it for you
To learn speaking, reading, writing,
And listening, too.

You'll read all kinds of things —
Stories, poems, and plays,
And texts that will help you understand
What your content teacher says.

Mary Lou McCloskey

Use this book to "grow" your English,
To talk about what you write and read.
Use it to learn lots of new words
And new reading strategies you'll need.

Good authors, good activities,
And especially your good teachers,
Can also help you learn grammar and writing,
And lots of other language features.

Lydia Stack

So please open this book
And learn everything you can.
Then write and show us how far you've come
Since you first began.

M.L.M. and L.S.

http://visions.heinle.com

UNIT 1

Mysteries

Stonehenge, John Constable, oil on canvas, 1776–1837.

View the Picture

1. Who do you think put the stone posts here?
2. Why do you think they were put here?
3. What mysteries do you know about?

In this unit, you will read a mystery, a legend, and informational texts about mysteries. You will also practice writing these forms.

The Loch Ness Monster

an excerpt from an informational book by Malcolm Yorke

Objectives

Reading Make inferences using text evidence as you read an excerpt from an informational book.

Listening and Speaking Present an interview.

Grammar Understand the conjunction *but*.

Writing Write a paragraph that describes.

Content Math: Understand length.

Use Prior Knowledge

Describe an Animal

Prior knowledge is something that you already know. Use your prior knowledge to help you understand what you do not know.

There are many different animals. What animals do you know about?

1. Work with a partner. Think of animals that you know about. Choose one.
2. Make a web. List what you know about the animal. Answer these questions.
   a. What does the animal look like?
   b. Where does the animal live?
   c. What does the animal eat?
   d. Does the animal fly? Swim? Run fast? Climb trees?

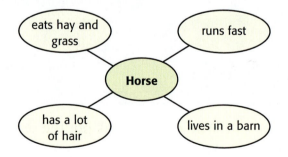

Build Background

Dinosaurs

Background is information that can help you understand what you hear or read.

Dinosaurs were animals that lived millions of years ago. Some were very large. Others were very small. Some ate meat. Others ate plants.

SCIENCE

Content Connection

This is a picture of a *Tyrannosaurus rex*. It was a very large dinosaur that ate meat.

Build Vocabulary

Use Language Structure to Find Meaning

When you learn new words, you **build your vocabulary.**

You can use **language structure** to figure out what a word means. Language structure is the way language is organized. Authors often make statements in one sentence and give an example in the next sentence. The information in the second sentence will help you figure out the meaning of words.

Khalid <u>adores</u> carrots. He eats them every day.

The second sentence tells us that Khalid eats carrots every day. This probably means that he likes carrots a lot. You can guess that *adores* means "likes a lot."

Read these sentences. Use the second sentences to figure out the meanings of the underlined words.

1. The men <u>searched</u> for it. But they never saw it again.
   a. looked　　**b.** caught
2. Some scans showed <u>huge</u> objects in the lake. The objects were bigger than sharks but smaller than whales.
   a. very large　　**b.** very small

The Heinle
Newbury House
Dictionary

Activity Book
p. 1

Student
CD-ROM

Text Structure

Informational Text

The **text structure** of a reading is its main parts and how they fit together.

"The Loch Ness Monster" is an **informational text.** An informational text gives facts about a topic. Look at the chart. It shows the features of an informational text. Look for these elements as you read or listen to "The Loch Ness Monster."

Informational Text	
Details and Examples	Details and examples explain the topic.
Experiences	Experiences are things that happened to real people.
Visuals	Visuals are pictures that help readers understand.

Student
CD-ROM

Reading Strategy

Make Inferences Using Text Evidence

A **reading strategy** is a way to understand what you read. You can become a better reader if you learn good reading strategies.

Authors do not always tell you everything. Sometimes you have to **make inferences.** When you make inferences, you guess using information that you know. You also use **text evidence.** Text evidence is in what you read.

1. Read this sentence.

A man comes into the room. He is wearing a wet raincoat.

2. Now read these sentences. Which one is an inference that you can make from the sentence in **1**?
   a. It is raining.
   b. The man is cold.

Make inferences as you read "The Loch Ness Monster." Write your inferences in your Reading Log.

Reading Log   Student
CD-ROM

THE LOCH NESS MONSTER

an excerpt from an informational book
by Malcolm Yorke

1　"Dad! Dad! What's that in the **loch?**" shouted Jim Ayton. It was a calm summer's evening in 1963. Jim was working on his father's farm on Loch Ness, a lake in **Scotland,** when he looked up to see a strange **creature** moving silently down the lake. It was huge! Jim had never seen anything like it before.

2　Two men nearby heard Jim's shouts and rushed to join him and his father. The excited group wanted a closer look. They ran to the lake, climbed into a boat, and headed straight toward the creature.

> ### Make Inferences Using Text Evidence
>
> You can make this inference: The two men and Jim's father have never seen a creature like this. What text evidence helps you make this inference?

Audio
CD 1, Tr. 1

3　The creature's head looked a bit like a horse's head, only bigger. Its neck stretched nearly 6 feet (2 meters), as tall as a full-grown man. Its **snakelike** body was as long as a bus. Could it be the **legendary** Loch Ness **monster** that people had talked about for years?

4　Suddenly the creature rose out of the water. Then it dived. An **enormous** wave hit the small boat. It rocked and **swirled** around. Had the creature seen the men? Was it about to attack?

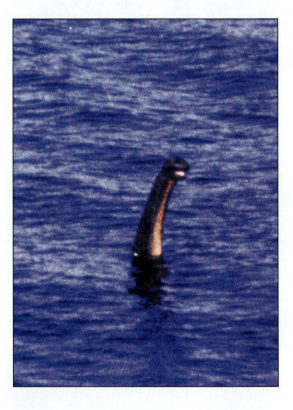

---

loch　a lake
Scotland　one of the nations in the United Kingdom
creature　a living thing
snakelike　long; looking like a snake
legendary　based on a story that is handed down over time

monster　a scary creature
enormous　very big
swirled　turned

5   A few seconds later the creature's head **reappeared.** It was farther away now. The monster seemed more **frightened** than **ferocious!** Then it was gone. The men searched and searched for it, but they never saw it again.

6   It was 20 years before anyone heard the story about what had happened that day. Jim and his father didn't think many people would believe them. But the Aytons and their friends are not the only people who **claim** to have seen this **mysterious** monster.

7   One of the earliest known **sightings** was made more than 1,400 years ago by Saint Columba, a traveling Irish holy man. **Legends** tell how, in 565 A.D., the saint saw a "water monster" attack a swimmer in Loch Ness. When the saint ordered it to leave the swimmer alone, the monster **retreated** immediately.

8   The Loch Ness monster first became famous in 1933, after a road was built around the steep sides of the Loch Ness valley. Tourists could now explore this **remote** area for the first time. It was not long before reports of monster sightings began appearing in newspapers all around the world.

9   **Spotting** the monster soon brought rewards. Newspapers would pay a lot of money for a photograph of the monster—even if it was **blurred!** Fortune seekers, scientists, and monster enthusiasts **swarmed** around the loch, all wanting to take the best monster picture ever.

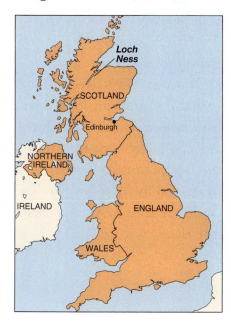

Make Inferences Using Text Evidence

Were many people interested in seeing the Loch Ness monster? Make an inference. What text evidence did you use to make this inference?

---

reappeared   appeared again, came back
frightened   scared
ferocious   very fierce or cruel
claim   say that something is true
mysterious   having no known cause
sightings   things that people see

legends   stories from long ago
retreated   moved away from
remote   far away from other places
spotting   seeing
blurred   not clear
swarmed   moved together in a large group

boats, each fitted with a **sonar** scanner, moved up the loch. What they discovered amazed them.

Make Inferences Using Text Evidence

You can make this inference: People want to know if the Loch Ness monster is real. What text evidence helps you make this inference?

10   Over the years, the searchers used more and more modern equipment. In 1972, an underwater camera produced a **close-up** of a strange object in the loch. When scientists used a special computer to **sharpen** up the image, this is what they saw. Could it be one of the monster's **flippers**?

11   The underwater photograph seems to show a flipper, but no one can be sure because the image is so **grainy.** It is hard to see or to take a photograph in the lake water because it is full of tiny pieces of peat, or dead plant material.

12   In 1987, a team of scientists searched the loch with high-tech equipment for a project called Operation Deepscan. A line of 19

13   Some scans showed huge objects moving deep in the lake. The objects were bigger than sharks but smaller than whales. Were they huge fish? Or was it a family of Loch Ness monsters? Again the **murky** water kept the scientists from knowing the answer.

14   Without clear pictures, scientists must rely on people's descriptions to know what the monster looks like. It seems that the creature has a long, thin neck, a **bulky** body with four flippers, and a long, powerful tail.

15   No animal living today fits this description. However, one **prehistoric** creature does.

---

close-up   a picture of something up close
sharpen   make better, make clearer
flippers   wide parts of the body on certain sea animals, used for swimming
grainy   unclear

sonar   a tool used to find things under water
murky   unclear and dark
bulky   large
prehistoric   the time before people wrote about history

Cryptocleidus (krip-toe-KLIE-duss) was a **plesiosaur:** a huge fish-eating **reptile** that lived in the sea. Some people think it looked a lot like the Loch Ness monster. However, *Cryptocleidus* is thought to have disappeared from the Earth 70 million years ago! Could it have lived on unnoticed?

Is the Loch Ness monster a **survivor** from the dinosaur age? Or were the people who saw it simply fooled by boats, logs, shadows, or giant **eels**? Could some of the sightings be the result of **practical jokes**? No one knows the truth—yet.

Make Inferences Using Text Evidence

What inference can you make about what *Cryptocleidus* looked like?

---

plesiosaur   a type of dinosaur
reptile   an animal that is cold-blooded and lays eggs; snakes and lizards are reptiles

survivor   something that still lives
eels   fish that look like snakes
practical jokes   tricks

About the Author

Malcolm Yorke (born 1938)

Malcolm Yorke has written more than 20 books. Many of these books are for young people. Yorke was once a college teacher. He taught people how to be teachers. Today, Yorke still writes books. He also paints and makes other kinds of art.

➤ What was Malcolm Yorke's purpose in writing about the Loch Ness monster? To entertain, to inform, or to persuade?

Beyond the Reading

Reading Comprehension

Question-Answer Relationships (QAR)

You can understand a selection better if you answer different kinds of questions.

"Right There" Questions
1. **Recall Facts** Where is Loch Ness?
2. **Recall Facts** When was the road built around Loch Ness valley?
3. **Recall Facts** What dinosaur does the Loch Ness monster look like?

"Think and Search" Questions
4. **Describe** Use your own words to describe what the Loch Ness monster looks like.
5. **Explain** What did Operation Deepscan discover?

"Author and You" Questions
6. **Draw Conclusions** Why do you think the newspapers paid a lot of money for pictures of the Loch Ness monster?

7. **Analyze Author's Perspective** Do you think the author believes there is a Loch Ness monster? Why do you think what you do?

"On Your Own" Questions
8. **Speculate** Do you think people will ever find the Loch Ness monster? Why or why not?
9. **Form Questions** What questions would you like to ask and research about this mystery? Write your questions. Then revise them.
10. **Connect Across Texts** Compare this reading with other mysteries that you have read about.

Activity Book
p. 2

Student
CD-ROM

Build Reading Fluency

Repeated Reading

When you **build reading fluency,** you learn to read faster and to understand better.

Repeated reading helps increase your reading rate and builds confidence. Each time you reread you improve your reading fluency.

1. Turn to page 6.
2. Your teacher or partner will time you for six minutes.
3. With a partner, take turns reading each paragraph aloud.
4. Stop after six minutes.

Listen, Speak, Interact

Present an Interview

When people listen and talk to each other, they **interact.**

During an interview, one person asks questions. Another person answers them.

1. Work with a partner. One student will be the interviewer. The other student will be Jim Ayton.
2. Work together to ask and answer questions.
   a. What were you doing when you saw the monster?
   b. What was the monster doing?
   c. How did you feel when you saw the monster?
3. Make up two more questions on your own. Share them with your partner. Then revise your questions.
4. Write each question on a note card. Write the answer on another card.

Question 1:

Interviewer: What did the Loch Ness monster look like?

Answer 1:

Jim Ayton: The monster was very big! It . . .

5. Use your note cards to present your interview to the class.

Elements of Literature

Use Visuals

Literature is something that you read. Writers use many different ways to express themselves. These ways are the **elements of literature.**

The **visuals** (pictures) in the selection show what the animals and places look like.

1. Work with a small group. Take turns reading paragraphs 3, 8, and 10 aloud. Look at the visuals.

2. Discuss the following questions:
   a. Did the visuals help you understand the text? Why or why not?
   b. Does it help to look at visuals before you read? Why or why not?

Activity Book
p. 3

Student
CD-ROM

Word Study

Analyze Compound Words

Words can have several parts. In this section, you will learn what the different parts mean.

A **compound word** is two words joined together to make one word. Use the meaning of each word to find the meaning of the compound word.

Treetop has the words *tree* and *top*. *Treetop* means "the top part of a tree."

1. Copy the chart in your Personal Dictionary.
2. Write the words that make up each compound word in your chart.

First Word +	Second Word ⇒	Compound Word
tree +	top ⇒	treetop
		underwater
		newspaper

3. Guess the definitions. Check your answers with your teacher.

Personal Dictionary   The Heinle Newbury House Dictionary   Activity Book *p. 4*   Student CD-ROM

Grammar Focus

Understand the Conjunction *But*

Grammar is the way that a language is put together.

A conjunction is a part of speech. It can combine two sentences into one compound sentence. The word *but* is a conjunction.

Sentence 1   **Sentence 2**

Carlos wanted to play. He had to finish his homework first.

Compound Sentence

Carlos wanted to play, **but** he had to finish his homework first.

The conjunction *but* shows **contrast**— how things are different. When you combine sentences with **but,** use a comma (**,**) after the first sentence. This helps make your meaning clear.

1. Find two sentences with the conjunction *but* in paragraphs 5 and 11. Write them on a piece of paper.
2. Combine these sentences with *but*. Be sure to use the comma correctly.
   a. I saw the monster. I couldn't take a picture.
   b. Some people don't believe in the monster. I do.

Activity Book *pp. 5–6*   Student Handbook   Student CD-ROM

From Reading to Writing

Write a Paragraph That Describes

In school, after you read literature, you often write about it. This section shows you how to do this.

Write a paragraph. Describe what the Loch Ness monster looks like.

1. Use the visuals to help you.
2. Review the selection to get ideas. Look at paragraphs 3, 11, and 13.
3. Draw a picture of the monster. Copy your paragraph below the picture.
4. Remember to indent your paragraph.

The Loch Ness monster looks like _____.

Its head looks like _____.

Its body looks like _____.

Its tail looks like _____.

Activity Book
p. 7

Student Handbook

Across Content Areas   MATH

Understand Length

Content areas are the subjects you study in school. Math, science, social studies, language arts, and other arts such as music and drawing are content areas.

Length tells you how long something is. People in the United States use a system called the **U.S. Customary.** Most people in the world use the **metric** system.

Work with a partner. Use the chart to answer the following questions.

1. Are inches shorter than feet?
2. Which is longer, a yard or a meter?
3. Are miles longer or shorter than kilometers?

U.S. Customary	Metric
1 foot = 12 inches	30.5 centimeters
1 yard = 3 feet	.9 meters
1 mile = 1,760 yards	1.6 kilometers

Note: "foot" changes to "feet" for numbers larger than 1 (for example: 2 feet, 3 feet).

Activity Book
p. 8

Mystery of the Cliff Dwellers

an excerpt from a textbook

Objectives

Reading Find the main idea and supporting details as you read an excerpt from a textbook.

Listening and Speaking Distinguish fact and opinion.

Grammar Use prepositional phrases.

Writing Write an informational text.

Content Social Studies: Read a population map.

Use Prior Knowledge

Talk About Your Community

A community is a city, town, village, or neighborhood where people live. What is your community like?

1. Work with a partner. Describe your community.
   a. What is the name of your community?
   b. Is your community big, small, or medium-sized?
   c. What does your community look like? Are there many trees? Are there tall buildings?
   d. What do you like best about your community? What do you like least?

2. Use a web to brainstorm things about your community.

What It Looks Like: It has many trees and parks.

What I Like Least: There is no movie theater.

Name of Community: Smallwood

What I Like Best: It has an art museum.

Size: It is small.

Build Background

Archaeologists

Archaeologists are scientists who study the ways people lived long ago. They study what the people ate, how they got food, and where they lived. Archaeologists often dig into the earth where people lived long ago to find artifacts—parts of houses, tools, and even garbage. They study these things to learn about the culture—the ways of living—of the people of the past.

Content Connection

SOCIAL STUDIES

Today, some archaeologists study artifacts in Mesa Verde National Park in Colorado. This park has many Native American houses from long ago.

Build Vocabulary

Learn Context Words by Grouping

As you read or listen to the audio recording of "Mystery of the Cliff Dwellers," you will learn new words related to land.

Work with a partner. Read the words and definitions. Match each word with the correct definition. Use a dictionary if you need to, or ask your teacher. Write your answers in your Personal Dictionary.

Words

1. mesa
2. cliff
3. farmland
4. mud

Definitions

a. land used to grow food
b. a high piece of land with a flat top (from the Spanish word for *table*)
c. a high piece of rock with a long drop
d. a sticky mixture of water and dirt

Personal Dictionary   The Heinle Newbury House Dictionary   Activity Book *p. 9*   Student CD-ROM

Text Structure

Informational Text

"Mystery of the Cliff Dwellers" is an **informational text.** It gives facts about a topic. This chart shows some features of this informational text.

"Mystery of the Cliff Dwellers" also includes **opinions.** Opinions are statements about what people think.

Informational Text	
Subject	what the text is about
Quotes	words that people have said; quotes usually have quotation marks (" . . . ") around them
Facts	information that is true
Definitions	the meanings of new words

Student
CD-ROM

Reading Strategy

Find the Main Idea and Supporting Details

The **main idea** is the most important idea in a paragraph or text. Usually, you can find the main idea in the first sentence of a paragraph.

Supporting details give information about the main idea. Usually, you can find supporting details in the middle of a paragraph.

Look for main ideas and supporting details as you read or listen to "Mystery of the Cliff Dwellers." Write them in your Reading Log.

Main Idea — Atlanta is a great place to live. It has lovely sunny weather. The Atlanta Braves baseball team is there. It's a great team. Also, Atlanta has a good train system called MARTA. — Supporting Details

Reading Log

Student
CD-ROM

The Mystery of the
Cliff Dwellers

an excerpt from a textbook

1   An **ancient** people lived high in the cliffs . . . then **disappeared.** Or did they?

2   Mystery **surrounds** the ancestral Pueblo people. It **swirls** around them like the dry wind of the high country where they lived. Why did they build their homes in the cliffs? Why did they **abandon** those homes? And who were they, really? Even their name is a mystery. The Navajo called them the *Anasazi*, which means "ancient **enemies.**" Today Pueblo Indians call them their Pueblo **ancestors.** No one knows what they called themselves.

> **Find the Main Idea and Supporting Details**
>
> What is the main idea of this paragraph?

Audio
CD 1, Tr. 2

---

ancient   very old

disappeared   went out of sight

surrounds   is all around something

swirls   moves in a twisting and turning motion

abandon   leave something behind

enemies   people who want to harm you

ancestors   people from whom you descend; for example, your grandparents, parents, and so on

3   A group of these ancient people settled at what is now Mesa Verde, in Colorado, about A.D. 550. At first they dug **pit houses** in the mesa, or flat-topped hill. Around the year 1200, they began moving off the top of the mesa into **high-altitude dwellings** they built of stone and mud under the cliff **ledges.** No one knows why they made this move. It may have been to **cultivate** more farmland. Some archaeologists think they moved for **protection.**

4   "The cliff dwellings seem safe to me," says Kathrine Warren, ten, of Durango, Colorado. "People could climb up and pull the **ladders** behind them so their enemies couldn't get to them."

Find the Main Idea and Supporting Details

The main idea of this paragraph is that the cliff dwellings seem safe. What detail does Kathrine Warren give to support this idea?

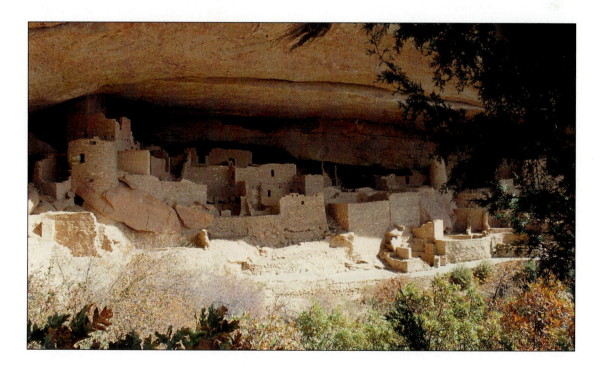

pit houses square houses that are dug into the ground	**cultivate** prepare land to grow food, trees, and flowers
high-altitude high above the ground	**protection** something that keeps you from being hurt
dwellings places where people live	**ladders** sets of steps used for climbing
ledges flat areas of rock that stick out	

5   Kathrine visited the **ruins** of Cliff Palace, one of the cliff dwellings, with Leighana Sisneros and Landon Wigton, both ten and from Durango. "It would have been **neat** to be an Anasazi kid," Leighana says. "But," Kathrine observes, "you wouldn't have had things like **lightbulbs,** and I would have missed reading books." Landon adds, "There weren't any grocery stores." But the ancestral Pueblo people didn't need grocery stores. They grew most of their own food. The men planted corn, squash, and beans on top of the mesa. They **conserved** water in the dry **climate** by building **dams** and **reservoirs.** The women ground the corn on metates (meh TAH tays), or **concave** stones, and cooked it in pottery they made with ridged surfaces. They often painted their serving bowls.

> ### Find the Main Idea and Supporting Details
>
> The ancestral Pueblo people did not need grocery stores. Which details support this idea?

---

ruins   broken parts of old buildings
neat   slang for "great"
lightbulbs   round glass parts of electric lights
conserved   saved
climate   the type of weather that a place has

dams   walls built across rivers to stop the water from flowing
reservoirs   bodies of water saved for use
concave   curving inward

6   "We climbed down into a kiva (KEE vuh)," says Landon. A kiva is an **underground chamber.** In its floor is a sipapu (SEE pah poo), or hole, symbolizing an opening between the **physical** world and the place where the Pueblo ancestors believed that life began.

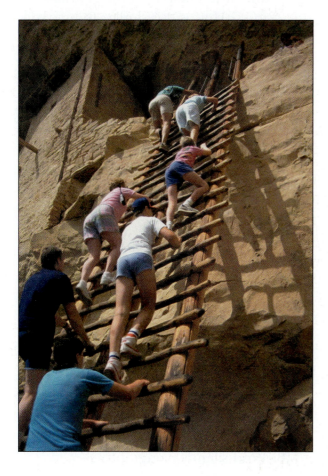

"Only the men were allowed in the kiva," Landon says. There they held religious ceremonies and gathered to talk, perhaps about the weather as people do today. By the late 1200s, the weather must have been on their minds a lot. Archaeologists know that for many years little rain fell in the region. By 1300 the cliff dwellings of Mesa Verde had been abandoned. "Maybe the people left because of the **drought,**" says Leighana. Some scientists agree. They think, too, that soil **erosion,** warfare, and disease may have driven them away. After so many years, the mysteries remain. But the ancient people probably did not **vanish.** Archaeologists and modern Pueblo people believe they **migrated** south. Today, through their **descendants**—the Pueblo Indians of Arizona and New Mexico—the ancient ones live on.   7

Find the Main Idea and Supporting Details

Archaeologists have many ideas about why the ancestral Pueblo people left Mesa Verde. This is a main idea of paragraph 7. What details support this main idea?

---

underground located below Earth's surface

chamber a room

physical related to objects in the real world

drought a time of little or no rainfall

erosion when soil washes away or blows away because of the weather

vanish disappear suddenly

migrated moved from one place to another

descendants your children, grandchildren, and so forth

Beyond the Reading

Reading Comprehension

Question-Answer Relationships (QAR)

"Right There" Questions

1. **Recall Facts** What did the Navajo call the ancestral Pueblo people?
2. **Recall Facts** About what year did a group of ancestral Pueblo people move to Mesa Verde?
3. **Identify** What is a kiva?
4. **Recall Facts** Who are the descendants of the ancestral Pueblo people?

"Think and Search" Questions

5. **Analyze Cause and Effect** Look at paragraphs 5–7. Why would a drought cause the ancestral Pueblo people to move?
6. **Analyze Cause and Effect** Name three reasons why the ancestral Pueblo people may have left the cliff dwellings.

"Author and You" Question

7. **Compare and Contrast** How did the ancestral Pueblo people get their food? How is this similar to how you get your food? How is it different?

"On Your Own" Questions

8. **Determine Distinctive Characteristics of Culture** In what ways is your culture different from the Anasazi culture?
9. **Determine Common Characteristics of Culture** In what ways is your culture similar to the Anasazi culture?

Activity Book
p. 10

Student
CD-ROM

Build Reading Fluency

Read Silently and Aloud

Reading silently for practice and reading aloud for expression are two important ways to become a fluent reader.

1. Listen to the audio recording of "Mystery of the Cliff Dwellers."
2. Follow along with the reading on page 18.
3. Read silently paragraphs 1–3 two times.
4. With a partner read aloud.
5. Your partner will time you reading aloud.

Listen, Speak, Interact

Distinguish Fact and Opinion

"Mystery of the Cliff Dwellers" includes quotes from people who are visiting Mesa Verde. Some of these quotes give facts, and some give opinions. Study the difference between facts and opinions.

Fact	You can show that a fact is true. Example: The moon comes up in the east.
Opinion	An opinion is what you believe or think. Example: The moon is beautiful tonight.

1. Work with a partner. One of you will read the quotes in paragraph 4 aloud. The other will read the quotes in paragraph 5 aloud.
2. As you read your quotes, your partner should not look at the reading.
3. Ask your partner to identify one fact and one opinion from the quotes.
4. Discuss your partner's answers.
5. Do the same thing with your partner's reading.

Elements of Literature

Write Quotes

"Mystery of the Cliff Dwellers" uses **quotes.** Writers use quotes to tell us the exact words that people say. Look at these quotes from paragraphs 5 and 6:

Landon adds, "There weren't any grocery stores."

"We climbed down into a kiva," says Landon.

The quotes can come before or after the name of the person who said the words.

How to Punctuate a Quote		
Quotation Marks	" . . . "	around the words the person says
Comma	,	• after the quote if the quote comes first • before the quote if the quote comes last

1. Ask a partner the following questions. Your partner should answer in complete sentences.
   a. What is your favorite food?
   b. What is your favorite color?
2. Write each answer as a quote.

Activity Book
p. 11

Student
CD-ROM

Word Study

Root Words and Suffixes

The word *archaeology* comes from two Greek words. The **root word** *archae* means "very old." The suffix (end of the word) *-logy* comes from a Greek word that means "word." In English, *-logy* usually means "study of."

The names of many sciences are formed from Greek words in this way. Guess what these sciences are about.

Root	Meaning	Suffix	Name of Science
bio	life		biology
geo	earth	+ logy	geology
entomo	insect		entomology

An **archaeologist** is a person who studies archaeology. Notice how this word is formed.

archaeology + ist

You drop the *y* and add *ist*.

Copy and complete these sentences in your Personal Dictionary.

1. A ＿＿ studies Earth.
2. A ＿＿ studies life.
3. A ＿＿ studies insects.

Personal Dictionary   Activity Book p. 12   Student CD-ROM

Grammar Focus

Use Prepositional Phrases

Prepositions are a part of speech. A preposition followed by a noun or pronoun is called a **prepositional phrase.**

One use of prepositional phrases is to say *where* something happens.

The people lived **in the cliffs.**

The prepositional phrase *in the cliffs* tells where the people lived.

Answer the following questions on a piece of paper. Use a prepositional phrase from the box in each of your answers.

in Mesa Verde	in the kiva
in the library	in the pool

a. Where are the students studying?
   They are studying ＿＿ .
b. Where is Marta swimming?
   She is swimming ＿＿ .
c. Where are the cliff dwellings?
   They are ＿＿ .
d. Where did the men hold ceremonies?
   They held them ＿＿ .

Activity Book pp. 13–14   Student Handbook   Student CD-ROM

From Reading to Writing

Write an Informational Text

Imagine that you are an archaeologist 500 years in the future. You are studying where you live today. Write an informational text that tells people about this home of the past. Write one paragraph.

1. Answer these questions:
    a. What is the place like? Is it an apartment or a house?
    b. What does it look like? How many rooms does it have?
    c. How many people lived there?
    d. How did the people live?

2. Use prepositional phrases that tell *where* something happened.

3. Exchange paragraphs with a partner. Proofread (look for errors in) your partner's paragraph.

Reading Log

Activity Book
p. 15

Student Handbook

Across Content Areas

SOCIAL STUDIES

Read a Population Map

To find the population of Native Americans in a state, look at the state's color on the population map. Find the same color in the legend. The numbers next to the colored square tell the population of Native Americans in that state.

Complete these research notes on a piece of paper.

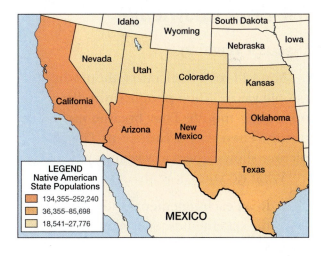

LEGEND
Native American
State Populations
- 134,355–252,240
- 36,355–85,698
- 18,541–27,776

> The states of _____ , _____ , _____ , and _____ have the most Native Americans. They all have between 134,355 and _____ Native Americans. The Native American population in _____ is between 36,355 and 85,698.

Activity Book
p. 16

Yawning

an informational text
by Haleh V. Samiei

Objectives

Reading Compare the text to your own experiences as you read an informational text.

Listening and Speaking Give an informational presentation.

Grammar Write dependent clauses.

Writing Write a paragraph using chronology.

Content Math: Read a bar graph.

Use Prior Knowledge

Discuss Yawning

You will read a selection about why people yawn. When people yawn, they open their mouth. They breathe in deeply. Then they breathe out. This picture shows a person yawning.

What do you know about yawning?

1. Read each statement below. Write *T* if the statement is true. Write *F* if the statement is false. Write your answers on a separate piece of paper.
   a. People yawn when they are tired.
   b. People yawn when they are bored.
   c. People yawn to stay awake.
   d. Some animals yawn.

2. Discuss your answers with another student.

Build Background

Oxygen

People and animals need oxygen to live. Oxygen is part of the air that we breathe. We cannot smell, taste, or see oxygen. When we breathe in, oxygen from the air goes into our bodies. Our bodies use this oxygen to do many things. For example, oxygen helps us turn food into energy.

SCIENCE

Content Connection

Fish also breathe oxygen. They get oxygen from the water that they live in.

Build Vocabulary

Identify Antonyms

An **antonym** is a word that has the opposite meaning of another word. For example, *little* and *big* are antonyms.

You can use the meaning of a word to find its antonym. You know that *little* means "not big." This helps you know that *big* is the antonym of *little*.

1. Copy the chart in your Personal Dictionary.
2. Write the correct antonym for each word. Choose one of these words:

   awake   calm   disagree

3. Ask your teacher or use a dictionary to find the meanings of any words that you do not know.

Word	Meaning	Antonym
little	not big	big
nervous	worried about something	
agree	have the same idea	
sleepy	tired	

Personal Dictionary

The Heinle Newbury House Dictionary

Activity Book *p. 17*

Student CD-ROM

Text Structure

Informational Text

"Yawning" is an **informational text.** An informational text gives facts and details about a topic. The chart shows some features of an informational text.

When you read an informational text, you learn new things. Read this reading selection slowly. This will help you understand the facts in it.

Informational Text	
Purpose	to teach us about something
Facts	give us information and details about the subject
Definitions	explain the meanings of new words

Student
CD-ROM

Reading Strategy

Compare the Text to Your Own Experiences

Everyone yawns sometimes. Try it right now. Open your mouth. Breathe in. Breathe out.

Can you remember times when you have yawned? Why do you think you did it? As you read the selection, compare what the author says about yawning to your own experiences. This strategy will help you better understand what you read.

As you read, ask yourself these questions:

1. What do I already know about what I am reading?
2. What is the new information that I am learning?

Student
CD-ROM

Yawning

an informational text
by Haleh V. Samiei

1   This article is going to **cast a spell** on you. As you read it, **pressure** will build behind your **ear drums,** and you'll lift your eyebrows and open your mouth wide. You'll hold this **position** for about six seconds as you take in a deep breath and then let a short one out.

2   Don't **panic.** It's just a **contagious** yawn. When you read about yawning, see someone yawning, or just think about yawning, you usually yawn yourself. But what's the purpose of yawning? Most people think that the answer is simple. You yawn when you're bored or sleepy. Some people think you yawn because you need **extra** oxygen. Is it true?

Compare the Text to Your Own Experiences

Do you yawn when you see other people yawning? What questions do you have about this?

3   Robert Provine, a scientist at the University of Maryland-Baltimore County, set out to find out. The first thing he did was to test whether people yawn when they're bored. Provine had no problem boring an unlucky group of people by making them watch a video of color-bar **patterns.** A different, lucky group got to watch a music video. No need to say that the people in the first group won the yawning contest.

Pressure

Audio
CD 1, Tr. 3

---

cast a spell   cause a special effect

pressure   force, tension

ear drums   parts inside the ear; they move so you can hear sound

position   where something is

panic   get very scared

contagious   able to be given to others

extra   more

patterns   designs of regular shapes and lines

4   To see if people yawn more when they're sleepy, Provine had his students keep a yawn **diary** for a week. Whenever they yawned, they had to write down the time. As you might guess, they yawned at night when they were tired and sleepy. But Provine also found that they yawned when they woke up in the morning.

5   When he thought about it, he realized that when people **stretch,** there's a good chance they'll also yawn. In fact, other scientists have also noticed that yawning and stretching are **linked.** For example, the muscles of people **paralyzed** on one side of their body **jerk** as they yawn, even though they can't make the muscles move **on purpose.**

6   People also yawn when they can't possibly be bored or sleepy. Sky divers yawn just as they're about to jump out of an airplane. Concert **violinists** yawn just before going on stage. Olympic athletes yawn just before a big **competition.** Provine thinks these people may be yawning because they're nervous. He thinks that when you're nervous, sleepy, bored, or have just awakened, yawning can help focus your attention.

> **Compare the Text to Your Own Experiences**
>
> Have you ever yawned when you were nervous? Explain.

---

diary a book where people describe what happened to them each day and how they felt

stretch make a body part longer by pushing it out

linked connected

paralyzed not able to move your body

jerk move suddenly

on purpose meaning to do something

violinists people who play the violin, a musical instrument

competition an event in which people try to do something better than one another, such as a race

Yawn stretches facial muscles.

Blood flows to brain.

Brain sends message to heart to beat faster, to body to sweat and fidget.

7   Ronald Baenninger, a scientist at Temple University, agrees with Provine. He and his wife Mary Anne, a scientist at The College of New Jersey, guessed that yawning helps you stay awake or become excited. They tested their guess by hooking up people to machines that **measured** changes in their bodies as they yawned. They found that as people yawned, they moved their **wrists** more than usual, they began sweating, and their hearts beat faster. This shows that these people were trying to stay awake, not fall asleep.

So what does yawning do that helps keep you **alert**? Provine thinks that by yawning, you stretch the muscles in your face and bring more **blood** to the **brain.** "It stirs things up," he says. The brain can then wake up the body through the **fidgeting,** sweating, and the faster heartbeat. You can see how this might help you stay awake at night, wake up in the morning, or become alert when you're bored or nervous.

8

Compare the Text to Your Own Experiences

Do you yawn when you are tired? How does this experience help you understand paragraphs 7 and 8?

Provine also tested whether people yawn to breathe in more oxygen. He had people breathe in a special mix of air that had less oxygen than usual. To get the oxygen they needed, people had to breathe faster. "We had people **huffing and puffing,**" he says. "But they didn't yawn any more than they did before."

9

---

measured   figured out how much

wrists   the part of the body between the hand and the forearm

alert   paying attention

blood   the red liquid pumped by the heart through the body

brain   the part of the body used for thinking and feeling

fidgeting   moving the body in a nervous way

huffing and puffing   breathing quickly and a lot

10   He didn't stop there. He also made people breathe in air that was *all* oxygen. They had more than enough oxygen in their blood, but they yawned just as much as before. So the idea that we yawn to get more oxygen can't be right.

11   But not everyone agrees with Provine and the Baenningers. Some scientists think that yawning has no **purpose.** They say that it's a **habit** left over from when you were **developing** as a baby in your mother's **womb** or one you **inherited** from our animal **ancestors.** Yawning might help get the face and jaw muscles of unborn babies working, and it might help animals stay alert.

Compare the Text to Your Own Experiences

Think about what you know about yawning. Do you think that yawning has no purpose? Explain.

12   It's **amazing** how difficult it is **get to the bottom of** something as simple as a yawn.

---

purpose   reason
habit   something that you do over and over
developing   growing
womb   the part of a woman's body where a baby can grow

inherited   received from
ancestors   people or animals from the past that you are related to
amazing   surprising
get to the bottom of   learn the truth about

About the Author

Haleh V. Samiei (born 1963)

Haleh V. Samiei lived in Iran as a child. She studied science in college. She also studied writing. Today, Samiei writes about science and health. She also writes articles for newspapers.

► How do you think Haleh V. Samiei learned about yawning? By talking to scientists? By reading books? Both? Why do you think she wrote this informational text?

Beyond the Reading

Reading Comprehension

Question-Answer Relationships (QAR)

"Right There" Questions

1. **Recall Facts** Who is Robert Provine?
2. **Recall Facts** Look at paragraph 3. What was the first thing that Robert Provine tested?
3. **Explain** Look at paragraph 7. What do Ronald and Mary Anne Baenninger think is the reason that people yawn?

"Think and Search" Questions

4. **Analyze Cause and Effect** What sometimes happens when you see another person yawn?
5. **Identify Steps in a Process** Look at paragraph 1. Identify the steps in yawning.

6. **Summarize** Look at paragraph 7. Name three things that people do when they yawn.

"Author and You" Question

7. **Evaluate Evidence** Why do you think people yawn?

"On Your Own" Questions

8. **Evaluate** Name two things that you learned from reading "Yawning."
9. **Compare Text Events with Experiences** Are your experiences with yawning similar to those discussed in the reading? Talk with a partner about his or her experiences.

Activity Book
p. 18

Student
CD-ROM

Build Reading Fluency

Rapid Word Recognition

Rapidly recognizing words helps increase your reading rate. It is an important characteristic of effective readers.

1. With a partner, review the words in the box.
2. Read the words aloud for one minute. Your teacher will time you.
3. Count how many words you read in one minute.

article	stretch	oxygen	bored	oxygen	article
breath	bored	stretch	oxygen	bored	oxygen
bored	diary	breath	article	diary	breath
oxygen	oxygen	bored	breath	article	diary
diary	breath	article	diary	stretch	bored

Listen, Speak, Interact

Give an Informational Presentation

Yawning is usually a reflex action—an action your body does that you can't really control. Two other reflex actions are sneezing and coughing.

Give an informational presentation about sneezing or coughing.

1. With a partner, decide which of you will present sneezing and which one will present coughing.
2. On your own, list facts about the reflex action that you chose. Answer these questions. Take notes on note cards.
   a. What happens in your body when you sneeze or cough?
   b. When do you sneeze or cough?

c. Can you sneeze or cough whenever you want to, or is it always a reflex action?
3. Present your information to your partner.
   a. Use the information on your note cards. Clarify your information with examples.
   b. Act out what sneezing or coughing is.
4. Take notes as you listen to your partner's presentation. Ask yourself these questions.
   a. Did I understand my partner's nonverbal messages?
   b. Did my partner give facts, opinions, or both?

Elements of Literature

Recognize Direct Address

The author of "Yawning" uses **direct address.** This means that the author speaks directly to the reader. The author uses the pronoun *you.* Look at this example from paragraph 1.

This article is going to cast a spell on you.

1. Reread paragraphs 1 and 2 of "Yawning."
2. Find three sentences that use the pronoun *you.* Write them in your Reading Log.

3. Why do you think the author uses direct address? Do you think that direct address makes the selection easier to understand?

Reading Log   Activity Book
p. 19   Student
CD-ROM

Word Study

Write Using Contractions

Contractions are two words that are joined together. You drop one or more letter from the second word. An apostrophe (') replaces the letters.

It**'**s just a contagious yawn.

First Word +	Second Word ⇒	Contraction
it +	is ⇒	it's

Notice that you drop the *i* in *is* when you form the contraction *it's*.

It's is different from *its*. *Its* is a possessive form.

I have a fish. Its name is George.

1. Choose the words that the underlined contractions come from.
   a. <u>You'll</u> lift your eyebrows and open your mouth wide.

      you will   you are

   b. People yawn just as <u>they're</u> about to jump out of an airplane.

      they can   they are

2. Write two sentences with contractions.

Activity Book   Student
p. 20   CD-ROM

Grammar Focus

Write Dependent Clauses

Dependent clauses have a subject and a verb. They are part of a complex sentence. The word *that* often begins a dependent clause.

I think **that** the answer is simple.

Here the dependent clause is *that the answer is simple*. The dependent clause tells what I think.

Look at the following pairs of sentences. Combine the two sentences into one sentence. Use a dependent clause with *that*. Underline the dependent clause. Be sure to start your sentences with a capital letter and end them with a period. Do not use a comma before dependent clauses starting with *that*.

1. Provine made the discovery. They yawned when they woke up.
2. Some scientists have a theory. Yawning has no purpose.

Activity Book   Student   Student
pp. 21–22   Handbook   CD-ROM

From Reading to Writing

Write a Paragraph Using Chronology

Chronology is the order in which events happen. Paragraph 1 of "Yawning" uses chronology. It describes the order in which things happen when you yawn.

1. Write a paragraph using chronology. Your paragraph will be about your morning routine.
2. Begin your paragraph with a sentence that tells what it is about.
3. Use time words such as *first, then, next,* and *last* to show chronology.
4. Write at least one sentence with a dependent clause with *that.*

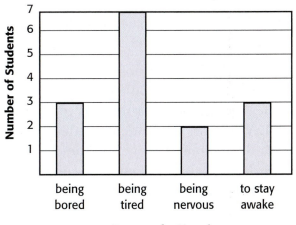

This is the routine that I follow every morning before school.
First, ~~~~~~~~~~~.
Then, ~~~~~~~~~~~.
Next, ~~~~~~~~~~~.
Finally, ~~~~~~~~~~~.

Activity Book
p. 23

Student
Handbook

Across Content Areas   MATH

Read a Bar Graph

A **bar graph** uses bars to show amounts. This bar graph shows the number of people who believe each reason for yawning. Across the bottom are the different reasons. On the left side is the number of people who gave each reason.

To read the bar graph, look at the reason at the bottom of a bar. Then find the numbered line that the top of the bar hits.

1. How many people think that we yawn because we are bored?
2. Which bars show the same number of people?
3. Which reason do the fewest number of people believe?
4. How many people gave reasons?

Number of Students (y-axis: 1–7)

Reasons (x-axis): being bored (3), being tired (7), being nervous (2), to stay awake (3)

Reasons for Yawning

Activity Book
p. 24

CHAPTER 4

The Sneak Thief

a mystery
by Falcon Travis

Objectives

Reading Use chronology to locate and recall information as you read a mystery.

Listening and Speaking Interpret text through dramatization.

Grammar Identify simple, compound, and complex sentences.

Writing Write dialogue in a mystery.

Content Language Arts: Learn words about the law.

Use Prior Knowledge

Discuss Rules

Rules are made to keep people safe. They tell us what we can and cannot do.

1. Work with a partner.
2. Copy this chart on a piece of paper.
3. Write the school rules that you know.
4. Write why each rule is needed.
5. Share your answers with the class.
6. Make a complete chart of rules to post in your classroom.

Rule	Why Rule Is Needed
No running in the halls.	So no one will fall down and get hurt

Build Background

Inspectors

Inspectors are types of police officers. They try to solve crimes. Crimes are actions that are against the law. Inspectors use clues to help them solve crimes. Clues are objects or facts that help answer a question.

SOCIAL STUDIES

Content Connection

Forensic doctors help solve crimes. They can get information by studying clues as small as a piece of hair.

Build Vocabulary

Learn Words Related to Train Travel

"The Sneak Thief" includes words related to train travel. Knowing the meanings of these words will help you understand the selection.

1. Copy the chart below in your Personal Dictionary.

2. Look at each word in the chart. Look at each word's meaning.
3. Write a sentence using each word.
4. Share your sentences with the class. Did you write similar sentences?
5. Look for these words as you read or listen to the audio recording of "The Sneak Thief."

Word	Meaning	Sentence
train station	a place where people go to get on the train	*I went to the train station.*
passenger	a person who rides in a train, car, boat, bus, or plane; it is not the driver	
ticket	a printed piece of paper that you buy; it lets you travel on a train, boat, bus, or plane	

Personal Dictionary   Activity Book *p. 25*   Student CD-ROM

Text Structure

Mystery

"The Sneak Thief" is a **mystery** story. Reading a mystery is like solving a puzzle. The chart shows the special features of a mystery.

Mystery	
Plot	The plot is the series of events in the story.
Problem	The story is about a question that needs to be answered.
Clues	Clues are details in the story that help answer the question.
Suspense	Suspense is the feeling of not knowing what is going to happen next.
Resolution	Resolution is the answer at the end of the story.

Student
CD-ROM

Reading Strategy

Use Chronology to Locate and Recall Information

Chronology is the order of events in a story. Notice chronology as you read. This will help you **locate** (find) and **recall** (remember) important information.

Authors often use words like *then, now, first, second, finally, before,* or *after* to show chronology.

1. Look at the timeline. The underlined words show chronology.

In 1998, we moved to San Diego.   Then we moved to Los Angeles.   Finally, we moved to Phoenix.

2. On a piece of paper, write these sentences in chronological order.
  a. Then my father hugged me.
  b. I woke up and went into the kitchen.
  c. Finally I remembered—it was my birthday!
  d. First my mother kissed me.
3. Look for words that show chronology as you read "The Sneak Thief."

Student
CD-ROM

The Sneak Thief

a mystery
by Falcon Travis

Audio
CD 1, Tr. 4

Use Chronology to Locate and Recall Information

What is the first thing that attracts Inspector Will Ketchum's attention?

1   Inspector Will Ketchum was **off duty.** He had just arrived at the train station to meet some friends, but their train was running an hour late. As he **strolled** across the main terminal, a man with the restless eyes of a **sneak thief** attracted his attention. Then he was lost in a sudden surge of passengers.

2   A few minutes later, the Inspector spotted the man, who was entering the station's coffee shop. Now he was carrying a leather **briefcase.** The man sat down at a **vacant** corner table, placing the briefcase between his chair and the wall.

3   The Inspector casually followed him in, sat at his table and, identifying himself as a police officer, asked if the man would mind stepping over to the **Station Master's** office to answer a few questions about the **ownership** of the briefcase that he had with him. The man claimed **indignantly** that the briefcase was his, but he agreed to go along.

4   In the Station Master's office the briefcase lay open on the desk, revealing a file of papers and an envelope containing about $200 in twenty-dollar bills.

---

off duty   not working
strolled   walked slowly
sneak thief   a person who steals, but tries to avoid being seen
briefcase   a small piece of luggage for holding books and papers

vacant   empty
Station Master   a person who watches over a train station
ownership   possession
indignantly   angrily

Use Chronology to Locate and Recall Information

What did Mr. Fink tell the Inspector *before* they opened the briefcase?

5   "Before we opened this briefcase, Mr. Fink," began the Inspector, "you told us it was definitely yours and that it contained only a couple of magazines. Now you **deny** that you are the owner. How do you explain that?"

6   Mr. Fink rubbed his chin and looked **puzzled.** "This definitely isn't the briefcase I handed in at the **checkroom** this morning," he said. "They must have given me someone else's. It looks exactly like mine, but I can see it isn't, now that it's open. My briefcase was locked and all it had in it were some magazines I was reading on the train. The owner of this briefcase shouldn't have left it open with all this money in it. If he got mine by mistake, he isn't going to be very happy about it."

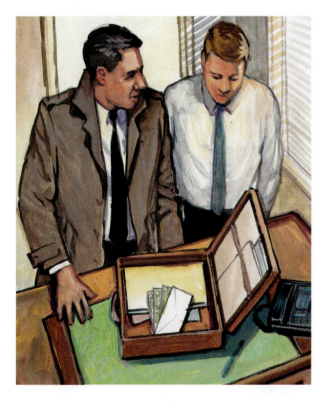

7   "I'm sure he won't be," said the Inspector. "What is more, he's probably wondering, as I am, why anyone would **check** a briefcase that had only a couple of magazines in it."

8   "That's easy to explain," said Mr. Fink. "I got to town this morning just before noon on one of those one-day round-trip **excursion** tickets—and I'll be going back tonight—if you don't make me miss my train. I was reading the magazines on the train. I brought my briefcase because I was hoping to find some **secondhand** books, but I didn't get to the bookstores because I met an old friend who invited me over to his house."

---

deny   say something is not true
puzzled   confused
checkroom   a place where you sign in your luggage

check   give for safekeeping
excursion   a short trip
secondhand   used by someone else before

9   "So that's when you checked your briefcase?"

10   "That's right," continued Mr. Fink. "I didn't want to carry it around with me, so I left it here and went to visit with my friend. Got my **taxi fare** paid both ways, had a great time and all I had to spend since I got off the train this morning was what they charged me at the checkroom."

11   "Lucky you," said the Inspector. "Now would you mind emptying out all your pockets and placing their **contents** on this desk?"

12   "I don't mind at all," said Mr. Fink, "I've got nothing to hide. The sooner you're satisfied, the sooner I can get going. I have to take this briefcase back to the checkroom and see if mine is still there."

Use Chronology to Locate and Recall Information

What does Mr. Fink say he did before he visited his friend?

13   Mr. Fink's statement and the contents of his pockets (shown at the left) were enough to tell Will Ketchum whether or not the suspect was telling the truth. If you have decided, too, turn to the SOLUTION . . . and see if you reached the same conclusion as the Inspector, and for the same reasons.

14   If you haven't been able to decide yet, look at the CLUES . . . for some **pointers** to the clues that helped the Inspector make up his mind.

15   **CLUES**
There is a clue in each of the following statements:

1. "My briefcase was locked."
2. "I got to town this morning just before noon on one of those one-day round-trip excursion tickets—"
3. "I was hoping to find some secondhand books."
4. "All I had to spend since I got off the train this morning was what they charged me at the checkroom."

---

taxi fare   the cost to ride in a taxi
contents   things found inside of something

pointers   pieces of advice

16 **SOLUTION**

The contents of the **suspect's** pockets do not include:
A key to the briefcase
The "return" part of the ticket
Enough cash (and no other way of paying) for buying books

17 Fink was **arrested** and **charged.** It was easy to find the owner of the briefcase. It turned out that he had put his case down while buying a newspaper, and in a matter of seconds it had **disappeared.** The sneak thief had **rehearsed** this story well, in case he was questioned, but he hadn't allowed for the contents of his pockets giving him away.

---

suspect a person who is thought to have committed a crime
arrested brought into police holding

charged blamed someone for something
disappeared gone out of sight
rehearsed practiced

About the Author — Falcon Travis

➤ Why do you think Falcon Travis wrote exactly what the characters said to each other? Does this make the characters seem real? Does this allow readers to learn the characters' thoughts?

Beyond the Reading

Reading Comprehension

Question-Answer Relationships (QAR)

"Right There" Questions

1. **Recall Facts** What was Mr. Fink carrying when he entered the coffee shop?
2. **Recall Facts** What was in the briefcase?
3. **Recall Facts** What type of ticket did Mr. Fink say he bought?
4. **Use Chronology to Locate Information** Use your knowledge of chronology to find the place in the story when the inspector asked Mr. Fink to empty his pockets.

"Think and Search" Questions

5. **Make Inferences** Why did Inspector Ketchum follow Mr. Fink into the coffee shop?

6. **Contrast** What did Mr. Fink say was in the briefcase? How was it different from what Inspector Ketchum found in the briefcase?

"Author and You" Questions

7. **Evaluate Evidence** Did Mr. Fink expect to be asked to empty his pockets? What tells you this?
8. **Make Judgments** Why did Mr. Fink look puzzled when Inspector Ketchum opened the briefcase?

"On Your Own" Question

9. **Evaluate** How do you think Mr. Fink felt after Inspector Ketchum found out that he was not telling the truth?

Activity Book
p. 26

Student
CD-ROM

Build Reading Fluency

Adjust Your Reading Rate for Quotations

Reading quotations helps you learn to adjust your reading rate. You must pause and read with expression. Reading with expression makes others want to listen to you.

Reread the conversation between Inspector Will Ketchum and Mr. Fink. Look for the quotation marks (". . ."").

1. With a partner, take turns rereading paragraphs 5–6 on page 43 aloud.
2. Read the quotations with expression.
3. Pause after each quotation.
4. Choose the quotation you like best.
5. Read it aloud in front of the class.

Listen, Speak, Interact

Interpret Text Through Dramatization

In "The Sneak Thief," the author uses dialogue, the actual words that characters say to each other. Read the story as a "Reader's Theater."

1. Work in groups of three.
2. Decide on roles. One person is the narrator. One person is the inspector. One person is Mr. Fink.
3. Dramatize the story by acting it out. As you read, show your understanding of the text and make your partners want to listen.
4. Show what the characters are thinking and feeling as you read their words.
5. Present your dramatization to the class.
6. Analyze your classmates' dramatizations. Are the characters believable?

Elements of Literature

Recognize Problem and Resolution

Most mysteries have a **problem** and a **resolution.** The **problem** is often a question that needs to be answered. The **resolution** is how a person solves the problem or answers the question.

Problem: Did Mr. Fink steal the briefcase?

Resolution: Inspector Ketchum uses clues. He figures out that Mr. Fink stole the briefcase. He arrests Mr. Fink.

1. Read these sentences. Decide whether they are problems or resolutions. Write your answers in your Reading Log.
   a. How can you learn more about outer space?
   b. You can read a book about outer space.
   c. You go to the movies first. Then you go to the park.
   d. Your friend wants to go to the movies. You want to go to the park. What should you do?
2. Write a sentence describing a problem that you have now or that you had in the past. Then write a possible resolution.

Reading Log   Activity Book
                  p. 27

Student
CD-ROM

Word Study

Apply Knowledge of Letter-Sound Correspondences

Some English words contain the letters *th*. These letters usually stand for a sound that is different from the sounds of *t* and *h*.

1. Listen as your teacher pronounces the *th* sounds in these words. Then repeat after your teacher.

<u>th</u>ief   <u>th</u>ing
<u>th</u>ree   tru<u>th</u>
<u>th</u>anks   too<u>th</u>

2. Practice reading these sentences with a partner.
  a. A man wi<u>th</u> <u>th</u>e eyes of a sneak <u>th</u>ief attracted his attention.
  b. Were <u>th</u>ere <u>th</u>ree magazines?
  c. Was <u>th</u>e suspect telling <u>th</u>e tru<u>th</u>?

Activity Book   Student
p. 28   CD-ROM

Grammar Focus

Identify Simple, Compound, and Complex Sentences

All sentences have **clauses.** A clause has a subject and a verb. A **subject** is who or what the sentence is about. A **verb** tells something about the subject.

There are three main sentence types: **simple sentence, compound sentences,** and **complex sentences.**

A **simple sentence** has one **independent clause.** An independent clause is a clause that can stand alone as a sentence.

You want milk.

A **compound sentence** has two or more independent clauses. These independent clauses are joined by a comma and a conjunction like *or, but,* or *and.*

You want milk, <u>but</u> I want juice.

A **complex sentence** has one independent clause and one **dependent clause.** A dependent clause is a clause that cannot stand alone as a sentence. Dependent clauses begin with words like *because, when, that,* or *although.*

<u>Although</u> you want milk, I want juice.

Copy these sentences on a piece of paper. Write whether each sentence is a simple sentence, a compound sentence, or a complex sentence.

1. Mai plays the piano, and Luis plays the drums.
2. When Ali is at home, Anna is at work.
3. Alta ran home with her brother.

Activity Book   Student   Student
pp. 29–30   Handbook   CD-ROM

From Reading to Writing

Write Dialogue in a Mystery

Many parts of "The Sneak Thief" have dialogue—what characters say to each other. However, the author does not use dialogue when he explains how Inspector Ketchum solves the crime. Write a dialogue between Inspector Ketchum and Mr. Fink for the solution of the crime.

1. Inspector Ketchum will explain what clues he used to solve the crime. Use the information in paragraph 16.
2. Mr. Fink will say why he is surprised that he was caught. Use information from paragraph 17.
3. Include how you think Mr. Fink feels after he is caught.
4. Reread paragraphs 6 to 8 of the selection. Use these as a model.

5. Use different sentence types— simple, compound, and complex.
6. Use correct punctuation for dependent clauses.
7. Use some chronology words such as *first, then, next,* and *after.*

> Inspector Ketchum said, "Mr. Fink, I know you stole the briefcase because you did not have _____, _____, and _____ in your pockets!"
>
> Mr. Fink said, "You caught me! I did not expect you to _____. I feel _____ because _____."

Activity Book
p. 31

Student Handbook

Across Content Areas

LANGUAGE ARTS

Learn Words About the Law

"The Sneak Thief" is about someone who broke the law (Fink) and someone who protects the law (Ketchum).

suspect: a person whom the police *think* committed a crime
criminal: a person who committed a crime
innocent: did not commit a crime
guilty: committed a crime

Copy these sentences. Complete each one with a law word.

1. The police aren't sure if the man stole the bicycle. He is still a _____ .
2. John Smith went to jail because he robbed a bank. He is a _____ .
3. Under U.S. law, you are _____ until you are proven _____ .

Activity Book
p. 32

CHAPTER 5

The Legend of Sleepy Hollow

a legend by
Washington Irving

adapted by
Jack Kelly

Objectives

Reading Identify imagery as you read a legend.

Listening and Speaking Talk about senses.

Grammar Use pronoun referents.

Writing Write a character description.

Content Social Studies: Read a timeline.

Use Prior Knowledge

Compare Oral Traditions

Most cultures and regions have stories that are very old. They are told from grandparent to parent to child. This is called the **oral tradition.** Examples are stories about La Llorona, Atlantis, Rip Van Winkle, and El Dorado.

1. With your class, talk about old stories that you know.
2. Make a chart of the oral traditions you and your classmates know. How are they the same? How are they different?

Oral Traditions	
Culture/Region of Origin	What the Story Is About

Build Background

Sleepy Hollow

The selection you will read takes place in Sleepy Hollow. Sleepy Hollow is a real town in the state of New York. It is a quiet town near the Hudson River with many parks and forests. The people who live in Sleepy Hollow like the town because it is peaceful.

SOCIAL STUDIES

Content Connection

The Dutch (people from The Netherlands) were the first Europeans to live along the Hudson River. They founded New York City and other cities and towns. One of them was Sleepy Hollow.

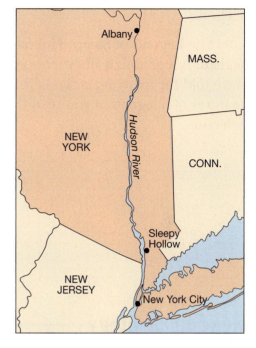

Build Vocabulary

Spell Frequently Misspelled Words

Some words are pronounced alike but have different spellings and meanings. Look at the example in the chart.

Copy these sentences in your Personal Dictionary. Fill in the blanks with *there, their,* or *they're*. Check your answers with a partner.

1. They didn't get up on time, so _____ late for school again.

2. I can't find my book. Oh! It's over _____ .

3. They have already finished _____ homework.

Word	Meaning	Example
there	a word used to start a statement or to indicate a place	**There** are many old stories in my culture. I'm going **there**.
their	possessive form of *they*	They told stories. **Their** stories were interesting.
they're	contraction of *they are*	My grandfather likes to tell stories. **They're** interesting.

Personal Dictionary

Activity Book p. 33

Student CD-ROM

Text Structure

Legend

"The Legend of Sleepy Hollow" is a **legend.** A legend is a story that people have told for many years. Look for these features of a legend as you read the selection.

Legend	
Tradition	The story is told from generation to generation.
Setting	The story takes place a long time ago, in a real place.
Amazing Characters and Events	The story is based on truth, but some characters and events are exaggerated or made up.

Student CD-ROM

Reading Strategy

Identify Imagery

Many writers use **imagery.** Imagery is writing that helps readers form **images** (pictures) in their minds. Imagery often refers to the senses: seeing, hearing, tasting, touching, or smelling.

He was a <u>tall</u>, <u>lanky</u> <u>young</u> man.

The words *tall, lanky,* and *young* help you picture the man in your mind.

Describing images can also help you learn and recall words.

1. Write these sentences from the reading in your Reading Log.

   His small head was perched on a skinny neck.

   The room would glow from the heat of a crackling wood fire.

2. Underline the words that help you form images in your mind.
3. Draw a picture for each sentence.
4. Share your pictures with a partner.

Reading Log   Student CD-ROM

THE LEGEND OF

Sleepy Hollow

by Washington Irving

adapted by Jack Kelly

Identify Imagery

Which words in this paragraph help you form pictures in your mind? Think of your image of this paragraph. Which words do you recall in the image?

1　When the good folk of Sleepy Hollow got together around the fire on dark and windy nights, their talk often turned to a **mysterious** being who had been seen riding along nearby roads.

2　"He was a **Hessian cavalryman** who lost his head in the Revolutionary War," one said. "A **cannonball** took it clean off."

3　"He's a ghost, the commander of all the evil spirits in these parts," another claimed.

4　Nobody knew for sure. But many a farmer, out late at night, would see this **apparition** go swooping past—an enormous, terrible figure mounted on a powerful **stallion**. He was the Headless Horseman!

5　"His body's buried in the churchyard," said one man, who claimed to be an expert on the subject. "At night he rides out to the battlefield where he was killed to look for his missing head. Toward dawn you'll see him go tearing through the Hollow as fast as he can ride. He has to get back to his grave before **daybreak**."

Audio
CD 1, Tr. 5

---

mysterious　not known
Hessian　a soldier from the nation of Germany
cavalryman　a soldier trained to fight on horses
cannonball　a metal ball that is shot from a large gun

apparition　a ghostly figure
stallion　a horse
daybreak　morning

6   One of those who listened most closely to these ghostly **tales** was Ichabod Crane. Ichabod was the town's schoolmaster, and a man who thought he knew a thing or two about ghosts himself.

7   Ichabod, indeed, looked something like a **crane.** He was a tall, **lanky** young man with long arms and legs, hands that **dangled** a mile out of his sleeves, and feet like shovels. His small head was perched on a skinny neck. He had huge ears and a long, pointed nose that made his head seem like a **weather vane** pointing the direction of the wind. Many said he looked like a scarecrow from some cornfield.

8   Now, Sleepy Hollow is one of the most peaceful spots in the world. It's a hidden valley along the Hudson River that's just as quiet and **drowsy** and dreamy as it can possibly be.

9   "This is a **haunted** spot," an old farmer whispered to Ichabod one night. "The sky is full of **meteors** and shooting stars. And there's nightmares that will slip into your dreams."

10   During the day, Ichabod didn't have time to think of ghosts and spirits. He was busy running his little one-room schoolhouse. If you went by on a warm drowsy day you might hear the **murmuring** voices of his pupils **reciting** their lessons.

> ### Identify Imagery
>
> Which words help you picture Ichabod Crane in your mind? Think of your image. Which words do you recall?

---

tales   stories
crane   a tall, long-necked bird
lanky   skinny
dangled   hung loosely
weather vane   an instrument that indicates wind direction

drowsy   sleepy
haunted   visited by someone or something as a ghost
meteors   large rocks or pieces of metal from outer space
murmuring   low and unclear sounding
reciting   repeating or saying aloud

11   Ichabod liked his pupils. . . . He always tried hard to keep on good terms with [their] families. . . . He had no choice. His salary was very small, and his **appetite** was very large.

Identify Imagery

What animal is Ichabod Crane compared to in this paragraph?

12   "What's for dinner?" were often the first words out of Ichabod's mouth. Though skinny, he could swallow a huge meal the way an **anaconda** snake does.

13   As part of his pay, he would room and take his meals with the farmers whose children went to his school. He lived with each family for a week, then moved on. Over the year, he made the rounds of the neighborhood, all his belongings tied up in a big cotton **handkerchief.**

14   Farmers in those days sometimes thought that schooling cost too much, or that schoolmasters were just lazy **drones.** To make the **burden** lighter, and to make himself useful, Ichabod would help his hosts with their chores whenever he could. He helped the farmers to make hay. He lent a hand when they **mended** their fences, took horses to water, drove cows to pasture, and cut wood for the winter fire.

---

appetite   desire for food
anaconda   a very large snake
handkerchief   a cloth used for wiping the nose or mouth

drones   people who live off others
burden   a responsibility or duty
mended   fixed

15 "Let me take care of the little lambs," he would say to the mothers. And he would sit for hours with one child on his knee, at the same time using his foot to rock another in its **cradle.**

16 One of Ichabod's great pleasures was to pass long winter evenings sitting by the fire with farmers' wives as they told tales of ghosts and **goblins.** They would talk while they spun wool and roasted apples in the fireplace.

17 "That field down **yonder** is haunted," someone would say.

18 "There's a goblin that lives under the bridge," another would claim. "I've seen him with my own eyes. . . ."

19 It was pleasant telling these tales while sitting **snug** in a chimney corner. The room would glow with the heat of the **crackling** wood fire. And of course no ghost dared to stick his head inside.

Identify Imagery

Which words in this paragraph help you form an image in your mind? Think of your image. Which words do you recall?

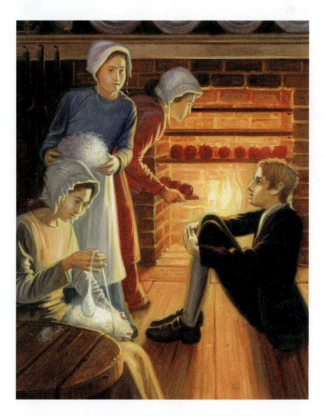

---

cradle   a small bed for a baby
goblins   make-believe creatures who do bad things
yonder   far away

snug   comfortable
crackling   making snapping or breaking noises

Identify Imagery

Which words help you picture the snowy evening?

20   But walking home **afterwards** was another story. Then all the **terrors** of the **fables** took form around the **timid** schoolmaster. Fearful shapes and shadows **loomed** along his path in the snowy evening. Seeing the light of a distant window, he wished he were back safe inside.

21   "Oh, keep away from me!" he would **exclaim.** But it was only a bush covered with snow, not a ghost.

22   "What was that?" he whispered. But it was merely the sound of his own feet breaking through the snow.

23   It got so that he **dreaded** even to look over his shoulder, in case someone was following him. But there was one spirit that Ichabod Crane feared more than any other. It was the one the old farmers' wives called the Galloping Hessian of the Hollow.

---

afterwards   at a later time
terrors   intense fears
fables   stories that have a lesson
timid   shy, scared

loomed   waited
exclaim   shout
dreaded   feared

Identify Imagery

What images are used to describe the glen? Think of your images. Which words do you recall?

24   Sometimes, very late at night, walking through some dark, shadowy **glen,** Ichabod would suddenly hear a rushing blast come howling through the trees.

25   "It's only the wind," he would tell himself. But he could never completely convince himself that it wasn't—the Headless Horseman!

---

glen   a low area of land between mountains or large hills

About the Author

Washington Irving (1783–1859)

Washington Irving was one of the first great writers in the United States. People all over the world know his stories. Washington Irving was born in New York City. He visited the Hudson Valley, and some of his greatest stories happen there. Washington Irving spent the last years of his life living near the town of Sleepy Hollow.

► Why do you think Washington Irving wrote "The Legend of Sleepy Hollow"? What questions would you ask Washington Irving?

Beyond the Reading

Reading Comprehension

Question-Answer Relationships (QAR)

"Right There" Questions

1. **Recall Facts** Who do the townspeople think the Headless Horseman is?
2. **Recall Facts** What is Ichabod Crane's job?
3. **Recall Facts** Where is Sleepy Hollow located?

"Think and Search" Questions

4. **Give Reasons** Why does the Headless Horseman appear?
5. **Give Reasons** Why does Ichabod Crane like to stay on the good side of the townspeople?

"Author and You" Questions

6. **Describe** What are three words that the author uses to describe Ichabod Crane?

7. **Make Inferences** Why is Ichabod Crane afraid when he leaves the homes of the farmers' wives?

"On Your Own" Questions

8. **Compare Your Experiences** Have you ever been afraid because of a scary story? Explain.
9. **Understand Setting** Do you think that Sleepy Hollow was a good place for the story to happen? Why or why not?
10. **Compare Legends** Do you know a legend similar to this one? How is it the same? How is it different?

Activity Book
p. 34

Student
CD-ROM

Build Reading Fluency

Read Silently

Reading silently for long periods of time helps you become a better reader. It helps you learn to read faster.

1. Listen to the audio recording of "The Legend of Sleepy Hollow."
2. Listen to the chunks of words as you follow along on page 54.
3. Reread paragraphs 1–4 silently two times.
4. Your teacher will time your second reading.
5. Raise your hand when you are finished.

Listen, Speak, Interact

Talk About Senses

"The Legend of Sleepy Hollow" uses imagery to help you form pictures in your mind. You use different senses to form these pictures. The five senses are touch, taste, smell, sight, and sound.

Touch	Taste	Smell	Sight	Sound

1. Work with a partner.
2. Read the sentences. For each sentence, decide which sense helps you form an image.
   a. The apples roasted in the fire.
   b. The room glowed with the heat of the crackling wood fire.
   c. The loud noise came howling through the trees.
   d. He had huge ears and a pointed nose.
   e. The bread was salty and sweet.
3. Copy the chart. Write the letters of the sentences in the columns.
4. Compare your answers to those of another pair of students. Use the names of the senses as you present. Are your answers the same as or different from the other pair's?

Elements of Literature

Analyze Setting and Tone

In "The Legend of Sleepy Hollow," Washington Irving tells us about the **setting** of the story—where it takes place.

We also learn about the main character, Ichabod Crane. Irving uses **tone** to tell us what he thinks about the character. His writing tells us what Ichabod is like.

1. With a partner, reread paragraphs 1 and 8. Then answer these questions.
   a. What kind of community is Sleepy Hollow? Describe the images of it that you have in your mind.
   b. This is a scary story. Why do you think the author describes Sleepy Hollow as he does?
2. What is Irving's tone in paragraph 7? Is it funny or serious?
3. Reread paragraphs 10 to 16.
   a. What do you learn about Ichabod?
   b. How would you describe him?
   c. What is Irving's attitude toward Ichabod? Does Irving suggest that Ichabod is a good teacher? Is he helpful?
4. Find other paragraphs in which Irving's tone tells you what he thinks about Ichabod Crane.

Reading Log   Activity Book   Student
                    p. 35   CD-ROM

Word Study

Identify Root Words and the Suffix *-less*

Many English words have a root word and a suffix. A **root word** is the main part of a word. A **suffix** is a word part added to the end of a root word. Adding a suffix can change the meaning of the root word.

The suffix *-less* means "without." The word *headless* has the root word *head*. *Headless* means "without a head."

1. Write the words in the box in your Personal Dictionary.
2. Circle the root word. Underline the suffix.

Words	Definitions
careless	without fear
heartless	without care
fearless	without a heart

3. Match each word with the correct definition. Check your answers in a dictionary.

Personal Dictionary   The Heinle Newbury House Dictionary   Activity Book p. 36   Student CD-ROM

Grammar Focus

Use Pronoun Referents

A **pronoun** is a word that takes the place of a noun. *She, her, I, me, he,* and *him* are examples of pronouns.

A **pronoun referent** is the noun that the pronoun replaces. In writing it is important to keep your pronoun referents clear.

<u>Marcos</u> is busy all day. <u>He</u> goes to school and then plays soccer.

The pronoun *He* takes the place of *Marcos*.

1. Copy these sentences on a piece of paper. Look at the underlined pronouns. Find the pronoun referent in the other sentence.

a. Sleepy Hollow is one of the most peaceful spots in the world. <u>It</u> is a hidden valley along the Hudson River.
b. Ichabod was the town's schoolmaster. <u>He</u> taught children all day.

2. Reread paragraph 2 of the reading. Find the referents for the pronouns *he* and *it*.

Activity Book pp. 37–38   Student Handbook   Student CD-ROM

From Reading to Writing

Write a Character Description

Washington Irving tells us what Ichabod Crane looks like. He uses adjectives such as *tall, lanky,* and *skinny.*

1. Choose a person that you know. This person can be a friend or family member. Or the person can be someone famous.
2. Write two adjectives that describe what this person looks like. Is the person very tall? Small? Beautiful?

> This person is named _____ . He/She is _____ as _____ . He/She is also _____ _____ . I think this person is very _____ .

3. Write a paragraph that describes this person. Remember to indent.
4. Use a dictionary or an online reference to check your spelling.
5. Be sure to use pronouns correctly and that the referents are clear.

Activity Book
p. 39

Student
Handbook

Across Content Areas

Read a Timeline

New York City, the largest city in the United States, had a different name when it was first settled. First study these facts.

a. In the 1500s and 1600s, Europeans explored North America.
b. The Netherlands sent explorers to North America.
c. The capital of The Netherlands is Amsterdam.
d. People from The Netherlands are called the Dutch.

Now look at the timeline and answer these questions.

1. What was New York City first called?
2. Why did they name it that?
3. How long did it take for the population to grow to 450 people?
4. When did the name change to New York?

Activity Book
p. 40

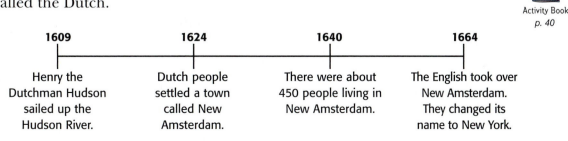

1609	1624	1640	1664
Henry the Dutchman Hudson sailed up the Hudson River.	Dutch people settled a town called New Amsterdam.	There were about 450 people living in New Amsterdam.	The English took over New Amsterdam. They changed its name to New York.

Listening and Speaking Workshop

Describe an Animal

Topic

In this unit, you read about the Loch Ness monster. Some people believe that the monster is a real animal. Choose an animal. The animal can be real or made-up. Describe your animal to the class.

Step 1: Choose or create your animal.

1. Draw a picture of your animal. Include details.
2. Write the name of your animal.

Step 2: List details about your animal.

1. Write words that describe your animal.
2. Use your senses to describe your animal. How does your animal look? Sound? Smell? Feel?
3. Write your answers in a Sense Chart like the one shown.

Animal	See	Hear	Smell	Touch
Loch Ness monster	large teeth, big eyes	loud noises	like the lake	wet scales

Step 3: Write descriptive sentences.

1. Reread paragraphs 3 and 4 of "The Loch Ness Monster" on page 6. Use them as models for writing.
2. Write five short sentences that describe your animal. Use the details in the Sense Chart.

   The Loch Ness monster has large teeth and big eyes. It also has scales.

   Remember pronoun referents. Here, the word *it* means "the Loch Ness monster."
3. Write one or two sentences about where your animal lives and what it eats.
4. Use a variety of sentence types.
   a. Make sure each sentence has a subject and a verb.
   b. Make sure your pronoun referents are clear.

Step 4: Review your sentences.

1. Answer the following questions:
   a. Do I have enough facts?
   b. Are my details interesting?
   c. Do my descriptions make sense?
2. Review your sentences. Write your sentences on note cards.

Step 5: Practice your description.

1. Practice with a partner. Take turns.
2. Use your note cards and drawing.
3. Speak slowly and clearly. Listen carefully as your partner speaks.
4. Have your partner fill out the Active Listening Checklist on a piece of paper. You fill out the Speaking Checklist.
5. Use the checklists to revise your work.

Step 6: Present your animal.

1. Speak slowly and clearly.
2. Record your presentation. Use the Presentation Checklist in your Student Handbook to evaluate your presentation.

✔ Active Listening Checklist

1. The description was very detailed / not detailed.
2. There was enough / not enough information about the animal.
3. I want to know more about ＿＿＿ .
4. I think this description could be more interesting if ＿＿＿ .

✔ Speaking Checklist

1. Did I speak slowly and clearly?
2. Were my details interesting?
3. Did I show my drawing?

Student Handbook

Viewing Workshop

View and Think

Analyze a Mystery Movie

Not all mysteries are stories in books. Many movies also are mysteries.

1. Watch a mystery movie. Ask your school librarian to pick one out.
2. Take notes as you watch the movie.
   a. Write the problem that the characters are trying to solve.
   b. List clues that you notice.
   c. Write your ideas about how to solve the problem. Your ideas may change as you watch.
   d. Note how the characters solve the problem. Were your ideas right?
3. Write a summary of the movie.

Further Viewing

Watch the *Visions* CNN Video for Unit 1. Do the Video Worksheet.

CNN Video

Writer's Workshop

Response to Literature: Compare Two Texts

Writing Prompt

In this unit, you read three informational texts, "The Loch Ness Monster," "Mystery of the Cliff Dwellers," and "Yawning." Write a report in which you compare and contrast two of these.

Step 1: Do research.

Do your research with a partner.

1. Reread the three texts. Make a chart. Organize the chart into three columns. Write the name of each text at the top of the columns. Use the chart to write a summary of the kind of information each text gives and how the author presents information.
2. Discuss the questions in the chart. Write "yes" or "no" for each reading.

3. Form additional questions. Revise your questions and add them to the chart.

Step 2: Choose your texts.

Decide which two texts you want to write about.

Step 3: Make comparisons and contrasts.

1. Choose the two comparisons and two contrasts from the chart that you think are the most important.
2. Write a sentence for each comparison and contrast. Examples: "Both 'Yawning' and 'The Loch Ness Monster' tell about an experiment." "'Yawning' tells about an experiment, but 'The Mystery of the Cliff Dwellers' does not."

Does the text . . .	The Loch Ness Monster	Yawning	Mystery of the Cliff Dwellers
. . . include historical background?	yes	no	yes
. . . tell about the experiences or opinions of ordinary people?			
. . . include descriptions?			
. . . include scientific information?			
. . . ask questions?			
. . . talk about an experiment?			

Step 4: Write your first draft.

1. Write your first paragraph.
   a. Name the two texts. Capitalize and punctuate the titles correctly to clarify meaning. Use capital letters for the first word and the important words, and put the title in quotation marks.
   b. Explain that informational texts use several ways of giving and explaining information.
   c. State that the two texts are both similar and different in the kind of information that they give and in how they do it. This is your **thesis statement**—the statement of your overall topic.
2. Write your second paragraph.
   a. State that the texts are similar in some ways. This is the **topic sentence** of this paragraph.
   b. Give examples to support this topic sentence. Use the two comparisons that you chose in Step 3.
   c. Use simple, compound, and complex sentences. Be sure to punctuate your independent and dependent clauses correctly.
   d. Use prepositional phrases, for example, "On page 8 of . . ."
3. Write your third paragraph.
   a. Write a topic sentence saying that the texts' features are different in some ways.
   b. Use the examples of contrast from Step 3.
   c. Make effective transitions between your sentences using words like *first, then,* and *finally.*

4. Write your conclusion.
   a. Say how these features can help the reader understand an informational text.
   b. Give your opinion. For example: Which text do you think has better features? Why? Use precise (exact) words in your answers.

Step 5: Revise.

1. Work with a partner. Listen as your partner reads your comparison to you.
   a. Is the right information in the paragraphs?
   b. Is the language precise?
2. Revise your text as necessary. You may want to:
   a. add or delete text
   b. elaborate unclear ideas
   c. combine sentences or ideas
   d. rearrange sentences

Step 6: Edit and proofread.

1. Proofread your story. Use a computer spell and grammar check, if possible.
2. Use the Editor's Checklist in your Student Handbook.

Step 7: Publish.

1. Type your final report on a computer or use your best handwriting.
2. Read your report to your class.

Student Handbook

Projects

These projects will help you learn more about real-life mysteries.

Project 1: Dramatize "The Legend of Sleepy Hollow"

In groups of three or four, act out part of "The Legend of Sleepy Hollow."

1. Reread paragraphs 1 to 5 of the story.
2. Study the main facts. Paraphrase them (tell them in your own words).
3. Each of you will be a person who lives in Sleepy Hollow. Imagine that you are sitting around a warm fire at night, telling scary stories.
4. As you speak, remember:
   a. Your purpose is to scare your friends. Speak in a way that does this.
   b. You are with family and friends. Speak in a way that shows this.
   c. Show that you are familiar with your audience and your topic.
5. As you listen, think about other speakers' purposes and perspectives—what they think or feel about the topic.

Project 2: Make a Poster About a Mysterious Place

Choose a mysterious place. Make a poster about it.

1. Choose one of these mysterious places or another one that you know about:
   a. Sleepy Hollow, New York
   b. Stonehenge, England
   c. Machu Picchu, Peru
2. Find pictures of your mysterious place. Use the name of your place to search on the Internet. Or make copies from books. Glue these pictures onto a poster.
3. Find facts about your mysterious place. Use reference books from the library or the Internet.
4. Organize and summarize the information you find in a chart.
5. Use your chart to write answers to these questions on your poster.
   a. What is the name of your mysterious place?
   b. Where is this place?
   c. Why is this place mysterious? What happened there?

Easter Island

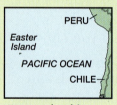

Easter Island is an island in the South Pacific Ocean.

Easter Island has very large sculptures. People are not sure who made the sculptures.

Further Reading

These books discuss mysteries. Read one or more of them. Write your thoughts and feelings about what you read in your Reading Log. Answer these questions:

1. What is the most interesting mystery that you read about?
2. What are some explanations for the mysteries that you read about?

Great Book of Whodunit Puzzles: Mini Mysteries for You to Solve

by Falcon Travis, Sterling Publications, 1993. This book provides several short mysteries that you can try to solve yourself. There is a section with clues to help you. There is also a solutions section.

The Legend of Sleepy Hollow

by Washington Irving, William Morrow & Company, 1990. Ichabod Crane is the schoolmaster in Sleepy Hollow. First, Crane hears the story of the Headless Horseman. Then he actually sees him!

Seven Wonders of the Ancient World

by Lynn Curlee, Atheneum, 2002. Read about the Seven Wonders of the World that have puzzled people for centuries. This book describes the Hanging Gardens of Babylon and the Great Pyramid at Giza.

Great Mysteries of the West

by Ferenc Morton Szasz (editor), Fulcrum Publishing, 1993. There are many mysteries in the western United States. This book discusses the disappearance of the Anasazi Indians. It also looks at rock art in the Southwest and the sea serpents of the Pacific Northwest.

Strange Stuff: True Stories of Odd Places and Things

by Janet Nuzum Myers, Linnet Books, 1999. This book talks about real-life mysteries such as quicksand and black holes. It also discusses Bigfoot and the Bermuda Triangle.

Wolf Rider

by Avi, Bradbury Press, 1986. This psychological thriller shows Andy, 15, trying to convince skeptical adults that the crank call he received truly is a murderer's confession.

Time Stops for No Mouse

by Michael Hoeye, Putnum Publishing Group, 2002. Mouse watchmaker Hermux Tantamoq leads a simple life until he meets Linka Perflinger, adventuress. Her disappearance leads him overnight into a life of detection and danger. A cosmetics tycoon, a newspaper reporter, and assorted other citizens of Pinchester contribute to the action and mystery. Hoeye follows this easy-to-read mix of suspense, wit, and fantasy with another, *The Sands of Time,* about the same characters on a desert adventure that nearly costs them their lives.

The Ghost in the Tokaido Inn

by Dorothy and Thomas Hoobler, Philomel Press, 1999. A jewel theft, a wise judge, the theater world, and 18th century Japan combine to make a Sherlock Holmes style mystery that is much more than a ghost story. Seikei, 14, would like to be a Samurai. While on a business trip with his merchant father he has the most challenging, suspenseful adventure of his life. He discovers that merchants can also exhibit Samurai attitudes.

Companion Web site

Reading Log

Heinle Reading Library
The Adventures of
Sherlock Holmes

UNIT 2

Survival

Ominous Coastline, photo by Sanford/Agliolo, 2000.

View the Picture

1. Describe what you see in this picture. How does it show survival?
2. Do you know any survival stories from current news or books you have read?

In this unit, you will read excerpts from three novels and two informational texts. You will learn about different survival problems that people can have. You will also learn to write these different forms.

CHAPTER 1

How I Survived My Summer Vacation

an excerpt from a novel
by Robin Friedman

Objectives

Reading Make inferences using text evidence and experience as you read an excerpt from a novel.

Listening and Speaking Predict a part of a story.

Grammar Use progressive tenses.

Writing Write realistic fiction.

Content Science: Identify food groups.

Use Prior Knowledge

Discuss Summer Experiences

In this chapter, you will read about a boy's experience during his summer vacation. Tell a small group about your summer.

1. Recall some interesting experiences you had one summer. Include both fun and difficult experiences.
2. Write your ideas on a note card. Look at the example.
3. Meet with a small group. Use your notes to tell about your experiences. Listen to your classmates tell about their experiences.

4. If you do not understand something, ask a classmate to clarify (to explain).

> *My Summer*
> - *My best friend moved away.*
> - *I went on a trip with my family.*
> - *I took care of my little sister.*

Build Background

Tofu

The main characters in the reading eat a food called tofu. Tofu is made from soybeans. Tofu is usually white, and it looks like cheese. Some people eat tofu because it is healthy. Many people who do not eat meat eat tofu instead.

Content Connection

Farmers in the United States grow a lot of soybeans. The major growing areas are in the midwestern and southern states.

States that Grow the Most Soybeans

Build Vocabulary

Use Precise Wording

Good writers use precise (exact and accurate) words. Here are some words from the reading. They are all about speech. Learning and using these words will help you write well.

Word	Meaning
yell	to shout
croak	to make a deep sound like that of a frog
enunciate	to speak clearly and precisely
interrupt	to stop someone from doing something, such as talking

Write the words and their meanings in your Personal Dictionary. Then write a sentence using each one. Use these situations.

1. Your brother wakes up in the morning and has a sore throat.
2. Your teacher gives you advice about an oral presentation that you are going to give.
3. You are at a soccer game and your team makes a point.
4. Your friend is talking, but you hear your father calling you.

Personal Dictionary   The Heinle Newbury House Dictionary   Activity Book p. 41   Student CD-ROM

Text Structure

Realistic Fiction

This reading, "How I Survived My Summer Vacation," is from a **realistic fiction** novel. Realistic fiction is a made-up story. However, it could happen in real life.

As you read the selection, notice the characters, setting, and events. Think about how these features make the selection seem realistic. Use your own experience to help you.

Realistic Fiction	
Characters	The people in the story do and say things that people do and say in real life.
Setting	The story happens in a place that could be real.
Events	The things that happen in the story could happen in real life.

Student
CD-ROM

Reading Strategy

Make Inferences Using Text Evidence and Experience

Writers do not always tell us directly what is happening in a story. They may write clues (details). These clues are **text evidence.** You can also use your **experience** to help make inferences.

1. Read this sentence. What inference can you make?

   Yeny was yawning and stretching in class.

   a. Yeny was up until 2:00 A.M. this morning.
   b. Yeny is never tired.

2. Use text evidence and your knowledge to make inferences as you read and listen to "How I Survived My Summer Vacation." Organize your ideas in a chart like the one here in your Reading Log.

Clues in the Text	My Own Experience	Inference
yawning and stretching	I often yawn and stretch when I am tired.	**?**

Reading Log

Student
CD-ROM

How I Survived My Summer Vacation

an excerpt from a novel
by Robin Friedman

1 I stared at my words until they began to **blur** into strange black shapes. A great opening line for a novel, I thought foolishly, grinning like an idiot and feeling oh-so-pleased with myself . . .

2 The next five minutes passed in slow motion while I struggled to think of another line. I stared out my window for **inspiration,** but our overgrown backyard offered up nothing. I looked at the roof, the fence, the driveway, the old oak tree, the herb garden.

3 Nothing. Absolutely nothing.

4 My eyes came to rest on the writing book next to me on the desk. GET RICH QUICK! the title screamed in bold, gold-stamped letters. *Write a Bestseller in Less Than a Year* it promised underneath the title in smaller type.

5 Less than a year? At this rate it would take a **century** . . .

6 I sighed.

7 If I was really going to write a novel this summer, then I had to write a second sentence. And a third, and a fourth, and a thousandth. But it was hopeless as usual, I thought in my **patented** grumpy way.

> **Make Inferences Using Text Evidence and Experience**
>
> Is the character finding it easy or hard to write his novel? What text evidence tells you?

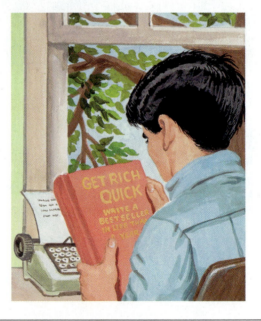

---

blur make it harder to see clearly

inspiration something that makes a person work hard or be creative

century 100 years

patented individual, very own (humorous usage)

8   A few more minutes passed as I silently **groped** for inspiration. A bushy-tailed squirrel raced across the lawn under my window, momentarily giving me an idea, but as soon as it was gone, so was my idea.

Make Inferences Using Text Evidence and Experience

How do you think the character feels right now? How does your experience help you make this inference?

9   "This isn't working," I said out loud. I pulled out the sheet of paper from my typewriter. I read the great opening line again, sighed again, and tore the paper into a million pieces. I fed another sheet of paper into the typewriter, trying to control my rapid breathing.

10   Stay calm, I told myself. It's going to be O.K. Panicking is for wimps.

11   The **aroma** of coffee began to drift into my room, which could only mean one thing. Dad was downstairs in the kitchen, preparing his signature breakfast dish: scrambled tofu with fig sauce.

12   Though all kids claim to have this problem, my parents are a *true* embarrassment to me.

13   "Jackie! **Grub**'s ready! Come on down!"

14   It was Dad, ready for breakfast at 9 A.M. on the dot, as usual. He always cooks precisely on the hour, whether it's lunch at 12 noon or dinner at 6 P.M. Mom says it's a **compulsion.** I say it's insanity.

---

groped   searched for something with the hands as if in darkness
aroma   a pleasant smell, especially of cooking

grub   informal word for food
compulsion   a need to do something that cannot be stopped

15   "Just a second!" I yelled down **irritably** . . .

16   I glared in the direction of the stairs, as if Mom and Dad were standing on the landing with their wheat-germ muffins and scrambled tofu with fig sauce in hand. Their idea of eating breakfast together on Saturday mornings has always gotten on my nerves, but this summer it was bugging me extra good . . .

17   Sighing again, I **dragged** my body down the stairs and into the kitchen, getting angrier with each step.

Make Inferences Using Text Evidence and Experience

How do you think Jackie feels about eating breakfast with his parents? What text evidence can you use?

18   "You know, I've been thinking," I said as I took a seat at the table. "I may be outgrowing Saturday morning breakfasts. After all, I'll be in high school next fall. I think we should reconsider its place in the family routine."

19   "Lighten up, Jackie," Dad replied, stirring his coffee. "Have a muffin." Though both my parents are committed to "healthful eating," Dad has a severe weakness for coffee, which he drinks black. I've never understood why he stirs it, since he never adds anything. Another compulsion, I guess.

20   I made a face as he passed me a plate of his **infamous, deformed**-looking, sawdust-tasting wheat-germ muffins. I might as well have been performing for my goldfish, though, because Dad didn't look at me. I passed the plate back to him, muffins intact.

---

irritably   in an annoyed or bothered way
dragged   pulled with difficulty

infamous   famous because of something bad
deformed   not in its normal shape or appearance

21   Have a muffin, he says. That was Dad's answer to everything. Well, it wasn't going to do the trick this time. It might have worked when I was ten or eleven, but now . . . I knew better. And I knew what I wanted. I had sworn . . . that by the end of the summer I'd have written the great American novel. I had wanted to be a writer ever since I was five years old. Writing was what I loved. I was great at it, in fact.

22   As if reading my mind, Dad turned to me and said, "Are you thinking about your great American novel again?"

23   I involuntarily clenched my fists but told myself to be cool.

24   Mom didn't seem to hear me or Dad. Before I could respond, she interrupted cheerfully. "We have great news for you," she said, pouring Chinese green tea into a little white cup.

25   My stomach muscles tensed as I waited to hear this so-called great news. I was sure it would be another **diversion** from my writing. Mom and Dad don't take my writing seriously. You'd think that being **editors** themselves, they would support me. But no.

Make Inferences Using Text Evidence and Experience

Does Jackie expect to like the news? Why or why not?

---

diversion a break from normal activity

editors people who correct, clarify, and shape written and recorded works

26   "You're going to love this, Jackie," Dad said in a **singsong** voice that reminded me of story time in kindergarten. "We're sending you to the best computer camp in the state this summer."

27   A few seconds of silence followed. "What?!" I finally said, in a voice that sounded like a frog croak.

28   "Diamond Jubilee Computer Camp," Mom said, enunciating each word carefully. "You'll love it. Guaranteed." She grinned at me. "If you do well, we'll even buy you a computer," she added in a playful tone.

29   I made a face. I didn't want a computer and I didn't want to go to Diamond Jubilee Computer Camp. I bet this camp started on Monday. They always sprang camp on me at the last minute—I should've known this summer would be no different.

30   Mom and Dad grinned at each other, then picked up their forks and started on the tofu. As far as they were concerned, the matter was closed. The only sound that followed was the **clink** of silverware against plates.

Make Inferences Using Text Evidence and Experience

How do you think Jackie feels about going to computer camp? What text evidence tells you this?

---

singsong a way of speaking in which the voice rises and falls with little change

clink a short, light, high sound

31   "Jackie, dear," Mom said, smiling gently, "your tofu's getting cold."

32   Well, as far as I was concerned, this summer I wasn't going to let them do it. "I am NOT going to computer camp," I said fiercely, rising from my chair in slow motion. "I'm not going to any kind of camp! Last year it was science camp, the year before it was tennis camp. No . . . more . . . camps! I'm staying in my room all summer and writing my novel!"

33   Both of them stared at me wordlessly, their forks frozen in midair.

34   "And I don't want any muffins—or tofu!"

35   With that, I **stormed** out.

Make Inferences Using Text Evidence and Experience

How does Jackie feel about his parents right now? What text evidence tells you?

---

stormed   moved in an angry way

About the Author   Robin Friedman (born 1968)

Robin Friedman started writing when she was a little girl. Friedman got the idea for "How I Survived My Summer Vacation" from listening. She listened to her husband tell stories with his friends. The stories they told about growing up were funny and interesting. Friedman was glad to have an idea for a novel.

► What strategy did Friedman use to write this novel? What is Robin Friedman's point of view—how she thinks and feels—about Jackie? How does this affect the way she wrote the text?

Beyond the Reading

Reading Comprehension

Question-Answer Relationships (QAR)

"Right There" Questions

1. **Recall Facts** What does Jackie want to do during his summer vacation?
2. **Recall Facts** What do Jackie's parents want him to do during his summer vacation?

"Think and Search" Questions

3. **Analyze Characters** Why is Jackie having trouble writing his novel?
4. **Make Inferences** Why is Jackie angry with his parents?

"Author and You" Questions

5. **Evaluate Ideas** Would you be annoyed if the adults in your family acted like Jackie's parents? Why?
6. **Make Judgments** Do you think Jackie should choose what he does during the summer, or do you think his parents should choose?

7. **Identify Author's Purpose** Why do you think the author wrote this story? To inform, to entertain, or to influence?

"On Your Own" Questions

8. **Speculate** Why do you think Jackie's parents want him to go to computer camp?
9. **Compare Your Experiences** How do Jackie's plans for the summer compare to yours?
10. **Compare Across Cultures** In your culture or region, how do young people usually spend their time when they are not in school? Compare and contrast your answer with the answers of students from other cultures or regions.

Activity Book
p. 42

Student
CD-ROM

Build Reading Fluency

Audio Reading Practice

Listening to the audio recording of "How I Survived My Summer Vacation" is good reading practice. It helps you to become a fluent reader.

1. Listen to the audio recording.
2. Follow along in your student book on page 76.

3. Listen to the phrases, pauses, and expression of the reader.

Listen, Speak, Interact

Predict a Part of a Story

You can make inferences to guess how characters feel. You can also make inferences to predict (guess) what will happen next.

1. Work with a partner. Reread paragraphs 33–35.
2. Talk about how you think Jackie's parents felt when Jackie stormed out of the kitchen. Were they surprised? Angry? Sad?
3. Use your knowledge to help you predict the next part of the story.

One of you will be Jackie's mother. One of you will be Jackie's father. Use actions and words to show what the parents do next.

4. As you speak, use language that is right for these things:
   a. Your audience—your "husband" or your "wife."
   b. Your purpose—to explore why your son left.
   c. The occasion—a difficult event for a family.

Elements of Literature

Analyze Plot

Plot is an important element in fiction. It is the events that happen in the story. The plot includes the **climax**—the most exciting moment in the plot. Copy this chart in your Reading Log.

Plot	tells the main events
	develops character through events
Climax	the most exciting moment

1. These sentences describe events from the story. Decide if each of them *tells a main event, develops a character,* or both. Support your answers.

   a. Jackie was working on his novel.
   b. His father called him down to breakfast.
   c. Jackie yelled irritably to his parents.
   d. Jackie's parents said they were sending him to computer camp.
   e. Jackie said that he wasn't going to computer camp, and he left the room.

2. Which of these sentences is the climax of the story?

Reading Log   Activity Book *p. 43*   Student CD-ROM

Word Study

Identify Words with Latin Roots

Many English words come from Latin. Read these dictionary entries. Look for the Latin roots at the end of the entries.

> **in·spi·ra·tion** /ˌɪnspəˈreɪʃən/ *n.* someone or something that makes a person work hard or be creative [Latin *spirare*, to breathe]

> **com·pul·sion** /kəmˈpʌlʃən/ *n.* a need to do something that cannot be stopped [Latin *pellere*, to drive]

1. Copy the dictionary entries in your Personal Dictionary.

2. Write the answers to these questions.
  a. What is the Latin root for *inspiration?* What does it mean?
  b. What is the meaning of the Latin root *pellere?*

| Personal Dictionary | The Heinle Newbury House Dictionary | Activity Book p. 44 | Student CD-ROM |

Grammar Focus

Use Progressive Tenses

Progressive tenses usually show that an action is going on at a point in time.

"This **isn't working**," I said out loud.

Mom and Dad **were standing** on the landing.

Use the present progressive to talk about actions that are going on now.

Present Progressive Tense		
Subject	**Auxiliary**	**Verb + ing**
I	am	
you/we/they	are	work**ing**
he/she/it	is	

Use the past progressive to talk about actions that were going on in the past.

Past Progressive Tense		
Subject	**Auxiliary**	**Verb + ing**
I/he/she/it	was	
you/we/they	were	work**ing**

Copy and complete these sentences.

1. Jackie _____ working on his novel now.
2. My parents _____ making breakfast when I came in.
3. It _____ raining when I got up.

| Activity Book pp. 45–46 | Student Handbook | Student CD-ROM |

From Reading to Writing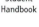

Write Realistic Fiction

In Listen, Speak, Interact you predicted a part of the selection. Now you will write what you predicted.

1. Recall the predictions you talked about with your partner.
2. Write this part of the story.
   a. Tell what Mom and Dad were doing when Jackie left the room. Use the progressive tense.
   b. Write dialogue that helps develop the characters of Mom and Dad.
   c. Write to discover a resolution to the conflict.

Mom and Dad were looking at each other. They were surprised. They didn't know what to say. Finally, Dad broke the silence. "What was that all about?" Dad asked.

"I don't have a clue," Mom replied. "Maybe Jackie is having a bad day."

Activity Book
p. 47

Student Handbook

Across Content Areas

SCIENCE

Identify Food Groups

Healthy foods contain **nutrients**—substances in foods that help our bodies grow and work.

1. Match each food group with an example.
2. With a partner, list other examples for each food group.
3. With your partner, create a form that you can use to interview other students about the things they eat. Organize your form according to the food groups.
4. Interview a few students. Revise your form if necessary. Interview a few more students. What did you find out?

Activity Book
p. 48

Food Groups	Examples
1. Breads, cereals, rice, and pasta	a. an apple
2. Meat, poultry, fish, beans, eggs, and nuts	b. a muffin
3. Dairy (foods made from milk)	c. tofu
4. Fruits and vegetables	d. cheese

CHAPTER 2

The Voyage of the *Frog*

an excerpt from a novel
by Gary Paulsen

Objectives

Reading Recognize tone and mood as you read an excerpt from a novel.

Listening and Speaking Conduct an interview.

Grammar Use the future tense.

Writing Write a story to resolve a problem.

Content Social Studies: Find compass directions.

Use Prior Knowledge

Talk About Dangerous Weather

Sometimes, bad weather can be dangerous. What are some types of dangerous weather? What problems can dangerous weather cause?

1. Work with a group. Make a chart like the one shown on a piece of paper.
2. List types of dangerous weather. Think about snow, rain, wind, and temperature.
3. List problems that dangerous weather can cause. Think about how it can hurt buildings, land, and animals.

4. Share your chart with the class. Work together to make one big chart on the board.

Dangerous Weather	Problems
a lot of rain	Land and houses can get covered with water.

Build Background

Sailboats

Sailboats are boats with sails—pieces of cloth that help boats move in the wind. Sailboats usually move in a zig-zag (like a *Z*). This means that sailboats turn in the water and change direction. Turning a sailboat helps the sails catch the wind.

 Content Connection

A **sailor** is a person who knows how to use a sailboat. A sailor controls the direction in which the boat moves.

Build Vocabulary

Use Reference Sources

A **reference source** can help you find the meaning of a word. A reference source is something that gives you information.

Use any of these reference sources as you read. Write words and definitions you learn in your Personal Dictionary.

Personal Dictionary

The Heinle Newbury House Dictionary

Activity Book *p. 49*

Student CD-ROM

Reference Sources	
Dictionary	A dictionary gives the definitions of words. It tells how words are pronounced. Some dictionaries also give information about usage and word origin.
Thesaurus	A thesaurus shows **synonyms** for words. Synonyms are words with similar meanings. (*Mad* is a synonym for *angry*.) Some thesauruses also show word usage.
Synonym Finder	A synonym finder is a book that lists many synonyms. Like a thesaurus, it may show word usage.
Software	Software is a tool you use on a computer. Some dictionaries and thesauruses are available as software. They may give meanings, pronunciations, derivations, and usage information.

Text Structure

Adventure Story

"The Voyage of the *Frog*" is a type of fiction called an **adventure story.** An adventure story tells about exciting or dangerous events. Look for these features of an adventure story as you read the selection.

Adventure Story	
Events	Exciting things happen in the story. Characters can be in dangerous situations.
Description	The author uses words to describe people and things. These words help readers make pictures in their minds.
Problem	The characters must resolve a difficult problem.

Student
CD-ROM

Reading Strategy

Recognize Tone and Mood

Authors can make us feel emotions. Two ways that writers do this are through **tone** and **mood.**

Tone is the feeling the author shows toward a character or a situation. For example, the author may approve of or be angry with a character.

Mood is the feeling the reader gets from the story. For example, the author might want to make the reader feel worried or scared.

Read the following sentences. Then choose the description that fits each one.

1. He was used to sailing alone. He was always prepared for any emergency.
   a. The tone is admiring.
   b. The tone is disapproving.

2. The room was full of little kids running around and having a good time. In the middle of it all was Rosa, with a big smile on her face.
   a. The mood is sad.
   b. The mood is happy.

Pay attention to tone and mood as you read and listen to "The Voyage of the *Frog*."

Student
CD-ROM

The
VOYAGE
of the
FROG

an excerpt from a novel

by Gary Paulsen

Audio
CD 1, Tr. 7

Prologue

This selection is about a boy named David. He is 14 years old. He goes out on a boat in the Pacific Ocean. A storm comes and throws the boat off of its path. David is alone in the boat. He does not know how he will survive.

1   It was then that he saw the ship—a small, older ship, coming out of the dusk, **aiming** almost at him but slightly off his bow, running with the wind and sea. Right there. A ship. Right in front of him. She had been running without lights but as soon as the people on deck saw him—there were three of them—they yelled and the lights came on and they started to pass not a hundred yards away, the people waving and yelling and laughing.

2   For a moment he couldn't say anything. He just didn't think it would happen this way. He didn't know for certain how it would happen, but not this way. Not so sudden. Suddenly he was saved. She was an old, very small **coastal freighter** but had been fixed up and repainted and she carried an American flag above her bridge.

3   "Hey," he **croaked.** They were going to pass him and leave if he didn't wake up. "Hey, hey, hey, hey, *hey!*"

Recognize Tone and Mood

What is the mood of the story at this point? Ask yourself, "What is David feeling?"

---

aiming   pointing at, directing toward
coastal   along the coast, where the land and water meet

freighter   a ship designed to carry freight, goods, or cargo
croaked   made a deep sound like a frog

4   He let go of the helm and waved with both arms, screamed, pointed at them and then at himself and at last they got the message and he heard the engines in the freighter **rumble** down to a stop west and slightly north of him.

5   He came about and let the *Frog* sail closer, came up into the wind and stopped about thirty yards away, rising and settling on the waves and swells. He looked up at the people on the rail.

6   "My name is David Alspeth," he yelled. "I was driven out to sea in a storm. . . ."

7   "It's him!" one of the young men yelled up at the **bridge** of the ship. "It's that kid they were searching for up off Ventura." He looked back down at David. "They had your picture in the paper and everything. Man, you are one heck of a distance from where they looked. They finally gave you up for dead, you know that?"

8   Well, I'm not, David thought. I'm not dead. Not even close. "Where am I?"

Recognize Tone and Mood

What is the tone of the story at this point? Ask yourself, "What is David's attitude toward the young man in paragraph 7?"

---

rumble make a low rolling noise

bridge the part of a ship where the officers stand to give orders

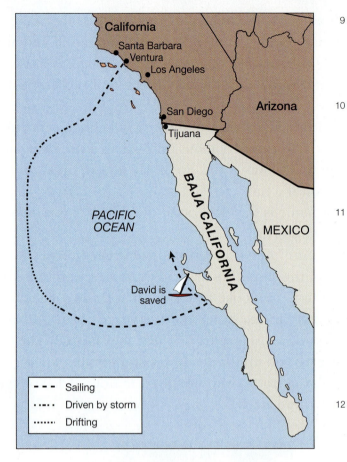

California
Santa Barbara
Ventura
Los Angeles

San Diego
Tijuana

Arizona

PACIFIC
OCEAN

BAJA CALIFORNIA

MEXICO

David is
saved

- - - Sailing
· · · · Driven by storm
· · · · · · Drifting

9   The man laughed. "About halfway down the coast of Baja. Maybe two hundred and fifty miles south of San Diego."

10   Another man came from the bridge, stepping down the ladder, to stand at the rail over the *Frog*. "I am Pierce. Henry Pierce. I am the captain."

11   David introduced himself—he almost added that he was the captain of the *Frog* but let it be. Captain Pierce was a heavy man, with round shoulders, gray hair, and pleasant eyes. It would sound **cocky,** smart-mouth to say that he, David, was captain of the *Frog*. But he felt like it.

12   "You gave everybody a rough time," the captain said. "They had planes and **choppers** looking for you."

13   "I was driven way south by the storm," David explained. "Way south. . . ."

14   "Well, you're all right now. We're down here to study whales but we're heading back tomorrow. We'll have you home in three to five days. . . ."

15   David closed his eyes, sighed, leaned back against the **boom** with his shoulder. That was it, then. He was done. He was saved. In three to four days he'd be home and there'd be a malt and a hamburger and his mother and father. . . .

Recognize Tone and Mood

What is the mood of the story at this point?

---

cocky feeling sure of one's importance and abilities
choppers helicopters

boom a long, horizontal pole that holds the bottom of a sail on a boat

16   "Get your **gear,**" the captain interrupted his dreaming, "anything you want to bring and we'll lower a ladder for you."

17   David looked up at him. "What about the *Frog*—what about the boat?"

18   The captain hesitated. "Well . . . we'll have to leave it."

19   "No." It came out before he could think. Just the word. "No."

20   The captain of the **research vessel shrugged.** "We haven't any choice. I haven't got any way to lift it aboard or a place to put it if we did. It's too big."

21   "No." David shook his head. "We could tow her."

22   A small smile, a sad smile. "We couldn't pull it more than two or three knots and then it would probably tear the boat apart. Sailboats don't tow at all."

23   There was a pause; the *Frog* rolled in the swells. The captain stared down at him, the small smile still on his lips. David looked back up at him but wasn't seeing him, wasn't seeing anything; his mind rolled with memories, the shark, the killer whales, the storm, the moon pouring down the sails, the dolphin spinning up into the gold. . . .

Recognize Tone and Mood

What is the tone of this paragraph? Ask yourself, "Does the captain understand David's problem?"

---

gear equipment
research vessel a boat built for study

shrugged lifted his shoulders upward as a sign of not caring or not knowing

24   All of it in his mind. Then the sentence came. Leave the *Frog*.

25   Us. We. Leave her to float and die on the ocean. Alone. Leave her to **drift** and die alone on the ocean.

26   "No."

27   "What do you mean, 'no'?" the captain asked.

28   David shook his head. "I won't leave her. I won't leave the *Frog*."

29   "But there is no other way. . . ."

30   "I'll sail her." There, it was out. "I'll sail her home myself. I won't leave her to die . . . to sink. Alone. I'll go back with her."

31   "You know that it's three hundred and fifty miles back to Ventura? Against **prevailing** wind and **current**? You'll have to **tack** the whole way. It could take two, three weeks. More if you hit bad weather."

Recognize Tone and Mood

What is the tone of this paragraph? Ask yourself, "What does this paragraph tell me about David?"

---

drift   float, carried by wind or water currents
prevailing   usual, frequent

current   the flow
tack   change direction depending on the wind

32 David rubbed the wooden boom with one hand. The wood felt warm, smooth, alive. She was alive. The ship had blocked most of the wind but enough **flurried** around to make the *Frog's* sails slap a bit and they **jerked** the boom gently. There was no other way. "I got here with her and I'm going home with her. That's it."

33 Another long silence while the captain studied him, frowning. A gull which had been following the ship screeched and flew over, banking on a wind **eddy.**

Recognize Tone and Mood

What is the tone of this paragraph? Ask yourself, "What is the author saying about the captain?"

34 "I'd do the same," the captain said at last, **abruptly,** nodding. "By God I'd do the same. Well, is there anything we can do for you, young sailor?"

35 David thought for a moment. "Two things. First, can you call my parents by radio or something and tell them that I'm all right and that I'll be home . . . well, whenever I get there. Explain everything to them." He gave the captain their phone number.

---

flurried flowed lightly
jerked pulled quickly and sharply

eddy turning or swirling wind
abruptly in a sudden manner

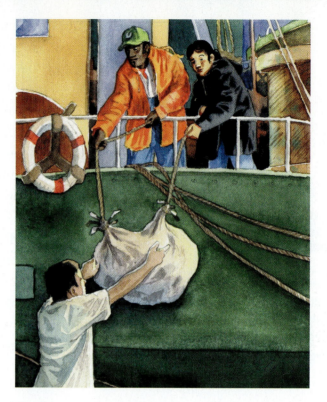

36   "Done."

37   "And the second thing is food and fuel for my stove. I don't have much food left. . . ."

Recognize Tone and Mood

What is the mood of the story at this point?

38   Before he could finish speaking, the other people on the boat, the whale researchers who had been standing silent all this time, started running in different directions and in ten or fifteen minutes had arranged a huge **bundle** of food and supplies on a blanket which they tied together and lowered to him into the **cockpit** of the *Frog*. David saw one can peeking through a corner as he put the heavy bundle below the cabin—the label said it contained a canned chicken. A whole chicken in one can.

39   "We put in a lot of extra goodies," a girl yelled down, laughing. "Be careful you don't get fat. There's also five gallons of water in a plastic jug."

---

bundle   things close together usually tied or fastened   **cockpit**   the area of a boat where the captain stands

Recognize Tone and Mood

What is the mood of the story in this paragraph?

40   David thanked them and they talked a little more—the captain told him to stand well off from shore, perhaps a hundred miles, to get good, steady wind—and then it was done. The captain went back up to the bridge, the engines changed their pitch, and the ship slid away into the dusk. As soon as it was clear, the wind hit the *Frog* and David was busy for a few moments **trimming** the sails and getting her going, and when he turned he could no longer see the ship except for the lights on her radar **mast**. . . .

41   He had some sailing to do.

---

trimming   placing the sails in the direction of the wind   **mast**   a pole on a boat to which the sails are connected

About the Author   Gary Paulsen (born 1939)

Gary Paulsen had an unhappy childhood. His family moved a lot because his father was in the army. He did not have many friends. A friendly librarian helped Paulsen find his love of reading. He once said that when this librarian gave him a library card, she gave him the world.

Gary Paulsen grew up to write many books for young adults. Most of his books are adventure stories. The main characters in his stories often must resolve problems.

► As you read or listened to "The Voyage of the *Frog*," did you determine Paulsen's purpose? Was it to inform, to entertain, to influence, or to express himself?

Beyond the Reading

Reading Comprehension

Question-Answer Relationships (QAR)

"Right There" Questions

1. **Recall Facts** Where is the *Frog* when the story begins?
2. **Recall Facts** Who is sailing the *Frog?*

"Think and Search" Question

3. **Recognize Cause and Effect** Why was David so far away from where he was trying to go?

"Author and You" Questions

4. **Compare Your Experiences** Why do you think David wants to stay with the *Frog?* How do you feel about something or someone that you have spent a lot of time with?

5. **Understand Author's Perspective** How do you think Gary Paulsen feels about David? How does he want you to feel about David?

"On Your Own" Questions

6. **Speculate** Why was David sailing the *Frog* by himself?
7. **Predict** Do you think David will make it home safely? Why or why not?
8. **Make Judgments** David decides to sail the *Frog* home rather than leave her behind to sink. Do you think this is a good idea? Why or why not?

Activity Book
p. 50

Student
CD-ROM

Build Reading Fluency

Adjust Your Reading Rate for Quotations

Reading quotations helps you learn to adjust your reading rate. You must pause and read with expression.

Reread the conversation between David and the man. Look for the quotation marks (" . . . ") around each conversation.

1. With a partner, take turns rereading aloud paragraphs 6–9 on page 91.
2. Read the quotations with expression.
3. Pause after each quotation.
4. Choose the quotation you like best.
5. Read it aloud in front of the class.

Listen, Speak, Interact

Conduct an Interview

Suppose David has returned from his voyage. People want to know about his experience. Conduct an interview about his experience. In an interview, a person asks another person questions.

1. Work with a partner. One of you will be the interviewer (the person who asks questions). One of you will be David.
2. Write questions that the interviewer will ask David. Use the following list to help you.
   a. What happened when you were on the *Frog?*
   b. Why did you decide to stay on the *Frog?*
   c. How did you feel when you came home?
3. Guess how David might answer each question. Use text evidence and your personal knowledge. Take notes on the answers.
4. Perform your interview for the class.
5. Listen as your classmates perform their interviews. Did you understand the major ideas? If not, ask your classmates questions.

Elements of Literature

Recognize and Analyze Problem Resolution

In fiction, one or more of the characters usually has a problem. The story is mostly about how the problem is resolved (worked out).

1. With a partner, reread the prologue of "The Voyage of the *Frog,*" on page 90. What is David's problem?
2. Now reread paragraphs 1 to 3. Is there a resolution to this problem? David thinks that his problem is resolved, but is it?
3. Reread paragraphs 16 to 18. What new problem does David have?
4. Reread paragraphs 19 to 30. What are David's choices?
5. Which choice does David take?
6. Do you agree with David's choice? Whether you agree or not, do you admire him?

Activity Book
p. 51

Student
CD-ROM

Word Study

Understand the Suffix *-ly*

A **suffix** is a group of letters added to the end of a word. A suffix can change the meaning of a word. It can also change a word from one part of speech to another.

Adverbs describe verbs (words that show action). Adverbs tell how an action happens. Many adverbs have the suffix *-ly*. The root word is usually an adjective. The suffix *-ly* changes an adjective to an adverb.

Sudden**ly** he was saved.

Adverbs can help make your writing vivid (interesting) and precise (exact).

Adjective	Adverb
sudden	suddenly

1. Copy the chart above in your Personal Dictionary.
2. Read these sentences.
   a. The captain said it abruptly.
   b. They jerked the boom slowly.
3. Write the adverbs that end in *-ly*. Write the adjective root word.

Personal Dictionary   Activity Book p. 52   Student CD-ROM

Grammar Focus

Use the Future Tense

One way to talk about events in the future is with *will*. In speech, *will* is often contracted as *'ll*. *Will not* is contracted as *won't*.

1. Find the sentences with the future tense in paragraph 30 of the reading. Copy them on a piece of paper.
2. The sentences are contracted forms. Rewrite them as full forms using *will* and *will not*.

Activity Book pp. 53–54   Student Handbook   Student CD-ROM

Statements with the Future Tense		
Subject	**will/will not**	**Verb**
I You He/She/It We They	**will** 'll **will not** won't	leave it.

From Reading to Writing

Write a Story to Resolve a Problem

Write an adventure story about a problem. The characters in your story will resolve the problem.

1. Use a Sunshine Organizer to help you plan your story:
   a. Who are the characters?
   b. What is the problem?
   c. When does the story happen?
   d. Where does the story happen?
   e. Why did it happen?
   f. How do the characters solve the problem?
2. Write a beginning, a middle, and an end. Indent each paragraph.

3. Use adverbs to make your writing vivid and precise.

Activity Book
p. 55

Student Handbook

Across Content Areas

Find Compass Directions

A **compass** is a tool that shows direction. **Compass directions** tell people which way they are going. The four main compass directions are **north, east, south,** and **west.** These are called the **cardinal directions.** North and south are opposite directions. East and west are opposite directions.

You can also name the directions between each cardinal direction. Northwest is between north and west. These are called **intercardinal directions.**

1. Copy this compass on a piece of paper.

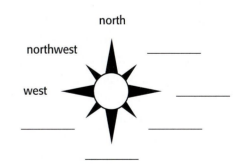

2. Label the directions with these words.
   a. northeast
   b. east
   c. south
   d. southwest
   e. southeast

Activity Book
p. 56

CHAPTER 3

Into the Reading

To Risk or Not to Risk

an informational text
by David Ropeik

Objectives

Reading Distinguish fact from opinion as you read an informational text.

Listening and Speaking Compare personal experiences.

Grammar Use present tense and subject-verb agreement.

Writing Write an informational text.

Content Science: Learn about psychology.

Use Prior Knowledge

Rate Risks

To take a risk means that you take the chance of getting hurt or losing something. For example, when you travel in a car, you take a risk of getting in an accident.

Some risks are bigger than others. The risk of getting into an accident is bigger while traveling in a car than in an airplane. This means more accidents happen in cars than in airplanes.

1. Copy the chart. Think about each risk listed. Write 1, 2, 3, or 4 next to each risk.
2. Share your chart with a small group. Did everyone rate the risks the same?

1	2	3	4
Small Risk	Some Risk	Risky	Very Risky

Risk	How Big
falling while using a skateboard	
getting a cold after visiting a friend with a cold	
getting bitten by a dog while running in the park	
getting lost while walking home from school	

Build Background

The Brain

We use two parts of our brains to decide if something is a risk. We use the **limbic system** and the **cortex.** The limbic system is the part of the brain that controls feelings and learning. The cortex is the part of the brain that controls thinking. We use the cortex to write and solve puzzles.

Content Connection

The limbic system works faster than the cortex. You may feel scared before you have time to think about why.

Build Vocabulary

Learn Vocabulary Through Reading

When you see a new word when you are reading or listening to the selections, there are several things you can do. Here are some of them.

1. Reread and review text.
   a. Reread sentences that have words you do not know. Adjust your reading speed to a slower rate so that you can pay more attention to the important ideas.
   b. Reread using context clues (words that are around the new word).
2. Use glosses (definitions).
   a. The definitions of boldfaced words are at the bottom of the reading selection pages.
   b. Review the definitions of any boldfaced words you do not know.

3. Use reference sources.
   a. You learned about reference sources in Build Vocabulary for Chapter 2. These include dictionaries, thesauruses, synonym finders, and software.
   b. Use reference sources to help you learn new words and clarify their meanings, pronunciations, derivations, and usages.
4. Write new vocabulary in your Personal Dictionary to help you remember new words.

Personal Dictionary

The Heinle Newbury House Dictionary

Activity Book p. 57

Student CD-ROM

Text Structure

Informational Text

"To Risk or Not to Risk" is an **informational text.** An informational text explains a topic. This selection explains how people respond to risk. Note the features of this informational text shown in the chart.

Look for questions and answers as you read "To Risk or Not to Risk."

Informational Text	
Facts	Facts are information that is true.
Questions	The text includes questions. The questions give clues about important ideas.
Answers	The text includes answers to the questions. The answers give details that support important ideas.

Student
CD-ROM

Reading Strategy

Distinguish Fact from Opinion

A **fact** is information that is true. A fact can be proven to be true. An **opinion** is a person's feelings about something. Opinions cannot be proven to be true. Read these sentences:

Jenny saw a movie. She thought the movie was very good.

Words like *think* and *feel* often express an opinion.

1. Are these sentences facts or opinions?
  a. That's a beautiful snake!
  b. Some snakes are poisonous.
  c. I think that snakes make great pets.

2. Look for facts and opinions as you read and listen to the selection. Write the facts and opinions in a chart.

Facts	Opinions
Jenny saw a movie.	She thought the movie was very good.

Student
CD-ROM

To Risk or Not to Risk

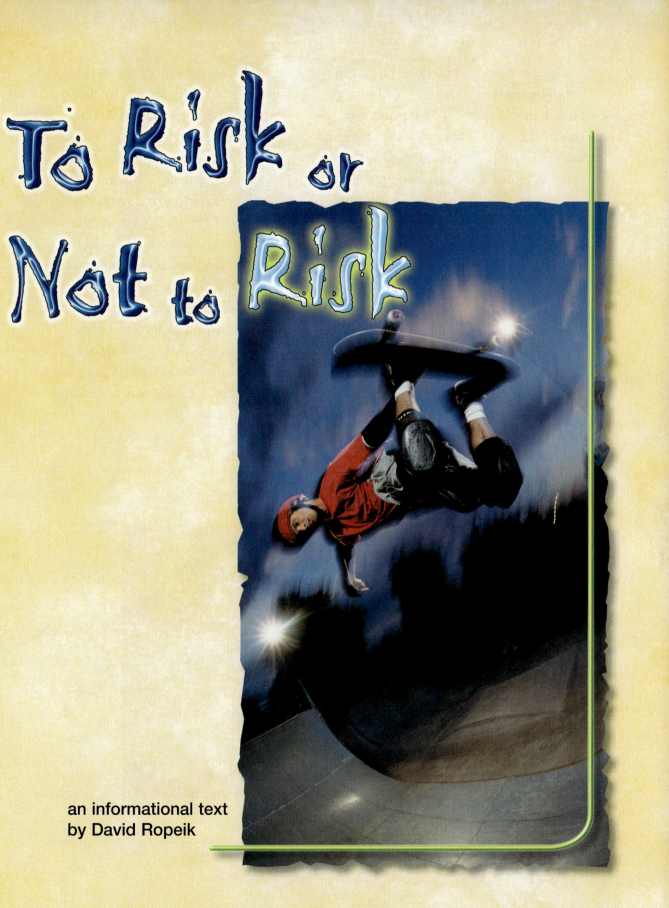

an informational text
by David Ropeik

1   The chances that you will be bitten by a **poisonous** snake are really low; about 1 out of every 40,000 people in this country is bitten each year. The chances of being bitten by a spider are pretty low, too. And the chances that anything bad will happen to you in the dark—except that you might trip and fall or bump into something—are far less than the chances that something bad will happen to you when the sun is out or the lights are on, which is when most of us are awake and active.

Distinguish Fact from Opinion

Is the statement "The chances of being bitten by a spider are pretty low" a fact or an opinion?

2   If the actual risk of these things isn't very big, why are we so afraid of them? Some scientists think our distant **ancestors** learned to be afraid of snakes, spiders and the dark millions of years ago. If you were living out in the savanna or in caves, snakes, spiders and the dark were bigger risks. So those who reacted fearfully to them survived and passed on their **genes**—and their fears—to us.

3   But why are many people also afraid of more modern risks that aren't that big? Like getting cancer from cell phones or dying from mad cow disease? Our distant ancestors didn't have cell phones or mad cows!

Audio
CD 1, Tr. 8

---

poisonous   causing harm or death by poison

ancestors   the people from whom one is descended (great-grandmother, father, and so on)

genes   the basic part of a living cell that contains characteristics of one's parents

And why don't people worry much about risks that *are* pretty big? Why do people refuse to wear seat belts in cars and continue to smoke?

4   It turns out that we react to most risks the same way we react to snakes, spiders and the dark: our fears are more important than the facts. But what makes us decide what to be afraid of and how afraid to be? To answer that question, scientists study the ways our fears seem to be at odds with reality. . . . And they've found some interesting patterns.

For example, suppose someone gives you two glasses, one filled with city tap water and the other with water bottled at a **rural** spring. Which would you drink? Surveys show that most people are less afraid of "natural" things than they are of **"artificial"** ones. Most people would pick the spring water, even though tests show bottled water often contains **bacteria** and other **impurities.**

5

Distinguish Fact from Opinion

Spring water is safer than water from a city tap. Is this a fact or an opinion? How can you tell?

---

rural   related to the countryside, not the city
artificial   made by humans, not made from
      natural things

bacteria   tiny living things; many cause diseases
impurities   dirty or bad things

6   Here's another example. Some people like to go **sky-diving.** It's risky, but they are choosing to take the risk themselves. Nobody's forcing them to do it. Most of us are less afraid of risks that we choose for ourselves, such as scuba-diving or skateboarding, and more afraid of risks we're forced to take, such as eating food that has been **genetically modified** or treated with chemicals.

> ### Distinguish Fact from Opinion
>
> Is the statement "I think skateboarding is safer than eating tomatoes treated with chemicals" a fact or an opinion? How can you tell?

7   Another factor that shapes our opinion of a risk is trust. If we trust the people who are supposed to protect us from the risk, we're more **inclined** to estimate it correctly. But if someone has an **untrustworthy** past, such as tobacco companies do, for example, there's a **tendency** to overestimate the risk by way of compensation.

8   Another factor that affects our fear of risks is familiarity. Is the risk new, or is it something we're used to? When a new risk comes along, like the West Nile virus now spreading across the U.S., we tend to overestimate it. But when the risk has been around for a while—say, the risk of riding a bike on city streets—we tend to underestimate it.

---

sky-diving   jumping out of an airplane and floating to the ground with the help of a parachute

genetically modified   changed or altered in something's genes

inclined   likely to
untrustworthy   dishonest
tendency   an inclination or habit

9   It also matters whether the risk comes with a benefit. Skiing is risky, but it's fun. **Vaccines** cause harmful reactions in a few people, but they protect most people against disease. If we think the benefit is greater than the risk, we're less afraid. But if we think the risk is greater, we're more afraid.

Distinguish Fact from Opinion

Explain how the statement "Skiing is risky, but it's fun" is both a fact and an opinion.

10   **Psychologists** call the next factor **dread.** Death by shark attack scares most of us more than death by car crash, even though the outcome is the same. That might seem foolish, since the risk of being killed in a car crash is far higher than the risk of being killed by a shark. But the more awful the **outcome,** the more afraid of it we are, and the more we overestimate the chances of it happening.

---

vaccines   medication taken to prevent many diseases
psychologists   people who study human and animal behavior

dread   a strong fear of something happening in the future
outcome   the effect or result

11   Here's a final **factor.** People are less afraid of risks when they feel in control. Most people aren't afraid of driving, even though the risk of an accident is **significant,** because they're holding the steering wheel and stepping on the gas pedal or the brakes, and so they have some control over what's happening.

12   Of course, these aren't the only factors that affect how we size up a risk. If the risk of harm is immediate, it seems bigger than if harm is **delayed.** Smoking is a good example of a delayed risk. If a great deal is known about the risk, we are less fearful than if there is little information. If the risk kills many at once, we fear it more than if it kills one at a time. If we've already been hurt, we're more afraid than if we have no painful memories.

13   You can probably come up with other **biases.** The more you think about it, the more interesting the psychology of fear becomes.

> ### Distinguish Fact from Opinion
>
> Does this paragraph contain facts or opinions?

14   Some people say that behaving this way is silly. They think we would make smarter decisions about risks if we just relied on the facts and not on our feelings. They say it shouldn't matter

---

factor   a fact to be considered
significant   large or meaningful

delayed   moved to a later time
biases   general tendencies

whether a risk is natural or artificial, **voluntary** or not, whether the risk is new or familiar, has benefits that **outweigh** the possible harm, or has a really nasty outcome. They say the only things that should matter are the facts: the likelihood of death or injury.

Distinguish Fact from Opinion

Does this paragraph contain facts or opinions? What words help you tell?

But the way our brains evolved, we may not have much choice. . . . Long before our ancestors had the highly developed, reasoning brains we have now, they could still recognize and respond to danger. And those **ancient** ways of staying safe are still at work. Our brains are actually built, biologically, to fear first, and think second. So when it comes to protecting ourselves, what we feel often matters more than what we think.

15

---

voluntary   done without being forced or paid
outweigh   to be more important than something else

ancient   very old

About the Author — David Ropeik (born 1951)

David Ropeik studies the risks that people take. He works at the Harvard Center for Risk Analysis. Harvard is a university in Cambridge, Massachusetts (near Boston). You can sometimes hear David Ropeik on the radio, talking about risk. He has also written a book about this topic.

Ropeik studied journalism in college. (Journalism is the study of gathering and reporting news.) He worked as a television news reporter. He also wrote science articles for newspapers. Ropeik has won important awards and honors for his work in journalism.

➤ Why did David Ropeik write this article for young readers? What do you think he wants people to learn from this article?

Beyond the Reading

Reading Comprehension

Question-Answer Relationships (QAR)

"Right There" Questions

1. **Recall Facts** What is a risk?
2. **Recall Facts** Do most people measure risks through the facts or through their fears?

"Think and Search" Questions

3. **Find Supporting Arguments** The text says that most people choose spring water over city water. How does this example show that people make choices because of their fears?
4. **Identify Cause and Effect** According to the author, how does trust affect people's opinions about risk?

"Author and You" Questions

5. **Connect Your Experiences** The author says people fear new risks more than familiar risks. Is this true for you? Give some examples.

6. **Identify Theme** The author says people are less afraid of risks that they choose. He also says that people are less afraid of risks when they feel in control. What is the common theme in these two examples?

"On Your Own" Questions

7. **Make Judgments** The author says that people fear immediate risks more than delayed risks. Do you think this is a good idea? Why or why not?
8. **State an Opinion** Do you think people should measure risk by the facts or by their feelings? Explain.
9. **Raise Additional Questions** Based on your knowledge, form additional questions about risk that are *not* answered in the reading.

Activity Book
p. 58

Student
CD-ROM

Build Reading Fluency

Read Silently

Reading silently is good practice. It helps you learn to read faster. An effective reader reads silently for greater periods of time.

1. Listen to the audio recording of paragraph 1 on page 106.
2. Listen to the chunks of words as you follow along.
3. Reread paragraph 1 silently two times.
4. Your teacher will time your second reading.
5. Raise your hand when you are done.

Listen, Speak, Interact

Compare Personal Experiences

"To Risk or Not to Risk" describes real risks that a person can take. Think about risks that you take every day.

1. List risks from the selection that you have taken, such as skateboarding.
2. List risks that you have taken that are not in the selection. For example, you may live in an area where there are many earthquakes.

3. Meet with a small group. Make a chart to compare your lists. Are many the same?
4. Talk about these risks. Which do you fear the most? Which do you fear the least? Why?
5. As you listen to your group members, distinguish between opinions and facts.

Elements of Literature

Identify Transition Words

Authors use **transition words** to connect ideas. These words help organize your sentences and paragraphs and blend them into larger units of text.

You can use transition words to contrast ideas. *But, however,* and *even though* are transition words. They show that you are about to read a different idea.

First Idea
Jo went to the party.

Second Idea
<u>However</u>, she did not have fun.

Usually, people have fun at parties. *However* shows that you will read a different idea: Jo did *not* have fun at the party.

1. Write these sentences in your Reading Log:
   a. Skiing is risky, but it's fun.
   b. Most people aren't afraid of driving, even though the risk of an accident is significant.
2. Circle the transition words. Then underline the ideas that are shown as different.

Reading Log   Activity Book
                        p. 59

Student
CD-ROM

Word Study

Identify Prefixes *over-* and *under-*

A **prefix** is a group of letters that is added to the beginning of a root word. A prefix may change the meaning of a root word.

The prefix *over-* means "too much." The prefix *under-* means "not enough."

1. Read the example in the chart.
2. In your Personal Dictionary, complete a chart like the one shown for each word pair.

Root Word	Over + Root	Under + Root
estimate: guess the amount of	overestimate: guess too much	underestimate: guess not enough
cook: heat food until done		
charge: to put a price on		

Personal Dictionary

The Heinle Newbury House Dictionary

Activity Book *p. 60*

Student CD-ROM

Grammar Focus

Use Present Tense and Subject-Verb Agreement

Use the present tense of verbs to talk about things that are generally true or that happen regularly.

Some people **like** to go sky-diving.

When a new risk **comes** along, we tend to overestimate it.

When the subject of a statement is *he, she,* or *it,* or a singular noun, you add an *s* to present tense verbs.

Choose the correct verb for each sentence.

1. He (give/gives) you two glasses.
2. Some people (say/says) that behaving this way is silly.

3. Psychologists (calls/call) the next factor dread.

Present Tense	
Subject	**Verb**
I you we they	work
he she it	work**s**

Activity Book *pp. 61–62*

Student Handbook

Student CD-ROM

From Reading to Writing

Write an Informational Text

Write an informational text to explain something you like to do or a place you like to visit.

1. Make an outline to organize your ideas.
2. Use questions to get readers involved.
3. Write answers to your questions. The answers should include details.
4. Make sure subjects and verbs agree.
5. Write two or three paragraphs.
6. Use the present tense. Be sure your verbs agree with your subjects.
7. Use transition words to help organize your paragraphs and to blend your paragraphs together.

Outline for Working Out

I. Working out is important.
  A. You feel better.
  B. You feel stronger.
II. There are many ways to work out.
  A.
  B.

Activity Book
p. 63

Student Handbook

Across Content Areas   SCIENCE

Learn About Psychology

Psychology is the study of how people act. People who study psychology believe these things affect how people act:

personality a person's qualities; what a person is like

environment where a person lives

habit a way of acting that a person often repeats without thinking

family background a person's family, including past generations

Match each sentence to the thing that affects how the person acts.

1. Alex keeps biting his fingernails.
2. Kasia is good at math. Her mother and aunt were also good at math.
3. Luis is a kind and creative person. However, he is not very patient.
4. Jim has lived in a large city his whole life.

Activity Book
p. 64

CHAPTER 4

Island of the Blue Dolphins

an excerpt from a novel based on a true story by Scott O'Dell

Objectives

Reading Paraphrase to recall information as you read an excerpt from a novel based on a true story.

Listening and Speaking Compare ways of working.

Grammar Identify the past and the past perfect tenses.

Writing Write instructions.

Content The Arts: List game rules in order.

Use Prior Knowledge

Distinguish Needs and Wants

Needs are things that people must have in order to live. Food is a need. *Wants* are things that people would like to have. A new CD is a want. What are some other needs and wants?

1. Work with a partner. Make a chart like this one.
2. List the needs that you must have in order to live.
3. Talk about your wants. List them in your chart.

Needs	Wants
food	a new CD

Build Background

The Lost Woman of San Nicolas Island

"Island of the Blue Dolphins" tells about a young Native American girl named Karana. Karana lived on San Nicolas Island in the 1800s. At first, she lived with her people, but they decided to leave. They got on a ship to go to California, but the ship left without Karana and her brother. Karana's brother died, and she was left alone. She lived there by herself for eighteen years.

Content Connection

San Nicolas Island is about 60 miles (97 kilometers) from Los Angeles.

Build Vocabulary

Locate Pronunciations of Unfamiliar Words

When you learn the meaning of a new word, learn its pronunciation from a dictionary or software, or ask your teacher. Look at this dictionary entry.

> **gnaw** /nɔ/ *v.* to keep biting at something over a period of time: *Rats gnaw through the cartons to get the food inside.*

1. Discuss these questions.
    a. How is the /n/ symbol pronounced?
    b. Is the /ɔ/ symbol a letter in the alphabet? Ask your teacher to pronounce it for you.
    c. How is *gnaw* pronounced?
    d. We say that the letter *g* in *gnaw* is silent. Why do we say that?
2. As you learn new words in the reading selection, learn their pronunciations.

The Heinle
Newbury House
Dictionary

Activity Book
p. 65

Student
CD-ROM

Text Structure

Fiction Based on a True Story

"Island of the Blue Dolphins" is **fiction.** Fiction is a story that includes made-up events and people.

The selection is **based on a true story.** It has events that happened to a real person in history. The features of fiction based on a true story are shown in the chart.

As you read "Island of the Blue Dolphins," think about events in the selection. Which events could have really happened? Which events seem to be made up?

Fiction Based on a True Story	
Main Character	• who the story is about • may act or look like a real person in history
Plot	• what happens in the story • similar to events that happened to a real person in history
Setting	• where the story happens • usually a real place

Student
CD-ROM

Reading Strategy

Paraphrase to Recall Information

When you **paraphrase,** you tell a part of a text in your own words. Paraphrasing helps you recall what you have read.

1. Read this paragraph. Then complete the paraphrase on a piece of paper.

The woman lived all alone on the island for 18 years. She had to build shelter, find food, and protect herself from wild animals.

Paraphrase Life on the _____ was very _____ . The woman had to provide everything for herself— _____ , _____ , and _____ .

2. As you read and listen to "Island of the Blue Dolphins," stop often to paraphrase.

Student
CD-ROM

Island of the Blue Dolphins

an excerpt from a novel based on a true story

by Scott O'Dell

Audio
CD 1, Tr. 9

Prologue

At this point in the story, Karana's brother has been killed by wild dogs. Karana is all alone on the island. She has to build a **shelter** for herself.

1   Many years before, two **whales** had washed up on the **sandspit.** Most of the bones had been taken away to make **ornaments,** but ribs were still there, half-buried in the sand.

2   These I used in making the fence. One by one I dug them up and carried them to the headland. They were long and curved, and when I scooped out holes and set them in the earth they stood taller than I did.

3   I put the ribs together with their edges almost touching, and standing so that they curved outward, which made them impossible to climb. Between them I wove many **strands** of **bull kelp,** which shrinks as it dries and pulls very tight. I would have used seal **sinew** to bind the ribs together, for this is stronger than kelp, but wild animals like it and soon would have **gnawed** the fence down. Much time went into its building. It would have taken me longer except that the rock made one end of the fence and part of a side.

> **Paraphrase to Recall Information**
>
> Paraphrase what Karana does in this paragraph.

---

shelter   a building that protects people

whales   large animals that live in the ocean; they look like very big fish

sandspit   a thin piece of sandy land, sticking out into the water

ornaments   things that are pretty rather than useful

strands   long thin pieces of something

bull kelp   large brown plants that grow below the sea

sinew   in the body, strong material that connects muscle to bone

gnawed   kept biting something for a long time

4   For a place to go in and out, I dug a hole under the fence just wide and deep enough to crawl through. The bottom and sides I **lined** with stones. On the outside I covered the hole with a **mat** woven of **brush** to shed the rain, and on the inside with a flat rock which I was strong enough to move.

5   I was able to take eight steps between the sides of the fence, which gave me all the room I would need to **store** the things I **gathered** and wished to protect.

6   I built the fence first because it was too cold to sleep on the rock and I did not like to sleep in the shelter I had made until I was safe from the wild dogs.

7   The house took longer to build than the fence because it rained many days and because the wood which I needed was **scarce.**

---

lined   put a border around
mat   a piece of material used on floors, in front of doors
brush   branches broken off from trees or plants

store   keep something to use later
gathered   collected, brought in
scarce   not a lot of

8   There was a **legend** among our people that the island had once been covered with tall trees. This was a long time ago, at the beginning of the world when Tumaiyowit and Mukat ruled. The two gods **quarreled** about many things. Tumaiyowit wished people to die. Mukat did not. Tumaiyowit angrily went down, down to another world under this world, taking his **belongings** with him, so people die because he did.

9   In that time there were tall trees, but now there were only a few in the **ravines** and these were small and **crooked.** It was very hard to find one that would make a good **pole.** I searched many days, going out early in the morning and coming back at night, before I found enough for the house.

Paraphrase to Recall Information

Paraphrase what Karana does in this paragraph. Use your own words.

10   I used the rock for the back of the house and the front I left open since the wind did not blow from this direction. The poles I made of equal length, using fire to cut them as well as a stone knife which caused me much **difficulty** because I had never made such a tool before. There were four poles on each side, set in the earth, and twice that many for the roof. These I bound together with sinew and covered with female kelp, which has broad leaves.

---

legend   a story from long ago
quarreled   argued
belongings   things you own
ravines   low areas in the earth with steep sides

crooked   bent, not straight
pole   a long rod, usually made of wood or metal
difficulty   trouble, problems

Paraphrase to Recall Information

Paraphrase this paragraph.

11   The winter was half over before I finished the house, but I slept there every night and felt **secure** because of the strong fence. The **foxes** came when I was cooking my food and stood outside **gazing** through the cracks, and the wild dogs also came, gnawing at the whale ribs, **growling** because they could not get in.

12   I shot two of them, but not the leader.

13   While I was building the fence and the house, I ate shellfish and **perch** which I cooked on a flat rock. Afterwards I made two **utensils.** Along the shore there were stones that the sea had worn smooth. Most of them were round, but I found two with hollow places in the center which I **deepened** and **broadened** by rubbing them with sand. Using these to cook in, I saved the juices of the fish which are good and were wasted before.

---

secure safe
foxes animals that look like small dogs with furry tails
gazing looking at something for a long time
growling making low, angry sounds

perch a small fish
utensils tools for eating food
deepened made deeper
broadened made broader, or wider

14   For cooking seeds and roots I wove a tight basket of fine **reeds,** which was easy because I learned how to do it from my sister Ulape. After the basket had dried in the sun, I gathered lumps of **pitch** on the shore, softened them over the fire, and rubbed them on the inside of the basket so that it would hold water. By heating small stones and dropping them into a mixture of water and seeds in the basket I could make **gruel.**

Paraphrase to Recall Information

Paraphrase this paragraph.

15   I made a place for fire in the floor of my house, **hollowing** it out and lining it with rocks. In the village of Ghalas-at we made new fires every night, but now I made one fire which I covered with **ashes** when I went to bed. The next night I would remove the ashes and blow on the **embers.** In this way I saved myself much work.

16   There were many gray **mice** on the island and now that I had food to keep from one meal to the other, I needed a safe place to put it. On the **face** of the rock, which was the back wall of my house, were several **cracks** as high as my shoulder. These I cut out and smoothed to make **shelves** where I could store my food and the mice could not reach it.

---

reeds   long stems of certain plants

pitch   a dark, sticky material; used to cover things so water does not go through them

gruel   hot cereal that is watery and not tasty

hollowing   taking out what is inside of something

ashes   powder left after something has burned

embers   a very hot piece of wood left after a fire

mice   very small animals; they often eat food that is left out

face   the front part of something

cracks   splits; breaks in a surface

shelves   flat pieces that are attached to a wall; used to hold objects

Paraphrase to Recall Information

Paraphrase this paragraph.

17   By the time winter was over and grass began to show green on the hills my house was **comfortable.** I was sheltered from the wind and rain and **prowling** animals. I could cook anything I wished to eat. Everything I wanted was there at hand.

Epilogue

Karana lived alone on the island for about 18 years. Someone finally found her. She was taken to California.

---

comfortable   something that is nice to be in or around   **prowling**   hunting quietly

About the Author

Scott O'Dell (1898–1989)

Scott O'Dell grew up in Los Angeles, California. O'Dell wrote more than 20 books for young people. Many of them tell stories about brave young people who face challenges and survive. O'Dell has said, "The only reason I write is to say something. I've forsaken [given up on] adults because they're not going to change, although they may try awfully hard. But children can and do change."

➤ What challenges do you think Scott O'Dell faced when he wrote "Island of the Blue Dolphins"? Why did he write the story?

Beyond the Reading

Reading Comprehension

Question-Answer Relationships (QAR)

"Right There" Questions

1. **Recall Facts** Where does the story take place?
2. **Recall Facts** Who is the main character in this story?
3. **Recall Facts** Why is she the only person on the island?
4. **Recall Facts** What does Karana use to make the fence?

"Think and Search" Questions

5. **Determine Sequence of Events** What is the first thing that Karana builds? Why does she build this first? What does she build next?
6. **Identify Cause and Effect** Why does Karana build the shelter?

"Author and You" Questions

7. **Analyze Character Traits** What kind of person is Karana? Describe her character traits.
8. **Make Inferences** How do you think Karana knew what materials to use for her projects?

"On Your Own" Questions

9. **Support Your Opinion** Do you think it would be hard to live on an island by yourself? What would you like about it? What would you not like? Explain.
10. **Connect Your Experiences** If you could take three things with you on an island, what would you take?

Activity Book
p. 66

Student
CD-ROM

Build Reading Fluency

Read Aloud to Engage Listeners

Reading aloud helps increase your fluency and expression. Learning to read with expression makes others want to listen to you.

1. Listen to the audio recording of "Island of the Blue Dolphins."
2. Turn to page 120 and follow along.
3. Pay attention to phrasing and expression.
4. With a partner, read aloud paragraphs 1–7 three times.
5. Select your favorite two paragraphs.
6. Read them in front of the class with expression.

Listen, Speak, Interact

Compare Ways of Working

In "Island of the Blue Dolphins," Karana must work alone to build her shelter. Do you think it is better to work alone or with other people?

1. Work alone. List as many states in the United States as you can.
2. Work with a small group. Again, list as many states as you can.

3. Talk about these questions:
   a. Did you list more states working alone or with the group?
   b. Did you have any problems working alone? Working with the group? Explain.
   c. Which did you like better: working alone or with the group? Why?

Elements of Literature

Compare and Contrast Themes and Ideas Across Texts

"Island of the Blue Dolphins" and "The Voyage of the *Frog*" have the same theme—survival. Both characters, Karana and David, have problems. Compare and contrast the theme and the idea of problem resolution in these two stories.

1. Read the following questions. Then reread both selections. As you read, take notes on these questions. You can add additional questions.
   a. What problems do the characters have?
   b. What is their most important problem?
   c. What help can they get from other people?
   d. What choices do they have?
   e. How do they resolve their problems?

2. Use your notes to complete a Venn Diagram.

Activity Book
p. 67

Student
CD-ROM

Word Study

Spell Frequently Misspelled Words

Some words are pronounced alike but have different spellings and meanings. Notice the differences between these words.

Word	Meaning	Example
two	the number 2	I needed **two** things—food and water.
too	more than enough; also	It was **too** cold to sleep on the rock. There were mice, **too**.
to	a preposition or a word used to introduce a verb	He sailed **to** the ship. It was too cold **to** sleep on the rock.

Copy these sentences in your Personal Dictionary. Fill in the blanks with *two, too,* or *to*. Check your answers with a partner.

1. May I please have _____ apples from the refrigerator?
2. Why? Because I want _____ eat them. I'm hungry.
3. No, not three. That's _____ many apples! I only want _____ !

Personal Dictionary   Activity Book p. 68   Student CD-ROM

Grammar Focus

Identify the Past and the Past Perfect Tense

All verbs have a **tense.** The tense tells you when an action happened.

The **past tense** describes an action that happened at a specific time in the past. The **past perfect tense** describes an action that happened before another action. *Both* of these actions have already happened.

happened first

Miguel <u>had finished</u> the book before I <u>started</u> it.

happened after

Most past tense verbs have *-d* or *-ed* at the end, such as *finished.* Past perfect tense verbs include *had* + a past participle.

1. Write the sentences below on a piece of paper. Underline the past tense verbs. Circle the past perfect tense verbs.
   a. After the basket had dried in the sun, I gathered lumps of pitch.
   b. I did not like to sleep in the shelter I had made until I was safe from the wild dogs.
2. Write two sentences, each one using the past tense and the past perfect tense.

Activity Book pp. 69–70   Student Handbook   Student CD-ROM

From Reading to Writing

Write Instructions

Write a short list of instructions explaining how to do something. Each step in the list tells the reader what to do. Use this as a guide.

1. Choose an activity to explain.
2. Think about how to do the activity. What steps must you take?
3. List the steps in chronological order (the order in which they happen).

How to Build a Fence on San Nicolas Island

○ **Step 1:** Gather whale ribs. You can find whale ribs buried in the sand.

○ **Step 2:** Gather some bull kelp. It is a plant that grows in the ocean.

○ **Step 3:** Put whale ribs in the ground next to each other.

Step 4: Tie the whale ribs together with bull kelp.

Activity Book
p. 71

Student
Handbook

Across Content Areas

THE ARTS

List Game Rules in Order

The Chumash were Native Americans who lived and worked together in villages. They also played games together.

The Game of *Payas*

Chumash boys and men played a game called *payas*. Two or more people could play *payas*. They used a large ring. Someone rolled the ring on the ground in a straight line. The players tried to throw a long stick into the middle of the ring. This was hard because the ring was moving. Players got 1 point if they got the stick into the middle of the ring. The player who got 12 points won the game.

Put the statements below in the correct order.

a. A player tries to throw a stick into the middle of the ring.
b. A player gets 1 point.
c. Someone rolls a ring on the ground in a straight line.
d. A player gets 12 points.

Activity Book
p. 72

CHAPTER 5

The Next Great Dying

an excerpt from an informational book by Karin Vergoth and Christopher Lampton

Objectives

Reading Identify cause and effect as you read an excerpt from an informational book.

Listening and Speaking Talk about conserving natural resources.

Grammar Recognize dependent clauses.

Writing Write an informational text.

Content Social Studies: Read a timeline.

Use Prior Knowledge

Think About Plants and Animals

No matter where you live, you see plants and animals. What plants and animals have you seen today? Which of these plants and animals do you see often? Which have you seen only a few times?

1. Work with a partner. Complete a chart like the one below.

2. List plants and animals that you have seen—around your school, in your community, in a movie, etc.
3. Which animal or plant do you think is special? Why?
4. Compare your chart with those of your classmates. Are there any unusual animals or plants listed?

See Often	Have Seen Only a Few Times
dogs	elephant
cactus	palm tree

Build Background

Endangered Species

An **endangered species** is a plant or an animal that is rare. There are very few of them. An endangered species is so rare that it may disappear from Earth within 20 years. There are thousands of endangered species in the world, for example, the Mexican grizzly bear, the giant panda, and the California condor.

Content Connection

SCIENCE

The ocelot is an endangered species. There are between 80 and 120 ocelots left in Texas.

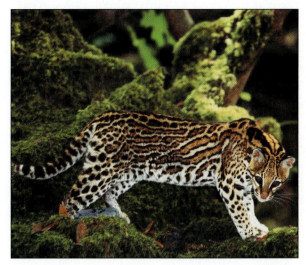

Ocelot

Build Vocabulary

Use a Word Wheel

"The Next Great Dying" has words that may be new to you. A Word Wheel can help you remember these new words.

1. Work with a partner. Look up *extinction* in a dictionary. Write the word and its definition in your Personal Dictionary.
2. Make a Word Wheel like the one here. Write the word *extinction* in one part of the Word Wheel.
3. List words related to *extinction* on a piece of paper.
4. Choose three words from your list to help you remember the meaning of *extinction*. Write these three words in your Word Wheel.

extinction

Personal Dictionary

The Heinle Newbury House Dictionary

Activity Book *p. 73*

Student CD-ROM

Text Structure

Informational Text

"The Next Great Dying" is an **informational text.** An informational text explains about a topic. The chart shows features of some informational texts.

Look for how the authors describe scientific processes. Does knowing about the scientific processes help you understand what you read?

Informational Text	
Topic	Many informational texts are about science topics.
Scientific Process	A scientific process is how scientists figure out something.
Facts and Examples	Facts and examples help to explain new ideas.
Definitions	The meanings of new words are given.

Student
CD-ROM

Reading Strategy

Identify Cause and Effect

A **cause** is the reason something happens. An **effect** is what happens because of the cause.

1. Read these two sentences. Which one is the cause, and which is the effect?
   a. The cat ran away.
   b. You teased the cat.
2. Notice causes and effects as you read and listen to the selection.
3. Use your Reading Log. Write causes and effects in a chart like the one here.

Reading Log   Student CD-ROM

The Next Great Dying

an excerpt from an informational book

by Karin Vergoth and Christopher Lampton

1   There are some things money can't buy. One of them is a live dinosaur. Try though you might, you'll never find a living dinosaur for sale. If you're lucky, you may find enough pieces of a dinosaur to put a **skeleton** together. If you have enough money, you may even be able to buy a dinosaur skeleton. Not long ago, the largest and most complete *Tyrannosaurus rex* skeleton ever found was bought at an **auction** by the Field Museum in Chicago for $7.6 million. But a **fossilized** skeleton, or a fossilized dinosaur egg, is as close as you'll ever get to owning the real thing.

Of course, everybody knows that   2
you can't buy a live dinosaur, or even find one. Dinosaurs lived on Earth a long time ago, but now they're gone. Nothing can bring them back. Dinosaurs became **extinct** 65 million years ago. They were wiped out by a deadly **catastrophe** that many scientists believe was **triggered** by a huge **comet** or **asteroid** crashing into Earth.

> ### Identify Cause and Effect
>
> What do many scientists think caused dinosaurs to become extinct?

Audio
CD 1, Tr. 10

skeleton   a body's bones

auction   a sale in which items are sold to the person who offers the most money

fossilized   when a dead animal or plant was buried and became hard like a rock

extinct   no longer in existence

catastrophe   a great disaster

triggered   caused

comet   an object made of dust, gas, or ice that travels in outer space

asteroid   a large rock in outer space

3   It wasn't only the dinosaurs that became extinct in this "great dying"; scientists estimate that up to 90 percent of all other **species** living at that time disappeared as well. Because so many species **died off** in a fairly short period of time, we refer to this great dying as a **mass extinction.** Scientists who study the **remains** of ancient life tell us that there have been five major mass extinctions in our planet's long history. Each one was caused by natural events, such as the changes in Earth's **climate** that caused the **ice ages** or the **impact** of comets and asteroids.

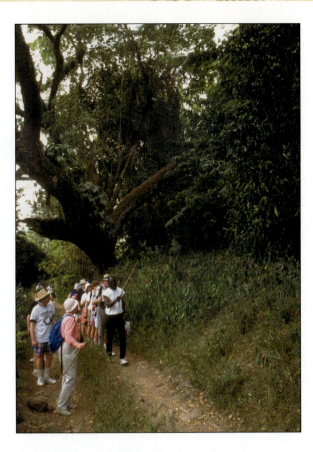

> ## Identify Cause and Effect
>
> What caused the five major mass extinctions in Earth's history?

4   We're in the middle of another mass extinction right now. Many people are calling it the "Sixth Extinction." But unlike past extinctions, this one isn't being caused by icy rocks from space or sudden changes in the climate. It is being caused by humans.

5   And it's happening much faster than the natural rate of extinction— the rate at which living things have disappeared over millions of years of Earth's history. It's difficult to say how much faster the present extinction is **progressing** because most of the species going extinct are unknown to science. Plus, scientists aren't really sure how many species there are on Earth.

---

species   groups of living things
died off   died one after another
mass extinction   the death of all animals or plants in many species
remains   parts or things that are left

climate   the type of weather that a place has
ice ages   periods of time when Earth was very cold and much of Earth's water turned to ice
impact   a hard hit
progressing   advancing, moving forward

Bald eagle

6   They've **identified** about 1 million different plants, animals, and other life forms, but that's just a drop in the bucket. Most scientists believe there are probably about 10 million species on Earth, and some think there may be as many as 100 million species.

7   So how many species are becoming extinct? Let's first consider the natural rate of extinction. If there were just 1 million species on Earth, and scientists could check up on each species every year to see if it was still surviving, they would **expect** that about one species would become extinct each year. Of course scientists can't **track** all species that closely—but they do **keep close tabs on** birds. There are about 10,000 species of birds. If birds were going extinct at the natural rate, one bird should be lost to extinction about every 100 years. What scientists are actually seeing is that one or more birds are going extinct each year. This means that the actual rate of extinction today is 100 times **greater** than the natural rate of extinction. That's **alarming!**

> ### Identify Cause and Effect
>
> Paragraph 4 says that humans are causing the "Sixth Extinction." Look at paragraph 7. What effect are humans having on birds?

---

identified   named
expect   think something will happen
track   follow the movement of something

keep close tabs on   notice what something is doing
greater   larger
alarming   shocking, scary

Taking all species of animals and plants together, scientists **estimate** that during the past century, the actual rate of extinction has been 100 to 1,000 times greater than expected. If there are indeed 10 million species on the planet, then 30 species are going extinct each day. In the next century, scientists predict the actual rate of extinction may be as much as 10,000 times greater than the natural extinction rate. In fact, some scientists warn that by the middle of the next century—about 50 years from now— half of all the species now living on Earth may be extinct. Another great dying is in progress—and very little is being done to stop it.

9

How did this mass extinction come about? Scientists do not need to **devise elaborate** theories to explain this twentieth-century disaster. The causes are all around them. Human beings— through **exploitation, neglect,** and overuse of Earth's resources—are engaged in **wholesale destruction** of the other living **organisms** on this planet. We are killing off our fellow species at an **appalling** rate.

Identify Cause and Effect

How are humans causing a mass extinction?

---

estimate   make a judgment about

devise   create, invent, think of

elaborate   complex, detailed

exploitation   using too much of something, usually in a greedy way

neglect   a state of not giving enough attention to something

wholesale destruction   very bad damage that affects many things

organisms   living things

appalling   shocking, very upsetting

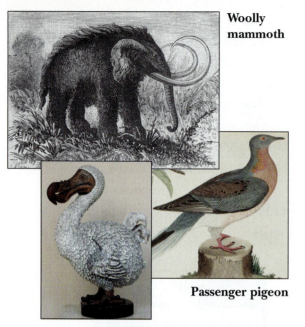

Woolly mammoth

Passenger pigeon

Dodo bird

10   When a species becomes extinct, no power on Earth can bring it back. Nothing can bring back the dinosaurs. If a particular species of bird, plant, or insect **ceases** to exist, no amount of money can bring it back. Extinction is forever. It's far worse than the death of an **individual** organism. When an individual dies, the children of that individual survive to carry on the species. But when a species becomes extinct, there are no children. The last dinosaurs left behind no **descendants**— neither did the woolly mammoth, or the dodo bird, or the passenger pigeon. Each of these creatures is now **absent** from Earth. If nothing is done, they will be followed into **oblivion** by the Bengal tiger, the California condor, and hundreds of other *endangered species*—species that are **teetering** on the **brink** of extinction at this very moment.

Dozens of species are nearing extinction right now. The African cheetah has been **displaced** from its natural home as humans **convert** its grasslands to pasture and farmland. The black rhinoceros is illegally hunted for its horns, which are used for medicines and dagger handles. The black-footed ferret was nearly starved out of existence when its food supply—prairie dogs—was **eliminated** by human hunting and disease. The cichlid, a small fish native to Lake Victoria in East Africa, was nearly wiped out when **non-native** Nile perch were introduced into the lake.

11

Identify Cause and Effect

The African cheetah is almost extinct. What is causing this?

---

ceases   stops an action

individual   one of a group

descendants   people or animals born into a certain family or group

absent   not present, missing

oblivion   nothingness

teetering   rocking back and forth in a dangerous way

brink   the top edge of a steep incline

displaced   removed

convert   change

eliminated   removed or gotten rid of

non-native   from somewhere else

12   These are only a few of the species now on the road to extinction. And though you have probably heard about some of the most **glamorous** species in danger of extinction, many others are unknown to all of us. These unidentified plants, insects, and **fungi** represent a valuable part of life on Earth.

> ### Identify Cause and Effect
>
> Many plants and animals are becoming extinct. What will be the effect of this?

---

glamorous   seen as interesting and exciting

fungi   living things that eat dead plants or animals and cannot survive apart from them

About the Authors

Karin Vergoth

Karin Vergoth helps adults and young people learn about science. She writes about science for magazines. Vergoth also works on a radio show about science. Today, Vergoth lives in Jersey City, New Jersey.

Christopher Lampton

Christopher Lampton has written more than 75 books about science. He has written about computers, the environment, and outer space. He also writes novels for young readers and adults. Lampton lives in Gaithersburg, Maryland.

➤ Why do you think Karin Vergoth and Christopher Lampton wrote "The Next Great Dying"? Did they want to entertain, inform, influence, or express themselves? Did they want to get readers to think about how humans are hurting the planet? Explain.

Beyond the Reading

Reading Comprehension

Question-Answer Relationships (QAR)

"Right There" Questions

1. Recall Facts When did dinosaurs become extinct?

2. Recall Details How many species have scientists identified so far?

"Think and Search" Questions

3. Identify List three species that the text says are nearing extinction.

4. Contrast How is the latest mass extinction different from the five other mass extinctions in Earth's history?

"Author and You" Questions

5. Evaluate Evidence Reread paragraph 9. What do scientists say are the causes of the latest mass extinction? Do you think the scientists are right? Why or why not?

6. Understand Authors' Perspective How do you think the authors feel about endangered species? What evidence can you find to support your answer?

"On Your Own" Questions

7. Support Your Opinion Do you think it is important to save endangered species? Why or why not?

8. Connect Your Experiences What are some things that you could do to protect endangered species?

9. Ask Questions What questions would you like to ask the authors of "The Next Great Dying"?

Activity Book
p. 74

Student
CD-ROM

Build Reading Fluency

Rapid Word Recognition

Rapidly recognizing words helps increase your reading rate. It is an important characteristic of effective readers.

1. With a partner, review the words in the box.

2. Read the words aloud for one minute. Your teacher will time you.

3. Count how many words you read in one minute.

pieces	caused	wiped	extinct	wiped	pieces
action	extinct	caused	wiped	extinct	wiped
extinct	estimate	action	pieces	estimate	action
wiped	wiped	extinct	action	pieces	estimate
estimate	action	pieces	estimate	caused	extinct

Listen, Speak, Interact

Talk About Conserving Natural Resources

Natural resources are things from nature that people use. We should try to conserve our natural resources—use less of them. How can we do this?

1. Work with a small group. Think of ways to conserve natural resources. For example, you could turn off the water while you are brushing your teeth.
2. List your ideas on a piece of paper. Does everyone in the group agree with all of the ideas?
3. Choose an idea you like. Present it to the class. Persuade your audience to do what you suggest.
4. As you listen to your classmates' presentations, take notes on these questions:
   a. What is the presenter trying to persuade me to do?
   b. Is the presenter giving examples and reasons?
   c. Did the presenter persuade me? Why or why not?

Elements of Literature

Analyze Deductive and Inductive Organization and Presentation

Sometimes authors tell you the point they want to make, and then they give you facts and examples to support it. This is **deductive** presentation and organization.

Read this deductive example.

"The doctor could tell that the man had a cold. He was sneezing and coughing."

Authors can also give you examples and facts first. This is **inductive** presentation and organization.

Here is the same information as before as an inductive example.

"The man was sneezing and coughing. The doctor could tell that he had a cold."

1. With a partner, read paragraphs 3 and 7 of the selection.
2. Is the presentation and organization of each paragraph inductive or deductive?
3. Talk about the choice of inductive and deductive presentation and organization. Would it make a difference if the author had switched them? Why?

Activity Book
p. 75

Student
CD-ROM

Word Study

Identify the Suffix *-ion*

A **suffix** is a word part added to the end of a word. A suffix sometimes changes the part of speech of a word. The suffix *-ion* changes a word into a noun (a person, a place, or a thing).

Extinct**ion** is forever.

Word	Suffix	Noun
extinct	+ -ion	→ extinction

Write these sentences in your Personal Dictionary. Complete the sentences. Use the underlined words to form a noun by adding the suffix *-ion*.

1. You always <u>distract</u> me from my work! You are a ____ .
2. Those men <u>construct</u> buildings. ____ is hard work.

Personal Dictionary   Activity Book p. 76   Student CD-ROM

Grammar Focus

Recognize Dependent Clauses

A **dependent clause** has a subject and a verb, but it cannot be a sentence on its own. It must be used with an independent clause. Many dependent clauses begin with the word *that*.

independent   dependent
clause   clause

<u>Scientists say **that** there have been five major mass extinctions.</u>

1. Write these sentences on a piece of paper.
   a. Everybody knows that you can't buy a live dinosaur.
   b. This means that the actual rate of extinction today is 100 times greater.
   c. They would expect that about one species would become extinct each year.
2. Underline the dependent clause.
3. Write your own sentence using a dependent clause with *that*. Do not use a comma to separate dependent clauses with *that* from the independent clause.

Activity Book pp. 77–78   Student Handbook   Student CD-ROM

From Reading to Writing

Write an Informational Text

Write an informational text that explains how people can consume fewer natural resources. Use what you learned in Listen, Speak, Interact.

1. Write an introduction, a body, and a conclusion.
2. Choose an inductive or deductive organization and presentation for each paragraph.
3. Use some dependent clauses with *that*. Punctuate them correctly.
4. Use the present and future tenses in some of your sentences.

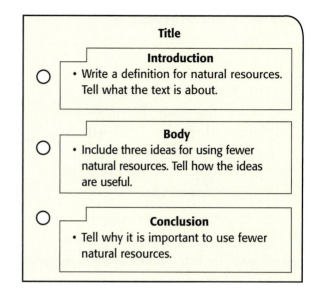

Title

Introduction
• Write a definition for natural resources. Tell what the text is about.

Body
• Include three ideas for using fewer natural resources. Tell how the ideas are useful.

Conclusion
• Tell why it is important to use fewer natural resources.

Activity Book
p. 79

Student
Handbook

Across Content Areas

SOCIAL STUDIES

Read a Timeline

A **timeline** lists events in the order in which they happened. The earliest event is usually on the left. The latest event is usually on the right.

Look at the timeline. It lists the dates when certain animals became extinct.

about 65 million years ago	about 10,000 years ago	about 1680	1914
Dinosaurs	The woolly mammoth	The dodo bird	The passenger pigeon

Answer these questions:

1. In what year did the passenger pigeon become extinct?
2. Which animal was the first to become extinct?
3. Did the dodo bird become extinct before or after the woolly mammoth?

Activity Book
p. 80

Listening and Speaking Workshop

Role-Play an Interview

Topic

In this unit, you read about scientists who study the survival of endangered species. Work with a partner. Role-play an interview with a scientist. Your interview will be about endangered species.

Assign roles. The interviewer asks questions. The interviewee is the scientist.

Step 1: Take notes on what you know.

1. Think about what you know about endangered species and extinction.
2. Ask your parents or a science teacher about endangered species.
3. Use resources in your library or on the Internet to find more information to add to your chart.
4. Organize your information in a chart.
5. Take notes on these topics:
   a. which animals are endangered today
   b. what people can do to save endangered species

Facts About Endangered Species	Causes of Extinction
About one bird species goes extinct each year.	Changes in climate

Step 2: Write your interview questions.

Use the chart and notes from Step 1 to write interview questions. Write each interview question on its own note card. Number each question.

Step 3: Answer the questions before role-playing the interview.

1. Work with your partner. Answer the interview questions. Use your notes from Step 1 to help you.
2. Write each answer on its own note card. Each answer note card should have the same number as the question it answers.

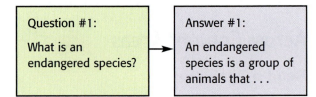

Question #1:
What is an endangered species?

Answer #1:
An endangered species is a group of animals that . . .

Step 4: Practice your interview.

The interviewer should:

1. Introduce the interviewee.
2. Use vocabulary about extinction in your questions.
3. Thank the interviewee at the beginning and end of the interview.

The interviewee should:

1. Answer the questions slowly and clearly.
2. Try not to read from the note card.

Step 5: Present your interview.

1. Speak slowly and clearly.
2. Look at your partner when you are speaking.

Step 6: Ask your classmates to evaluate your interview.

1. Ask your classmates to evaluate your interview by using the Active Listening Checklist. Then talk about how you could improve.

2. Ask your classmates to identify your purpose in speaking and major idea.
3. Ask your classmates, "What was the interviewee's perspective?"

Active Listening Checklist

1. Did the presenters speak too slowly, too quickly, or just right?

2. Did the presenters speak loudly enough?

3. Were the presenters' questions and answers interesting and correct?

Student
Handbook

Viewing Workshop

View and Think

Describe How Pictures and Diagrams Show Text Meaning

1. View the pictures or diagrams that appear with one of the selections in this unit. Choose your favorite one.
2. Answer the following questions.
   a. What does the picture or diagram show?
   b. How does the picture or diagram help you understand the text?

3. Think about other pictures or diagrams that could help readers. Draw one of these.
4. Describe your drawing to the class. Explain how it helps understanding.

Further Viewing

Watch the *Visions* CNN Video for Unit 2. Do the Video Worksheet.

CNN Video

Writer's Workshop

Response to Literature: Write a Survival Manual

Writing Prompt

Write part of a survival manual for new students at your school. A survival manual tells people how to survive or deal with a new or difficult situation. Here are some topics.

1. how to find the way around school
2. the most important rules
3. what to do if you need help
4. some things to do for fun

Step 1: Ask questions.

1. Think about these questions:
   a. What does a new student need to know to survive at your school?
   b. What problems would a new student face?
   c. How could a new student solve these problems?
2. Choose the most important problems.

Step 2: Find answers to your questions.

1. These resources can help you answer the questions in Step 1:
   a. teachers
   b. other students
   c. guidance counselor
   d. your school's student handbook
2. You might discover new questions as you answer other questions. Try to find answers to these new questions as well. For example:

Question: What do you do if you are sick and can't come to school?
Answer: An adult at home should call the office.
This leads to:
Question: What if you miss a test?
Answer: Talk to your teacher about making it up.
3. Write your answers in a chart.

How to Survive as a New Student at Sierra School	
Survival Problems	How to Solve These Problems
sick—can't come to school	adult at home—call the office
miss a test	talk to teacher—make up test

Step 3: Organize your survival manual.

1. You can use chronological order. What does a new student need to know first? Second? Next?
2. You may want to create a chart of Frequently Asked Questions.

Step 4: Write a first draft.

If possible, type your first draft on a computer.

1. Write a title for your survival manual.
2. Write an introductory paragraph to explain your purpose.

3. Include your chart of Frequently Asked Questions.

4. Write a conclusion. Explain why following your recommendations is important.

5. Use correct grammar.
   a. Begin sentences with words such as *another problem, also,* or *finally* to show new ideas.
   b. Be sure that your present tense verbs agree with their subjects.
   c. Vary your sentences by using dependent clauses.

How to _____

Introduction

This manual will help you _____

_____

Frequently Asked Questions

QUESTION: _____

ANSWER: _____

QUESTION: _____

ANSWER: _____

Conclusion

These points are important because

_____

Step 5: Add pictures.

Also include visuals (photographs, drawings, or diagrams). These visuals should help readers understand. For example, you might show a map of your school.

Step 6: Revise and edit your draft.

1. Exchange drafts with two classmates. Ask your classmates these questions:
   a. Is my manual useful and correct?
   b. Have I used simple language?
   c. Is there anything that you do not understand?
   d. Did I make spelling, punctuation, or grammar mistakes?
   e. Is my manual organized clearly?
2. Make any changes that are necessary. You may want to:
   a. add or delete text
   b. elaborate ideas
   c. combine text
   d. rearrange text
3. Use resource materials (dictionary, thesaurus, your Student Handbook) to help you revise and edit.

Step 7: Publish your survival manual.

1. Make a final draft. Use your best handwriting if you are writing your report by hand. Check for spelling and grammar mistakes if you are using a computer.
2. Make a cover page for your survival manual. The cover page should have the title and your name.
3. Invite the principal and the guidance counselor to read your survival manual. Ask if you can give them to new students.

The Heinle Newbury House Dictionary

Student Handbook

Projects

These projects will help you learn more about survival. Work alone, with a partner, or with a small group. If you need help, ask a teacher, a parent, or your school librarian.

Project 1: Research an Endangered Species

Learn about an endangered species. Choose one listed in "The Next Great Dying," or you may choose another one.

1. Find information in several sources in your school library. You can also search the Internet to find information. These search words are helpful: *endangered species, extinction.*
2. Gather information on these topics:
    a. the name of the animal or plant
    b. places where it lives today
    c. where it used to live
    d. interesting information
    e. why it is endangered
3. Make a poster about your animal or plant. Include the information you learned and pictures.
4. Use punctuation and capitalization to enhance your message.

Project 2: Summarize a Real-Life Survival Story

In Chapter 4, you read about the Lost Woman of San Nicolas Island. Find another story about a real person who survived a hard situation. Then summarize this real-life survival story.

1. Find a true survival story. Try these resources:
    a. Find a book in your school library. Ask the librarian for help.
    b. Look in current newspapers or magazines.
    c. Ask family members or friends.
2. Summarize the person's story. Write one or two paragraphs. Be sure to cite your sources.
3. Include pictures to help tell the story.
4. Present your summary and pictures to the class. You might record the summary on audio or video. You might also use presentation software. Add music to create an exciting mood.

AFRICAN CHEETAH

It lives in sub-Saharan Africa today. It used to live in most of Africa, in southern Asia, the Middle East, and India.

It eats small antelopes.

It can run 70 miles per hour!

Further Reading

The following books discuss the theme of survival. Choose one or more of them. Write your thoughts and feelings about what you read in your Reading Log. Take notes about your answers to these questions:

1. Think about the situations that the people faced. How would you feel if you faced these situations?
2. Have you ever been in situations like the ones you read about? Explain.

How I Survived My Summer Vacation: And Lived to Write the Story

by Robin Friedman, Cricket Books, 2000. Jackie wants to write a novel during the summer before he starts high school. But he cannot get past the first sentence! He asks his friends for help and ideas.

Voyage of the Frog

by Gary Paulsen, Yearling Books, 1990. David gets caught in a storm as he is trying to sail his boat, the *Frog*. After the storm ends, David must figure out how to get back home on his own.

Island of the Blue Dolphins

by Scott O'Dell, Scott Foresman, 1987. Karana, an American Indian girl, is left behind on her tribe's island. This story tells how Karana survives alone on the island for 18 years!

Backwater

by Joan Bauer, G.P. Putnam, 1999. Ivy, at age 16, finds great fascination in tracking and recording her family's history, especially after she discovers an eccentric aunt she's never met. Her attempt to interview Aunt Jo involves mountaineering, storms, shifting lake ice, and other adventures.

Climb or Die

by Edward Myers, Hyperion Press, 1996. This book tells the story of Danielle and her brother, Jake. Their family's car crashes in the Rocky Mountains during a snowstorm. Danielle and Jake must climb a mountain to find help for their parents.

Far North

by Will Hobbs, Morrow, 1996. Fifteen-year-old Gabe enrolled in a school in Canada's Northwest Territories so that he could be closer to his dad, an oil-field worker. Instead, he got an airplane accident, the friendship of two Dene Indians, a grizzly bear, starvation, extreme cold, and a blizzard. Breathless action and the Canadian landscape pervade Gabe's struggle to survive.

Memory Boy

by Will Weaver, HarperCollins, 2001. It's 2008, two years after a massive volcano completely changes life in the United States as we know it. Miles, sixteen, and his family leave the city to find refuge in their country cottage, only to find it inhabited by other desperate people who refuse to leave. Miles remembers enough from a school project to work out another refuge for his family.

The Extreme Survival Guide

by Rory Storm, Element Books, 1999. This compilation of tips and accounts about surviving disasters and emergencies draws from situations that actually happened around the globe.

Companion Web site   Reading Log

Heinle Reading Library
The Swiss Family Robinson

Journeys

Railroad Observation Car Heading West, photo, Franklin McMahon, 20th century.

View the Picture

1. A journey is a long trip. What kind of journey do you think these people are taking?

2. Why do you think these people are on this journey?

In this unit, you will read several selections about journeys. You will read a poem, a story, a science fiction story, informational texts, and a historical story. You will also learn the elements of these writing forms and how to write them yourself.

CHAPTER 1

Into the Reading

I Have No Address

a poem
by Hamza El Din

Objectives

Reading Recognize figurative language as you read a poem.

Listening and Speaking Draw and present images based on text.

Grammar Use apostrophes with possessive nouns.

Writing Write a poem using figurative language.

Content Science: Learn about migration of birds.

Use Prior Knowledge

Talk About Journeys

When you make a journey, you travel to different places. You may travel to a different country or another city. You may travel to the beach or the grocery store.

1. Work with a partner. Talk about a place where you have traveled.
2. Use a Sunshine Organizer to answer these questions. Write the answers next to the triangles.
   a. Where did you go?
   b. Who went with you?
   c. When did you go there?
   d. Why did you go there?
   e. What did you do there?
   f. How did your journey change you?

Who? What? When? Where? Why? How?

A Place Where I Have Traveled

Build Background

Song Sparrows

Sparrows are small birds. They live in many places around the world. There are many different types of sparrows. The song sparrow is one type. They are called song sparrows because they sing songs. In some places, these songs tell us that spring has arrived. Song sparrows live in North America. You may even see them in your own backyard.

SCIENCE

Content Connection

Many sparrows **migrate**—move from one place to another. They move to warmer, southern areas in the fall, when the weather gets cool. They move back to northern areas in the spring, when the weather gets warm.

Build Vocabulary

Identify Multiple-Meaning Words

Some words can mean more than one thing. These words are called **multiple-meaning words.** You can figure out what these words mean by reading the words around them (the context).

Read each sentence. The underlined words are multiple-meaning words. Choose the correct definition.

1. Anna lived in different countries and learned different <u>tongues</u>.
   a. parts of your mouth that help you talk and taste food
   b. spoken languages

2. We cannot go swimming. The <u>waves</u> are too high.
   a. raised areas of water that move across the surface of the sea
   b. hand signals

3. The fishermen <u>cast</u> their nets into the water.
   a. assigned a part in a play or movie
   b. threw

The Heinle Newbury House Dictionary

Activity Book *p. 81*

Student CD-ROM

Text Structure

Poem

"I Have No Address" is a **poem.** A poem is a type of writing that expresses feelings or ideas. The chart shows the features of this poem.

Think about how these features help the author show feelings and ideas.

Poem	
Stanzas	The poem is organized in groups of lines.
Images	The author describes people, places, and things.
Free Verse	The words at the end of lines do not rhyme (do not have the same ending sounds).
Repetition	Words and ideas are repeated (said more than once). This shows strong feelings or important ideas.

Reading Log   Student CD-ROM

Reading Strategy

Recognize Figurative Language

Authors often use **figurative language** to describe people, places, and things. Figurative language is not literal. That is, it does not mean exactly what the individual words mean. Look at this example:

The idea was a flash of light in my brain.

This does not mean that there was a real "flash of light." It means that the idea came quickly, like a flash of light.

This kind of figurative language is called a **metaphor.** A metaphor describes one thing as if it is another thing.

Metaphors are often used in literary writings, especially in poems. You will understand poems better if you look for them as you read or listen.

In your Reading Log, write the metaphors that you find as you read or listen to the audio recording of "I Have No Address."

Reading Log   Student CD-ROM

I Have No Address

a poem
by Hamza El Din

Audio
CD 2, Tr. 1

Recognize Figurative Language

What is the metaphor in this stanza?

1   I am a sparrow with a white heart and a thousand tongues.
    I fly around the **globe**
    Singing for peace, love and **humanity**
    In every place.
    I have no address.

2   My address is lines **ornamented** by dreams, beating hearts
        united by smiling hope
    For people who wish good for other people all the time.
    I sing, smile and cry.
    My tears wash away pain
    In every place.

3   Our paths are boats of longing, turning round and round
        with us—
    One day to the east, another to the west, to **tranquil**
        moorings.
    And when the waves go against us and cast us away,
    Then the echo of my sounds at midnight will be a dock at the
        shore of tranquility,
    In every place.

---

globe   the world
humanity   the state or condition of being human
ornamented   decorated

tranquil   calm, peaceful
moorings   places where something, especially a boat,
        can be tied and made secure

Recognize
Figurative
Language

What is the
metaphor in this
stanza?

4   The day we join hands with others' hands, our **universe** is
    A rose garden blooming in the holy night.
    It contains us, with hope, love and **alleluias.**

5   And I am the sparrow on the branch.
    I sleep, dream and fly happily
    In every place.
    I have no address.

---

universe   the stars, planets, other heavenly bodies, and   **alleluias**   expressions of joy
       all of space

About the Author

Hamza El Din (born 1929)

Hamza El Din was born in Sudan, a country in Africa. When El Din was a young boy, his village was flooded (covered with water). He and his family were forced to leave their home. When El Din was in college, he began singing. He also learned to play the oud, a stringed instrument from Africa and the Middle East. Today El Din travels all over the world, playing and singing his music for others.

► Hamza El Din moved as a young boy. Do you think this event affected his poetry? How do the main ideas and details in his poem support your ideas?

Beyond the Reading

Reading Comprehension

Question-Answer Relationships (QAR)

"Right There" Questions

1. **Recall Facts** What type of bird does the author describe himself as?
2. **Recall Facts** What does this bird do?
3. **Recall Facts** What does the rose garden contain?

"Think and Search" Questions

4. **Understand Figurative Language** What does the author mean by the metaphor "a dock at the shore of tranquility"?
5. **Understand Figurative Language** What does "a dock at the shore of tranquility" have to do with the bird's song?

"Author and You" Questions

6. **Identify a Recurrent Theme** Where does the sparrow sing?

7. **Understand Characterization** Why do you think the author chose a bird to represent himself?
8. **Describe Mental Images** What image do you have of the address in stanza 2?
9. **Appreciate Writer's Craft** Choose a stanza that you like. Explain how the way it is written helps you enjoy it.

"On Your Own" Questions

10. **Understand Figurative Language** What do you think the author means by "Our paths are boats of longing, turning round and round with us—"?
11. **Understand Author's Perspective** What do you think the author wants for everybody?

Activity Book
p. 82

Student
CD-ROM

Build Reading Fluency

Echo Read Aloud

Effective readers learn to read with feeling. Echo reading helps you read with feeling and expression. Your teacher reads a line. Then the class reads (echoes) the same line aloud. Turn to page 156.

1. Listen to your teacher read.
2. Read the same line aloud with expression.
3. Continue listening and reading.

Listen, Speak, Interact

Draw and Present Images Based on Text

The poet (author of the poem) writes descriptions of people, places, and things. He writes about a bird flying around the world. He also writes about people holding hands.

Descriptions help you draw **images** (pictures) in your mind. When you read or listen to the poem, what pictures do you make in your mind?

1. Listen to the audio recording of the poem.
   a. What effect did the reader's interpretation have on you?
   b. How did the words affect you?
2. Reread the poem. Pay attention to the images you make in your mind.
3. Draw one of these images on a piece of paper.
4. Read the poem aloud to the class. Ask your classmates, "Which words from the poem does my drawing show?"

Elements of Literature

Recognize Style, Tone, and Mood

Authors use several elements of literature to create an effect on the reader. Three of these are **style, tone,** and **mood.** Read the meanings in the chart.

Reread "I Have No Address" and answer these questions in your Reading Log.

1. The author uses first-person narration as an element of style.
   a. What effect does this have on you?
   b. Explain how the effect would be different if the poem was in third-person narration.
2. What is the author's tone? Is it negative or positive?
3. What is the mood? Do you feel sad? Hopeful? Disappointed? Happy?

Element	Meaning
Style	how authors use language to express themselves
Tone	the author's attitude (how the author feels) toward the topic
Mood	the feeling that you get from reading a text

Reading Log

Activity Book
p. 83

Student
CD-ROM

Word Study

Recognize the Suffix -ity

A **suffix** is a group of letters added to the end of a word. A suffix changes the meaning of a root word.

Singing for peace, love, and huma**nity**

The root word of *humanity* is *human* (a person). When the suffix *-ity* is added, the meaning of the word becomes "condition or state of" being human.

If the root word ends in *e*, drop the *e* before adding *-ity*.

1. Copy the chart in your Personal Dictionary.

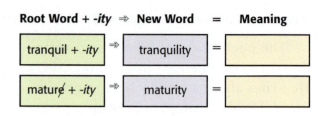

Root Word + *-ity* ⇒	New Word	=	Meaning
tranquil + *-ity* ⇒	tranquility	=	
mature + *-ity* ⇒	maturity	=	

2. Write the meaning of each word with the suffix *-ity* in the boxes.
3. Use a dictionary to check if your ideas are correct.

Personal Dictionary   The Heinle Newbury House Dictionary   Activity Book p. 84   Student CD-ROM

Grammar Focus

Use Apostrophes with Possessive Nouns

Possession means belonging to someone. An apostrophe (') shows possession when used with a noun and sometimes the letter *s*.

The poet**'s** tears wash away the pain.

Use the chart to learn when to use *'s* with a noun, and when to just use *'*.

Add apostrophes to the underlined words.

1. The two <u>brothers</u> room is messy.
2. The <u>womens</u> coats are in the closet.

Most Nouns

Singular Noun	Add 's	Possessive Singular Noun
poet	's	poet's
Plural Noun	**Add '**	**Possessive Plural Noun**
poets	'	poets'

Plural Nouns that Do Not End in *s*

Plural Noun	Add 's	Possessive Plural Noun
children	's	children's

Activity Book pp. 85–86   Student Handbook   Student CD-ROM

From Reading to Writing

Write a Poem Using Figurative Language

Write a poem about a person you know. The poem can be serious or funny.

1. Separate your poem into stanzas.
2. Use figurative language to describe the person. Reread stanza 1 on page 156 as a model.
3. Use free verse. The words at the end of lines do not need to rhyme (have the same ending sounds).
4. Repeat words to show strong feelings or important ideas.
5. Use some possessive noun forms.

6. Choose how to present your poem in writing. Use handwriting, printing, or a special font on a computer.

(Title of Poem)

(Name) is a _____.

(He or She) does _____ and _____.

(He or She) has _____ of _____.

(Name) is a _____.

VISIONS
Activity Book
p. 87

Student
Handbook

Across Content Areas

SCIENCE

Learn About Migration of Birds

When birds **migrate,** they travel from one area to another. This is called **migration.** Some birds travel thousands of miles during their migration. They do this in order to find warmer temperatures, more food, and more water. For example, some North American birds migrate south to Central and South America. The birds' migrations give them warmer temperatures, more food, and more water.

Most migrating birds follow the same **migration route.** A route is a path of travel. The same routes are used every year.

Complete each sentence with a word from the box.

migrate	south	route

1. In the spring, some birds _____ from Mexico to parts of Canada.
2. Groups of sparrows fly through our town every April. Our town must be on the birds' migration _____ .
3. The birds began migrating in October. They traveled _____ to Central America.

VISIONS
Activity Book
p. 88

CHAPTER 2

Into the Reading

The Voyage of the Lucky Dragon

an excerpt from a novel
by Jack Bennett

Objectives

Reading Paraphrase to recall information as you read an excerpt from a novel.

Listening and Speaking Have a debate.

Grammar Identify subject and object pronouns.

Writing Write to solve a problem.

Content Social Studies: Describe countries on a map.

Use Prior Knowledge

Talk About Problems

We must often face problems in our lives. Sometimes we can resolve our problems. Sometimes we cannot. Trying to resolve problems helps us learn and grow.

1. Think about a problem in your life that you had to resolve. Use these questions to help you brainstorm:
   a. Did you ever have problems getting used to a new place?
   b. Did you ever have problems getting along with a friend?
   c. Did you ever have problems understanding schoolwork?
2. Use a Cluster Map to organize your notes.

3. Work with a partner to compare and contrast your problems. Interpret your partner's verbal and non-verbal messages (what he or she says and does).

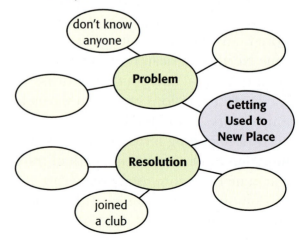

Build Background

Vietnam

Vietnam is a country in Southeast Asia. For many years Vietnam was divided into North Vietnam and South Vietnam. North Vietnam had a communist government. South Vietnam did not have a communist government.

The communists wanted to control both parts of Vietnam. This led to a war between North Vietnam and South Vietnam. A war within a country is called a **civil war.** The war ended in the 1970s. North Vietnam and South Vietnam became one country with a communist government.

Content Connection

In a **communist** country, the government usually owns all of the land and businesses.

Build Vocabulary

Learn Words Related to Emotions

The words below relate to **emotions** (feelings). Read the words and their definitions. Then complete each sentence with the correct word. Write in your Personal Dictionary.

shocked felt a lot of surprise

anxiously in a worried way

delighted very happy, pleased

mournfully in a very sad way

guilty a feeling of having done something wrong

1. "My dog ran away," he said ___ .
2. Sasha was ___ to get a new bike.
3. I wish I had never said those hurtful words. I felt ___ .
4. He never thought this would happen. He was ___ .
5. Juan did not study yesterday. He took the test ___ .

Personal Dictionary   Activity Book *p. 89*   Student CD-ROM

Text Structure

Historical Fiction

"The Voyage of the Lucky Dragon" is **historical fiction.** Historical fiction is a made-up story that is set during a real time in history. Look at the features of historical fiction in the chart.

Look for details that tell you about the setting of the story. Use the **prologue** (introduction) to help you learn about background events in history. Analyze the story plot to see the characters' problems and how they resolve them.

Historical Fiction	
Setting	The story is set in a real place and time.
Characters	The characters may be made-up. Some characters may also be real people.
Plot (Series of Events)	Historical fiction stories combine made-up events with events that really happened.

Student CD-ROM

Reading Strategy

Paraphrase to Recall Information

When you tell a part of a reading selection in your own words, you **paraphrase.** This can help you recall what you have read. Read this example:

Text from the Reading Selection:
She came back in a few seconds, her face pale. "Father," she said. "Please come. There's a—a young man to see you. He's strange—"

Paraphrase:
She came back right away. She looked scared. She asked her father to come because there was a young man who wanted to see him. She thought he looked odd.

When you paraphrase, follow these steps:

1. Read the text several times until you understand it.
2. Close your book.
3. Write your paraphrase.
4. Check your paraphrase against the text. Revise your paraphrase to include all of the important information.

As you read or listen to "The Voyage of the Lucky Dragon," paraphrase some of the paragraphs.

Student CD-ROM

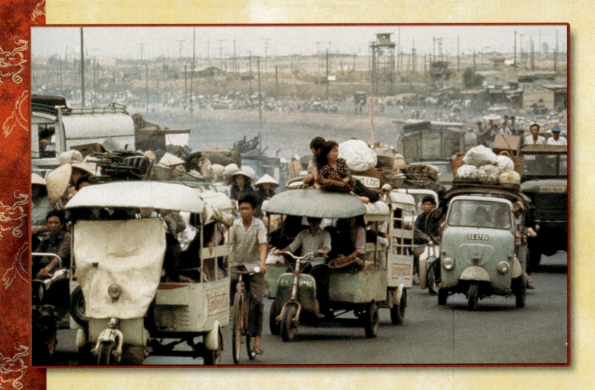

The Voyage of the Lucky Dragon

an excerpt from a novel
by Jack Bennett

Audio
CD 2, Tr. 2

Prologue

This story is about a family in Vietnam. The time of the story is the late 1970s. The Vietnam War has ended. The communists have taken control of the government. They have also taken control of all the businesses in Vietnam.

When this reading begins, the family receives a visitor. This visitor is a young man who works for the new government in Vietnam.

Paraphrase to Recall Information

Paraphrase this paragraph.

1   There was no letter from Phan Thi Chi's father the next day. But that evening, while the whole family was having supper around the big table in the back room, a young man came into the shop. He **rapped rudely** on the counter and Ly ran out to serve him.

2   She came back in a few seconds, her face **pale.** "Father," she said. "Please come. There's a—a young man to see you. He's strange—"

3   Phan Thi Chi and his wife got up **hastily,** their food unfinished. Ah Soong, Uncle Tan and Quan and Ly exchanged uneasy glances. Then, with one accord, they crowded into the narrow, short passage between the back room and the shop.

---

rapped   struck or hit
rudely   without manners

pale   lacking color
hastily   quickly

Paraphrase to Recall Information

Paraphrase this paragraph.

4   The strange young man was quietly dressed in a white short-sleeved shirt, black trousers and black shoes. He was about twenty-two or twenty-three; no older. His young face held **authority** and, as he glanced around the little shop, a cold **contempt.** He put back in his pocket a card he had just showed Phan Thi Chi and glanced at the expectant faces crowding the passage.

5   "Family?" he asked.

6   "Yes," said Phan Thi Chi. After all, he thought, **defensively,** Ah Soong is family.

7   The young man unfolded a sheet of typewritten paper.

8   "You are Phan Thi Chi, shopkeeper, of thirteen Bach Dang, Gia Dinh?"

9   "Yes."

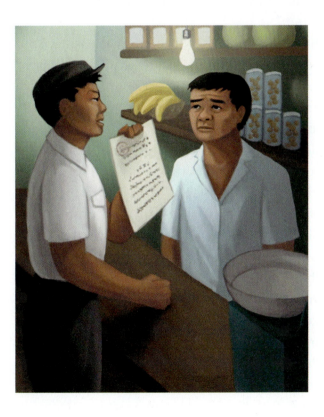

10   "You have heard of the government **decree** of March twenty-three?"

11   "It is only March twenty-four today and I have heard no news all day."

12   "From March twenty-three—that is yesterday—all trading and business operations by **bourgeois** elements of the population are **abolished.** Do you know what that means?"

---

authority   power to command
contempt   disfavor
defensively   protectively

decree   an official order
bourgeois   middle class
abolished   stopped

13   "Yes," said Phan Thi Chi quietly. "It means you take my shop away from me."

14   "That is right. This shop is now owned by the state. You will remain in control of it until the state sends a manager to take over."

15   "How do I and my family live?"

Paraphrase to Recall Information

Paraphrase this paragraph.

16   There was suddenly a deadly **hush** in the room: it was as though everyone had stopped breathing. Out in the street a dog barked suddenly. It seemed very loud. The young man read from his piece of paper:

17   "Phan Thi Chi will be sent to a re-education camp in Ho Chi Minh City. After showing progress, he will be sent to a New Economic Zone in An Gian Province—"

18   "I know nothing about farming," said Phan Thi Chi.

19   The young man **shrugged.** "You'll learn. It will be part of your re-education."

20   "And my family?"

21   "Your wife will go to a re-education centre at Long Tanh. Your children will be sent to a New Economic Zone at Le Minh Xuan."

22   "Will we be allowed to visit each other? To write?"

---

hush silence   **shrugged** raised one's shoulders to express doubt

23   The young man shrugged again.

24   "I don't know. That depends on the **authorities,** I suppose."

25   Phan Thi Chi felt himself growing angry despite the cold fear that gripped him.

Paraphrase to Recall Information

Paraphrase this paragraph.

26   "What about the rest of my family?" He pointed to Ah Soong, her face **inscrutable,** to Aunt Binh and Uncle Tan. Uncle Tan balanced on his **crutch,** his eyes on the young man.

27   The young man consulted his paper again.

28   "I have no instructions about these people," he said. He looked at Uncle Tan.

29   "Where did you lose your leg?"

30   "It's buried at Hue."

31   "With a lot of Americans and **traitors,**" said the young man.

32   Uncle Tan just stared at him. The young man folded his paper and put it in his pocket.

33   "Well, I have no instructions about you, one-leg. Nor about these two ladies—" he nodded at Ah Soong and Aunt Binh.

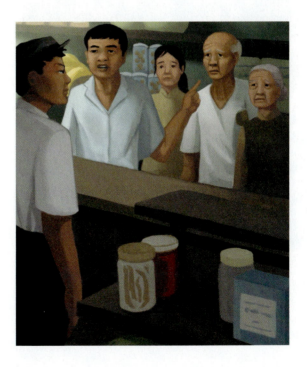

---

authorities   those in control
inscrutable   difficult to understand

crutch   a tool to help someone walk
traitors   people who betray their country

Paraphrase to Recall Information

Paraphrase this paragraph.

34 "No doubt you will hear from the authorities soon enough." He turned to the **ashen-faced** Phan Thi Chi. "You may operate your shop until the state official arrives. That may take a few days or a week. You must not sell any goods which have been **declared** subject to state control—"

35 "How do I know what they are?"

36 "You must find out. Don't ask me how. But you must find out. Go to the Public Security Bureau. It is a serious offense to trade in state-controlled goods, you know."

37 And then he was gone, leaving a shocked silence which Phan Thi Chi was the first to break.

38 "Shut the door," he said to his wife. "Quan, shut the back door. Lock it. Then all come upstairs, to the roof. Nobody can hear us there."

39 When they were all on the roof, **dodging** Ah Soong's washing, he told them of his plan to escape to Rach Gia, and start a new life on his old father's boat. When he had finished talking, he watched their faces anxiously.

40 Quan was the first to speak. To his father's **relief,** he was delighted. Quan was a strange boy sometimes, with his own ideas.

---

ashen-faced gray, gloomy
declared said out loud

dodging avoiding
relief ease from discomfort

41   "When do we go?" was all he said. "I'd love to be a fisherman—"

42   "You mustn't forget your schoolwork," said his mother. "There'll be a school at Rach Gia, you know—"

43   "Not like the one here, I hope," said Ly, **wrinkling** her nose.

44   "Things will be different in Rach Gia," their father promised them. "It's a little village. People are different down there."

45   "If I like working on the boat, I might become a marine engineer," said Quan. "Eh, mother? I could see the world!"

Paraphrase to Recall Information

Paraphrase this paragraph.

46   "I don't like the sea," said Aunt Binh **mournfully.** "I went out on a junk at Da Nang. I got sick. And boat people aren't like us. But don't worry about me, please. I know I have to do as I'm told."

47   "No you don't," said Phan Thi Chi rather **cruelly.** "You can always go to one of their New Economic Zones, and learn to be a rice-farmer."

48   Aunt Binh turned her head away, sniffling quietly, and Phan Thi Chi felt guilty.

---

wrinkling   folding or shrinking
mournfully   sadly

cruelly   in a mean way

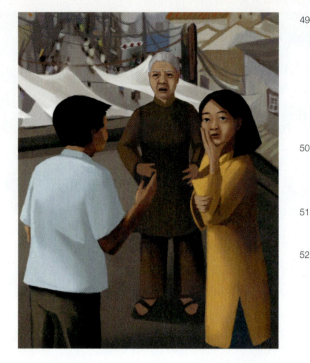

49   "Well, if that is decided then, I'd better go and get some food ready for the trip," said Ah Soong, as though Phan Thi Chi had announced that a bus was waiting to **whisk** them to Rach Gia on the instant.

50   Phan Thi Chi cleared his throat **nervously** and his wife glanced at him with a sly smile.

51   "Ah, well," said Phan Thi Chi, and the old woman looked at him sharply.

52   "We—ah, I, had thought, Ah Soong, that, ah, you—well, it could be a rough life down at Rach Gia and ah, well, we don't know what sort of house we will find, you know, and so—"

53   "And so you thought I'd go back to China! At my age! After nearly half a **century** in Vietnam! What nonsense!"

54   "Now just listen, Ah Soong," said Phan Thi Chi nervously, rolling a desperate eye at his wife, who was **gazing steadfastly** over the rooftops as though entranced by some sight in the general direction of the National Assembly Building.

Paraphrase to Recall Information

Paraphrase this paragraph.

55   "Besides," said Ah Soong, "besides the fact that I haven't written to my family in China for years, have you forgotten who runs the country now? When I left it was the Kuomintang, and now it is the **communists.** Well, I didn't like the Kuomintang when I was a girl in China, and I don't like what I've seen of the Vietnamese communists. Why should the Chinese communists be different? Or better? No, I'm coming with you. I have some money of my own.

---

whisk   take away

nervously   uneasily, uncomfortably

century   a time period of 100 years

gazing   staring

steadfastly   steadily

communists   members of the Communist Party; a social system marked by the common ownership of goods and services

Besides—" and the old woman drew herself up and glanced **scathingly** at the rest of the family, "you couldn't get on without me! Now I have things to do." And she shuffled off downstairs, leaving Phan Thi Chi embarrassed behind a flapping wet sheet.

56   "I told you," said Ly's mother after a short silence.

57   "Are you coming, Uncle Tan?" asked Quan.

58   Uncle Tan twirled his crutch.

59   "I saw a movie about a one-legged **pirate** once," he said with a grin. "And he had only one eye, too. Yes I'm coming."

60   So it was decided.

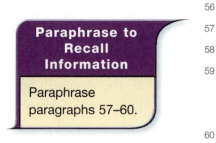

Paraphrase to Recall Information

Paraphrase paragraphs 57–60.

---

scathingly   extremely harshly

pirate   one who robs at sea

About the Author   Jack Bennett

Jack Bennett has traveled all over the world writing for magazines and newspapers. He has also written books for adults and children. He wrote a novel for young adults called *The Lieutenant.*

➤ How do you think Jack Bennett got the information he needed to write this story? Why do you think he wrote it?

Beyond the Reading

Reading Comprehension

Question-Answer Relationships (QAR)

"Right There" Questions

1. **Recall Facts** Where does the story take place?
2. **Recall Facts** On what day is Phan Thi Chi supposed to hand over his shop?
3. **Recall Facts** What city does Phan Thi Chi plan to take his family to? Why?

"Think and Search" Questions

4. **Explain** How long will it be before the government manager will take over?
5. **Analyze Plot** Why would the government want to take Phan Thi Chi's shop?
6. **Recognize and Analyze Problem Resolution** How does the family resolve their problem? Do you think this is the best resolution? Explain.

"Author and You" Questions

7. **Recognize Character Traits** How do you think the young man feels about telling Phan Thi Chi his shop will be taken from him? What text evidence do you find?
8. **Recognize Character Traits** Why is Quan excited about leaving?

"On Your Own" Questions

9. **Predict** What do you think might happen to Phan Thi Chi if he does not turn over his shop?
10. **Predict** Do you think life will be easy for the family in Rach Gia? Why?

Activity Book
p. 90

Student
CD-ROM

Build Reading Fluency

Read Silently and Aloud

Reading silently for practice then reading aloud helps you read with expression and understanding.

1. Listen to the audio recording of "The Voyage of the Lucky Dragon."
2. Follow along with the reading on page 166.
3. Read silently paragraphs 1–3 two times.
4. With a partner read aloud.
5. Your partner will time you reading aloud.

Listen, Speak, Interact

Have a Debate

When people have a **debate,** they give arguments to support different opinions. When you debate, you do not always agree with the opinions you are arguing for.

1. Work in a group of four. Divide into two sides:

   Side 1: Argue that Phan Thi Chi and his family should leave their home.
   Side 2: Argue that Phan Thi Chi and his family should stay at their home.

2. Each side lists reasons—with evidence, elaborations, and examples—to support their argument on note cards.

3. Present your debate to the class. One debater from Side 1 presents one or two arguments. Then one debater from Side 2 speaks. Then the other debater from Side 1 gives more arguments. Finally the other debater from Side 2 speaks.

4. As a class, analyze the debates. How believable and persuasive were the debaters?

Elements of Literature

Recognize Mood

Authors use words to create a **mood.** A mood is a feeling that the reader gets from the text. Happiness, sadness, and anger are examples of mood.

> There was suddenly a deadly hush in the room: it was as though everyone had stopped breathing.

These sentences create a mood of **suspense.** Suspense is a feeling of fear and nervousness from not knowing what will happen next. The words *suddenly* and *deadly hush* create this mood.

1. Match each sentence with the mood it creates.

happiness   anger   sadness

   a. Phan Thi Chi felt himself growing angry.
   b. Quan was the first to speak. To his father's relief, he was delighted.
   c. Aunt Binh turned her head away, sniffling quietly, and Phan Thi Chi felt guilty.

2. With a partner, discuss how these moods add to the effect of the text. Do you understand the characters and the story better because of the moods?

Activity Book
p. 91

Student
CD-ROM

Word Study

Analyze the Prefix *un-*

A **prefix** is a group of letters added to the beginning of a word. A prefix often changes the meaning of a root word. You can learn the meaning of a word if you know the meaning of a prefix.

The word **un**finished has the prefix *un-*. This prefix means "not." The root word is *finished*. When the prefix *un-* is added to *finished,* the meaning becomes "not finished" (not done).

Copy and complete the chart in your Personal Dictionary. For the meaning, choose a word from the box above the chart.

false	sad	different

un- +	Word ⇒	New Word	Meaning
un- +	finished ⇒	unfinished	not finished, not done
un- +	happy ⇒		
un- +	true ⇒		
un- +	common ⇒		

Personal Dictionary   The Heinle Newbury House Dictionary   Activity Book *p. 92*   Student CD-ROM

Grammar Focus

Identify Subject and Object Pronouns

A **pronoun** is a word that is used in place of a noun. *I, you, it,* and *them* are examples of pronouns.

A **subject pronoun** can be used as the subject of a sentence.

An **object pronoun** is used after some verbs or after a preposition.

1. Copy the sentences below on a piece of paper.
2. Underline the subject pronouns and circle the object pronouns.
   a. He just stared at her.
   b. I got sick.
   c. You will remain in control of it.

Subject Pronoun	Object Pronoun
I	me
you	you
he/she/it	him/her/it
we	us
they	them
Examples:	**Examples:**
He lives with Aunt Binh.	Phan Thi Chi lives with *her.*
She walked between Tan and Quan and us.	She walked between *them* and *us.*

Activity Book *pp. 93–94*   Student Handbook   Student CD-ROM

From Reading to Writing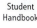

Write to Solve a Problem

The family of Phan Thi Chi has a problem. Write how they will solve their problem.

1. Work with a partner. Decide how the story will end.
2. Answer these questions to help you brainstorm:
   a. What happened while the family traveled to Rach Gia?
   b. What happened when the family arrived in Rach Gia?
   c. Was the family happy living in Rach Gia? Why or why not?
3. Write three paragraphs. Make sure your story has a beginning, a middle, and an end.
4. Give your story a title.
5. Be sure that you use subject and object pronouns correctly.
6. Use possessive nouns. Be sure to use the apostrophe correctly.

Activity Book
p. 95

Student
Handbook

Across Content Areas

Describe Countries on a Map

First, look at the map on page 163. Then read this paragraph. Pay attention to the words in bold type.

Thailand is a country in Southeast Asia. It **borders** four other countries, Laos, Cambodia, Myanmar, and Malaysia. Thailand **lies between** Laos **to the north and east,** Cambodia and Malaysia **to the south,** and Myanmar **to the west.** Thailand has a **coast** on the South China Sea.

Now use the map on this page to write a similar paragraph about the state of Georgia.

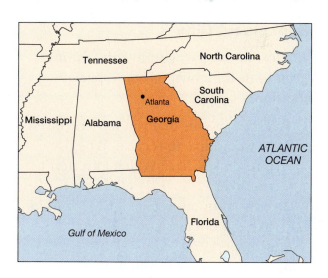

Tennessee

North Carolina

South Carolina

•Atlanta

Mississippi Alabama Georgia

ATLANTIC OCEAN

Florida

Gulf of Mexico

Activity Book
p. 96

CHAPTER 3

The Time Bike

an excerpt from a
science fiction novel
by Jane Langton

Objectives

Reading Predict as you read an excerpt from a science fiction novel.

Listening and Speaking Give a presentation.

Grammar Write using contractions.

Writing Write a description.

Content Social Studies: Learn about time zones.

Use Prior Knowledge

Think About Gifts

Most of us enjoy getting gifts—things given to us for a birthday or a special occasion.

1. Think of gifts that you have received or would like to receive. Which gifts do you like? Which gifts don't you like?
2. Write your answers in a Cluster Map like the one here on a piece of paper.
3. Share your ideas with a small group.
4. Tell why you like and do not like different gifts.

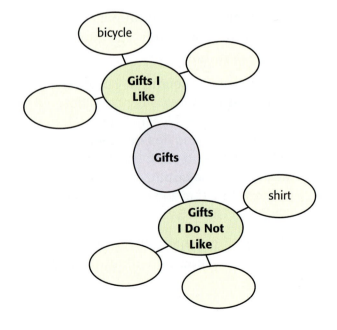

Build Background

Time

People use time to tell when things happen. Time tells us when things happened in the past, are happening in the present, and will happen in the future. Clocks and watches help us measure time within a day. They tell us seconds, minutes, and hours. We use calendars to measure days, months, and years.

Sundial

SOCIAL STUDIES

Content Connection

Long ago, some people used **sundials** to tell time. Sundials were placed outdoors. People told time by looking at the sun's shadow on the sundial.

Build Vocabulary

Use Context to Understand New Words

You can learn the meaning of a word by finding clues in its **context.** The words and sentences that surround a word are its context.

There was a sound, a kind of whispering underlined{murmur}.

The words *sound* and *whispering* can help you figure out the meaning of *murmur. Murmur* means a "a low sound."

1. Use context to guess the meaning of the underlined words.

a. In the dark it gleamed a little, the way his old rocket model had glowed in the dark.
b. It sparkles like a diamond.
c. The bike was a failure. It didn't work.

2. Use a dictionary to check if your ideas are correct.

3. Write the words and their meanings in your Personal Dictionary.

Personal Dictionary   The Heinle Newbury House Dictionary   Activity Book *p. 97*   Student CD-ROM

Text Structure

Science Fiction

In this chapter, you will read **science fiction.** A science fiction story is not a true story. It uses ideas from science and technology to show how life, usually in the future, could be different. Look for these features of science fiction as you read the selection.

Science Fiction	
Characters	the people in the story
Scientific Ideas	imaginary scientific inventions or discoveries that affect the characters
Plot	events that might happen in the future, usually based on scientific ideas

Student CD-ROM

Reading Strategy

Predict

When you **predict** something, you guess what will happen next. You can use clues in the text to predict what will happen in a story. Read this paragraph:

> It was a hot summer day. Alex had been running. He was tired and thirsty. He saw a water fountain in the park ahead. He slowed down and turned.

What do you think Alex will do next? This is predicting.

Clues	Alex is thirsty. He sees a water fountain in the park.
You Can Predict	Alex will walk to the park. He will drink water from the water fountain.

1. Study the title page of the reading selection on page 181. What does the title tell you? What does the picture tell you?
2. Predict what will happen in the story. Record your answers in your Reading Log.
3. Review what you predicted when you finish the selection. Were you right?

Reading Log   Student CD-ROM

The Time Bike

an excerpt from a science fiction novel

by Jane Langton

Audio
CD 2, Tr. 3

Prologue

This story takes place in Concord, Massachusetts. The main character is an eighth grader named Eddy Hall. The expensive new bike that Eddy gets for his birthday is stolen. He receives another bike from his mysterious uncle, Prince Krishna from India. Eddy is disappointed with this bike. He thinks that it looks old and out of style. However, he soon learns that you cannot always judge something by how it looks.

1   Three days went by, and the bicycle from India was still in the front hall beside the stairs, in the way.

2   "Eddy," said Uncle Freddy, "would you move it? Why not put it on the front porch where you kept the other one? But lock it to the railing this time."

3   So it won't be stolen? Eddy smiled grimly. Who would steal such a dumb old bike? But even so, he didn't put it on the front porch where anybody could see it. He found a perfect hiding place for it, a shadowy **triangular nook** next to the coat closet under the front hall stairs.

4   It was just the right size, and it had a **crimson** velvet curtain on a **drawstring** that hid his skateboard and Uncle Freddy's old golf bag and a croquet set with a couple of broken mallets.

Predict

Eddy doesn't like this bike. Do you think he will change his mind?

---

triangular like a triangle
nook a small room

crimson red
drawstring a string that moves a curtain

5   **Laboriously,** Eddy carried the old stuff up to the attic. Then he wheeled his **shameful** new bicycle into the space behind the curtain.

6   In the dark it gleamed a little, the way his old rocket model had glowed in the dark because **phosphorescent** stuff was mixed with the plastic. His embarrassing new bicycle must be coated with phosphorescent paint.

Predict

Predict what Eddy will find out about this bike.

7   It trembled slightly under his hands as he propped it upright, almost as if it were alive. Little sparkles flickered around the rims of the wheels. And there was a sound, a kind of whispering **murmur.**

8   Eddy pulled the curtain aside to let in light and peered at the dial mounted on the handlebars. It wasn't a

speedometer—it was a clock. And there was a dome-shaped bell on top, just like the one on an old-fashioned alarm clock. The whole thing looked just like a clock in a cartoon, the kind that bounces up and down when the alarm goes off.

9   He looked more closely at the dial. How weird! It didn't say 1, 2, 3, 4, all the way to 12. In fact, there were two dials. The words printed on them were very small. One said:
    Days
and the other:
    Years

---

laboriously requiring hard work
shameful embarrassing
phosphorescent a quality that makes something glow

murmur a low, unclear sound
speedometer an instrument that measures how fast something is going

10   There were a great many little marks around the circle of the Days dial—probably 365 of them, decided Eddy, one for every day of the year.

11   The Years dial was different. It went from 0 to 10 to 100 to 1,000 to 10,000 to 100,000. A hundred thousand years! What did it mean, a clock that told the time in thousands of years?

Predict

Predict what the tab switch will do.

12   And there was a **tab** at the side, some sort of on-off switch. No, it wasn't an on-off switch, it was a plus-and-minus switch. What did that mean, plus and minus?

13   "Why, Eddy," said Aunt Alex, suddenly appearing in the front hall with Eleanor, "what a lovely headlight. It sparkles like a diamond."

14   "It does?" Eddy looked. The rocket-shaped headlight on the front **fender** was just one more thing that was out of style. He tried to turn it off, but there was no switch.

15   "It reminds me of something," said Eleanor, narrowing her eyes, staring at it through her big glasses.

16   Eddy knew what she was thinking of—the big jewel that had once been part of the stained-glass window in the attic, that huge chunk of glass that had turned out in the end to be a diamond, a real diamond, so valuable that it was beyond price. "It's not much good without a switch," he said. "The battery will run down any minute."

---

tab   a projection or flap attached to something else   **fender**   a part of a bike that protects the wheel

17   "The one in back is pretty too," said Aunt Alex, bending low over the rear fender, where the red reflector shone in the light of the desk lamp. "It's like a ruby, a real ruby." She stood up and smiled at Eddy. "It's like a bicycle from fairyland."

Predict

What do you think Eddy will do next?

18   Then she went into the kitchen with Eleanor, and Eddy went back to studying his new bicycle with more interest than before.

19   He climbed on the seat to see what it felt like and dropped the curtain again. Now he was alone in the dark with the bike. In front of him the headlight shone on the wall of the coat closet, making a bright pattern like a star.

20   To his surprise it felt good to **perch** erect, high above the floor. It was sort of **majestic** and **dignified,** like riding an elephant.

21   Something white twirled in front of him—the tag on the handlebars. Eddy reached for it, but it kept fluttering and twisting. Finally he got it between his fingers. Pulling open the curtain he looked at the tag. One side still said *Srinagar, Kashmir.* The other said:

TIME BIKE

22   *Time Bike!* What did that mean?

23   He could hear Aunt Alex talking quietly from the kitchen with Eleanor, who was complaining loudly about Amanda Upshaw's party.

---

perch   sit, usually on a high place
majestic   showing greatness

dignified   noble, honorable

24   "I still don't have an **invitation!** Becky's got one. Lisa's got one. It's only me, I'm the only one that hasn't got one. I mean, they've all got invitations already, all the best kids!"

25   There was a pause and then Aunt Alex said, "What do you mean by 'best kids'?"

26   "Oh, you know, Aunt Alex. They're— oh, I don't know. If you could see them, you'd know what I mean."

27   "I see," said Aunt Alex.

28   Eddy stopped listening. What if he set the dial of the clock for some time in the past, like six months ago? Maybe it really was a time bike. Maybe it would really take him back to last December. Dreamily, he put his fingers on the setscrew that moved the hand of the dial that counted days.

Predict

What do you predict will happen next? Do you predict the bike will take Eddy to the past?

29   Then he came to his senses. The idea was too scary. He should think it over first and then try it very carefully. Those people in fairy stories who were given three wishes always got in trouble. They wasted all three because they didn't think. He would be more careful.

30   But at that instant the little **rooster** in the backyard crowed noisily, and the silly cuckoo popped out of the clock and squawked.

31   Eddy's hand jerked. The bicycle jiggled, and the bell went *ding*. There was a flash of lightning in the little round mirror on the handlebars, and a humming noise from the wheels as if they were going around.

---

invitation   a card or letter that asks someone to come to an event

rooster   a male chicken

32   It was only for a moment. Then the vibration stopped. The **dinging** stopped. Eddy got off the bike and opened the curtain.

33   Through the **oval** window in the front door he could see the trees across the road, and the grass in the front yard. Everything was green. It was still June, not last December.

34   The bike was a failure. It didn't work. It wasn't a time bike. The strange dials didn't mean anything at all.

35   Aunt Alex and Eleanor were still talking in the kitchen.

36   "What do you mean by 'best kids'?" said Aunt Alex.

37   "Oh, you know, Aunt Alex. They're—oh, I don't know. If you could see them, you'd know what I mean."

38   "I see," said Aunt Alex.

Predict

What do you predict will happen after this part of the story?

---

dinging   light ringing   **oval**   shaped like an egg

About the Author

Jane Langton (born 1922)

Jane Langton has been writing for more than 40 years. She is best known for writing adult mysteries. She also writes fiction for young adults. Langton lives in Massachusetts, and many of her stories take place there. Langton says she enjoys putting realistic characters into this setting.

► Why do you think Jane Langton wrote this story? Was it to entertain, inform, or persuade?

Beyond the Reading

Reading Comprehension

Question-Answer Relationships (QAR)

"Right There" Questions

1. **Recall Facts** Where did the mysterious bike come from?
2. **Recall Facts** How were the two dials labeled?
3. **Recall Facts** What did the two sides of the bike's tag say?

"Think and Search" Questions

4. **Draw Conclusions** Why was Eddy embarrassed by the bike?
5. **Explain** What happened to his last bike?
6. **Analyze Character Changes** How does Eddy's point of view change during the story?

"Author and You" Questions

7. **Draw Conclusions** Why do you think Eddy hesitated to use the bike?
8. **Identify Elements** What makes the bike different?
9. **Draw Conclusions** What happens at the end of the story?

"On Your Own" Questions

10. **Predict** What do you predict Eddy will use the bike for?
11. **Predict** Do you think time travel will be possible in the future? Explain.

Activity Book
p. 98

Student
CD-ROM

Build Reading Fluency

Repeated Reading

Repeated reading helps increase your reading rate and builds confidence. Each time you reread, you improve your reading fluency.

1. Turn to page 182.
2. With a partner, take turns reading each paragraph aloud.
3. Your teacher or partner will time six minutes for you.
4. Stop after six minutes.

Listen, Speak, Interact

Give a Presentation

In the selection, Eddy learns that his bike can travel in time. Suppose you had a Time Bike.

1. Decide where you would go if you had a Time Bike. Would you go to a certain time and place in history? A certain time and place in your life?
2. Answer these questions on a piece of paper:
   a. Where would you like to go? What is the time and place?
   b. Why do you want to go to this time and place?
   c. What is life like in this time and place?
   d. What do you want to do when you are there?
3. Present your answers to the class.
4. As you listen to your classmates' presentations, take notes.
5. With a partner, compare your notes on one classmates' presentation. Are your perceptions of the presentation the same or different?

Elements of Literature

Recognize Foreshadowing

In fiction, authors often give the reader clues about what will happen later in the story. This is called **foreshadowing.**

You know that Eddy didn't think that his bike was special at the beginning of the story. Read this sentence about the bicycle in paragraph 7:

> It trembled slightly under his hands as he propped it upright, almost as if it were alive.

Ordinary bicycles don't tremble, and they don't seem to be alive. This tells us that this might be a special bicycle after all.

Write answers to these questions in your Reading Log.

1. What other examples of foreshadowing about the bicycle do you find in paragraphs 7 and 8?
2. Reread paragraphs 31 and 32. What do these paragraphs foreshadow?

Reading Log   Activity Book
                      p. 99

Student
CD-ROM

Word Study

Study the Prefix *bi-*

A **prefix** is a group of letters added to the beginning of a word. A prefix may change the meaning of a word.

The word ***bi****cycle* has the prefix *bi-*. *Bi-* means "two." *Cycle* is the root word of *bicycle*. The word *cycle* means "wheel." When *bi-* is added to *cycle,* the word *bicycle* is formed. A bicycle is a vehicle with two wheels.

Match each of the following words with the correct definition. Use a dictionary if you need help.

1. *bicultural*
2. *biweekly*
3. *bilingual*

a. able to speak two languages
b. made up of two cultures
c. happening every two weeks

The Heinle Newbury House Dictionary

Activity Book p. 100

Student CD-ROM

Grammar Focus

Write Using Contractions

Some auxiliary verbs can be made into a **contraction.** An apostrophe (') replaces the letters that are taken out. Look at the chart.

The word *not* can be contracted with any auxiliary verb:

Did you do your homework? No, I <u>didn't</u>.

Would you travel in time? No, I <u>wouldn't</u>.

The contraction of *will* + *not* is *won't.*

1. Copy paragraph 24 on a piece of paper, but change all of the contracted forms to full forms.
2. Write a sentence for each contracted form in the chart.

Auxiliary Verb	Contracted Form	Example
am	'm	I'm a student.
is	's	She's a student.
are	're	We're students.
have	've	I've eaten sushi.
has	's	He's eaten sushi.
had	'd	I'd already done my homework.
will	'll	They'll be there.
would	'd	I said I'd be there.

Activity Book pp. 101–102

Student Handbook

Student CD-ROM

From Reading to Writing

Write a Description

Write a paragraph that describes a place in the past. You may write about the place you presented in Listen, Speak, Interact, or you may write about another place. This paragraph will be a part of a larger piece of writing. It can be a letter, journal entry, narrative, memoir, or other form of writing. Decide which form you want to use.

1. Include information that answers these questions:
   a. What is the name of the place?
   b. Where is the place?
   c. What is the time and date?
   d. What people and things would you see in this place?
   e. What do people do there?

2. Use figurative language to help readers picture the place in their minds.
3. Find information in your school library or on the Internet. Use the name of the place as a keyword (for example, "Ancient Rome").
4. List the sources you use to write your paragraph. Check your Student Handbook for the correct form.
5. Place a drawing or a photograph below your paragraph. The picture should help readers understand your description.

Activity Book
p. 103

Student
Handbook

Across Content Areas

Learn About Time Zones

A **time zone** is an area that has the same time. Most of the United States is in four time zones. These time zones are called Eastern, Central, Mountain, and Pacific.

Suppose it is 11:00 P.M. in New York City. Then it is 10:00 P.M. in Chicago.

Use the map to answer the questions:

1. It is 3 P.M. in New York City. What time is it in Denver?
2. It is 10 P.M. in Los Angeles. What time is it in Chicago?

Activity Book
p. 104

Why We Can't Get There From Here

an informational text
by Neil de Grasse Tyson

Objectives

Reading Reread and record to learn and recall as you read an informational text.

Listening and Speaking Listen to an informational text.

Grammar Use comparative and superlative adjectives.

Writing Use multiple resources to write a research report.

Content Math: Solve a time problem.

Use Prior Knowledge

Talk About Ways to Travel

There are many ways to travel. For example, you can travel by car or bicycle.

1. Brainstorm a list of ways to travel.
2. Choose your two favorite ways. Use a Venn Diagram to show how they are the same and how they are different.

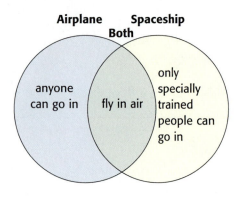

Airplane   **Spaceship**

Both

anyone can go in   fly in air   only specially trained people can go in

3. Tell your partner about these ways to travel, and listen to your partner's response. After your partner speaks, summarize what he or she said.
4. With your class, organize a chart of all the ways to travel.
5. Take a survey. Organize a record of how many students have traveled each way.
6. Ask and answer questions like these to compare ways of travel.
   a. Which way of travel is the most popular? Why?
   b. Which is the least popular? Why?

Build Background

Space

Space is the area outside the atmosphere of Earth. (The atmosphere is the air that is around Earth.) In space there are stars, moons, and planets. Planets, like Earth, move around a star such as the sun. Some planets are very hot. They are close to the sun. Some planets are cold. They are far away from the sun.

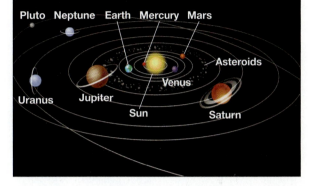

Pluto Neptune Earth Mercury Mars
Asteroids
Venus
Uranus Jupiter
Sun Saturn

SOCIAL STUDIES

Content Connection

Neil Armstrong was the first person to walk on the moon. This was in 1969.

Build Vocabulary

Apply Knowledge of Root Words

You can expand your vocabulary by looking for words made from root words that you already know. Read this example:

The spaceship was **unmanned.**

In the word *unmanned,* **man** is the root word. Remember that the prefix *un-* means *not,* so an *unmanned* spaceship is one with no people on it.

1. In your Personal Dictionary, copy these words. Underline the root words. Guess the definitions.
   a. earthly
   b. typically
   c. roughly

2. As you read or listen to the selection, look for root words to help you understand and to expand your vocabulary.

Personal Dictionary

The Heinle Newbury House Dictionary

Activity Book p. 105

Student CD-ROM

Text Structure

Informational Text

"Why We Can't Get There From Here" is an **informational text.** An informational text explains a topic. Look at the chart. It shows some features of an informational text that are in the selection.

Informational Text	
Facts	true information about the topic
Examples	details that show how information is true
Pictures	visuals that help readers see examples of important ideas

Student
CD-ROM

Reading Strategy

Reread and Record to Learn and Recall

As you read an informational text, you can take special steps to learn and recall new information. These steps will help you in your other courses, especially science and social studies.

As you read "Why We Can't Get There From Here," follow the steps in the chart.

Step	What to Do
1. Preview questions	Look over the text. Ask yourself: What do the title and headings tell me? What do I know about this topic?
2. Read	Read to find answers to your questions.
3. Reread	Go back and read again, slowly and carefully. Reread aloud if you do not understand.
4. Record	Take notes on important facts.

Student
CD-ROM

Why We Can't Get There From Here

an informational text by Neil de Grasse Tyson

1   Space. Why can't we get there from here? Well, one problem is the distance to the nearest star. Space is **vast** and empty beyond all earthly **measure.** When **Hollywood** movies show a starship cruising through the **galaxy,** they typically show points of light (stars) drifting past like **fireflies** at a rate of one or two per second. But the distances between stars in the galaxy are so great that a spaceship would have to be traveling roughly 500 million times faster than the **speed of light** for the stars to rush by like that.

The Moon is far away compared with where you might go in a jet airplane, but it sits at the tip of your nose compared with anything else in the **universe.** If Earth were the size of a basketball, the Moon would be the size of a softball some ten **paces** away—the farthest we have ever sent people into space. On this scale, Mars (at its closest) is a mile away. Pluto is 100 miles away. And Proxima Centauri, the star nearest to the Sun, is a *half-million miles* away!   2

> ### Reread and Record to Learn and Recall
>
> Reread paragraph 1. What question is the author going to answer?

Audio
CD 2, Tr. 4

---

vast   large

measure   an amount of something

Hollywood   a city in the state of California where lots of movies are made

galaxy   a large group of stars and planets

fireflies   insects that light up

speed of light   the rate at which light moves

universe   all of space including galaxies, stars, and planets

paces   steps

3   Let's **assume** money is **no object.** If a spaceship **sustained** the speed needed to escape Earth—seven miles per second—the trip to the nearest star would last a long and boring *100,000 years!* Too long, you say?

4   How about a spaceship that travels as fast as *Helios B,* the U.S.-German **solar probe** that was the fastest-ever **unmanned** space probe? Launched in 1976, it was clocked rising through 42 miles per second (150,000 miles per hour) as it accelerated toward the Sun. This craft would cut the travel time to the nearest star down to a **mere** 15,000 years—*three times the length of recorded human history.*

5   What we really want is a spaceship that can travel near the speed of light. (*Helios B* was traveling at only one-fiftieth of one percent of the speed of light.) How about 99 percent the speed of light? All you would need is *700 million times* the energy that **thrust** Apollo **astronauts** toward the Moon!

Reread and Record to Learn and Recall

Take notes on the important facts in paragraphs 4 and 5.

Reread and Record to Learn and Recall

Reread this paragraph aloud. What is the most important thing you learned?

---

assume   believe something is true

no object   not a problem; not worth anything

sustained   kept up or maintained

solar probe   a small spacecraft sent to study the Sun

unmanned   having no crew or passengers

mere   small, only

thrust   forced

astronauts   people trained to fly a spacecraft

6   But, wait, that's not quite right. As **Einstein** correctly **predicted,** when your speed increases, so does your **mass,** forcing you to spend even more energy to **accelerate** your spaceship to near the speed of light. A back-of-the-envelope **calculation** shows that you would need at least *ten billion times the energy used for our Moon voyages!*

7   No problem. These are very **clever engineers** we've hired. But now we learn that the closest star known to have planets is not Proxima Centauri, but one that is much farther, about 15 light-years away. Einstein showed that,

while traveling at 99 percent of the speed of light, you will age at only 14 percent the pace of everybody back on Earth, so the round trip for you will last not 30 years but about four. On Earth, however, 30 years actually do **pass by,** and *everybody has forgotten about you!* . . .

Reread and Record to Learn and Recall

Record what this paragraph means. Use your own words.

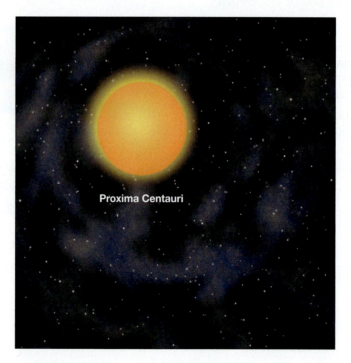

Proxima Centauri

Einstein a great scientist
predicted guessed, based on knowledge
mass the measure of a solid body
accelerate increase speed

calculation math
clever smart
engineers people who design or construct structures
pass by go on

8   Given . . . the great distances involved, it is unlikely we will travel to the stars. What we need, but may never have, is a **breakthrough** in our scientific understanding of the **structure** of the universe, so that we might **exploit** shortcuts through the **space-time continuum**—perhaps through **wormholes** that connect one part of the **cosmos** to another. Then, once again, reality will become stranger than fiction.

> **Reread and Record to Learn and Recall**
>
> Reread the author's preview question in paragraph 1. Can you answer it now? If not, reread the selection. Read slowly and carefully. Record your answer.

---

breakthrough   an advance or discovery
structure   the way parts are put together
exploit   use or develop
space-time continuum   how space and time work together

wormholes   holes that lead somewhere else in space
cosmos   everything that is in space

About the Author

Neil de Grasse Tyson (born 1958)

As a young boy Neil de Grasse Tyson was interested in space. He got a telescope so that he could look at the planets and stars.

Tyson wrote his first book about space in 1989. He makes his books about space easy to understand. He wants his books to be fun for people to read.

► How did Tyson organize "Why We Can't Get There From Here"? Did he use cause and effect? Did he use inductive or deductive presentations? (See page 141.) Give examples.

Beyond the Reading

Reading Comprehension

Question-Answer Relationships (QAR)

"Right There" Questions

1. **Recall Facts** What star is nearest the Sun?
2. **Recall Facts** What is the name of the fastest-ever unmanned space probe?
3. **Recall Facts** Where is the farthest distance a person has been in space?

"Think and Search" Questions

4. **Identify** What speed would be best for a spaceship to reach another planet?
5. **Evaluate Evidence** What is stopping us from reaching other planets?

"Author and You" Questions

6. **Summarize** What is the author's main point in this selection?

7. **Identify Author Challenges** What challenges did the author face in writing this selection?

"On Your Own" Questions

8. **Present Opinions** Do you think humans will ever travel to the other planets? Support your opinion.
9. **Present Opinions** Would you like to travel to another planet? Why or why not? Record your thoughts as a journal entry.
10. **Find Similarities and Differences Across Texts** Compare and contrast this reading with "The Time Bike." How is it similar? How is it different?

Activity Book Student
p. 106 CD-ROM

Build Reading Fluency

Adjust Your Reading Rate to Scan

When you scan you adjust your reading rate to read fast. Scanning means looking at the text for key words to help you answer questions. Work with a partner. Read aloud key words as you look for information. Write your answers on a piece of paper.

1. If Earth were the size of a basketball, how far away would Pluto be from Earth?
2. How many miles per hour does the spaceship *Helios B* travel?
3. What did Einstein predict?
4. What is the closest known star to the sun?

Listen, Speak, Interact

Listen to an Informational Text

Listen to the audio recording of "Why We Can't Get There From Here" and do the following:

1. First determine what you want to listen for. Do you want to gain information, solve a problem, or enjoy?
2. As you listen, take notes on the major ideas.
3. Listen for the way the speaker uses sounds and intonation to give meaning.
4. Write down two new vocabulary words that you learned.
5. With a partner, discuss how well you understood the recording. Ask your partner to help you with things you did not understand. Listen again and try to understand more.
6. Write a summary of the selection in one paragraph.
7. Compare your summary with your partner's.
8. Think about your experiences and knowledge. How do these relate to the selection? Discuss this with your partner.

Elements of Literature

Analyze Organization and Presentation of Ideas

In "Why We Can't Get There From Here," the author presents information in several ways.

Record answers to these items in your Reading Log.

1. Find an example of a question that the author asks the reader. What effect does this question have on you?
2. Find an example of comparing and contrasting. How does this help you understand?
3. The author uses a deductive presentation: He says that people can't go to faraway stars. Then he gives the reasons. Work with your teacher and the class to list the reasons.

Ways to Organize and Present Ideas

Questions	The author asks questions to the reader.
Compare and Contrast	The author shows how things are the same or different.
Deductive Presentation	The author makes a general statement and then gives reasons or details to show why the statement is true.
Inductive Presentation	The author gives examples and then states a conclusion based on the examples.

Reading Log   Activity Book
p. 107

Student
CD-ROM

Word Study

Identify the Suffixes *-er* and *-est*

To compare one thing to another, you add the suffix *-er* to an adjective. This is the **comparative** form of the adjective.

This risk is great**er** than that one.

To show that something is the most of its kind, you add the suffix *-est* to an adjective. This is the **superlative** form.

Proxima Centauri, the star near**est** to the Sun . . .

This means that no other star is nearer.

1. Reread paragraph 1 on page 196. Find one example of a comparative adjective with the suffix *-er.*
2. In the same paragraph, find one example of a superlative adjective with the suffix *-est.*

Personal Dictionary

The Heinle Newbury House Dictionary

Activity Book *p. 108*

Student CD-ROM

Grammar Focus

Use Comparative and Superlative Adjectives

In Word Study, above, you learned that adding the suffixes *-er* and *-est* to an adjective allows you to compare two or more things. They make your writing more precise.

Most Short Adjectives:
Add *-er* or *-est* to the adjective

Adjective	Suffix	Comparative Superlative	Changes
great	-er -est	greater greatest	
close	-er -est	closer closest	drop the e
noisy	-er -est	noisier noisiest	change y to i

Long Adjectives:
Use *more* or *most*
in front of the adjective

Adjective	Superlative
interesting	more interesting most interesting
beautiful	more beautiful most beautiful
difficult	more difficult most difficult

1. Write one comparative sentence and one superlative sentence with the adjectives *fast* and *strange.*
2. Write one comparative sentence and one superlative sentence with the adjectives *clever* and *important.*

Activity Book *pp. 109–110*

Student Handbook

Student CD-ROM

From Reading to Writing

Use Multiple Resources to Write a Research Report

You should do research on a topic before you write about it. There are many research resources that you can use.

1. Brainstorm science topics you would like to know more about.
2. Think of at least three keywords that you can look up. For example, if your topic is the planet Mars, your keywords might be *Mars*, *planets*, and *solar system*.
3. Do your research. Use your keywords to find information about your topics. Use at least two of the resources listed in the chart. Take notes on what you find.
4. Be sure to cite your sources using the correct format shown in your Student Handbook.
5. Write your report in three paragraphs.
6. Use comparative and superlative adjectives to make your writing more vivid and precise.

Research Resources	
Type of Resource	**Description**
Encyclopedia	general information in alphabetical order; often available on CD-ROM
Atlas	a book of maps
Thesaurus	lists of words with similar meanings (synonyms)
Dictionary	alphabetical list of words with meanings, pronunciations, and origins
Newspapers and Magazines	current and recent events
Internet	many kinds of information
Experts	anyone who knows about the topic, such as a teacher or a librarian

Student Handbook   Activity Book
                          p. 111

Across Content Areas

MATH

Solve a Time Problem

Work with a small group to solve this time problem.

> Juan has to be at his grandmother's house in Los Angeles at 3:00 P.M. He lives 240 miles away. He can travel there at 60 miles per hour. What time should he leave home to get there on time?

Make up another time travel problem. Have a classmate solve it.

Activity Book
p. 112

The California Gold Rush

an excerpt from an informational book by Pam Zollman

Dame Shirley and the Gold Rush

an excerpt from a historical novel by Jim Rawls

Objectives

Reading Compare and contrast as you read an excerpt from an informational book and a historical novel.

Listening and Speaking Present the story of a journey.

Grammar Use adverbs.

Writing Compare and contrast two reading selections.

Content Science: Learn about natural resources.

Use Prior Knowledge

Talk About Challenges

A challenge is something difficult that you must do. Climbing a mountain is a big challenge. Learning to skate is a smaller challenge.

Draw a web to organize your ideas about a challenge.

1. Think about a challenge you have met. Write this in the center.
2. Read these questions and write the answers in the web.
   a. Where did the challenge happen?
   b. When did it happen?
   c. Why did you accept the challenge?
   d. How did you get ready?
   e. How did you feel afterward?

3. Share your challenge with the class.

It took place at school.

It happened last year.

Run a mile in five minutes

I felt very good.

I was on the track team.

I trained for three months.

Build Background

The Frontier

Before the 1800s, land west of the Mississippi River was called the frontier. Mainly Native Americans lived on this land. Settlers began to move to the frontier in the early 1800s. These settlers were called pioneers.

The land of the frontier had many natural resources. Natural resources are things from nature that people use. Some natural resources are trees, water, and metals, such as gold. Gold was a very important natural resource in California.

Content Connection

The Mississippi River is located in the center of the United States. It is one of the longest rivers in the world. It runs 2,350 miles.

Build Vocabulary

Study Words Systematically

One way to study the meanings of words is to make a word list.

1. Study these words that are useful in your social studies classes.
   a. Make a section in your Personal Dictionary. Copy the chart.
   b. As you read, fill in the meanings of the words. Use a dictionary or ask your teacher.
2. Look through a newspaper or a magazine. Find current articles on natural resources. Read the articles and add new words to your list.

Social Studies Vocabulary	
Word	**Meaning**
covered wagon	a large wagon covered with cloth
mining	
ranch	
stagecoach	
mule	

Personal Dictionary   The Heinle Newbury House Dictionary   Activity Book p. 113   Student CD-ROM

Text Structure

Nonfiction and Historical Fiction

"The California Gold Rush" is **nonfiction.** Nonfiction tells about real people and events. It also includes facts.

"Dame Shirley and the Gold Rush" is **historical fiction.** Historical fiction is a made-up story that happens during a real time in the past.

Look for features of nonfiction and historical fiction as you read.

	Nonfiction	Historical Fiction
Characters	real people	real people and/ or made-up people
Setting	real time and place	real time and place
Events	real events to tell the story	real events and made-up events to tell the story

Student CD-ROM

Reading Strategy

Compare and Contrast

When you **compare,** you notice how two or more things are similar. When you **contrast,** you notice how two or more things are different.

You can use a Venn Diagram to compare and contrast bananas and apples. Bananas and apples are similar because they are types of fruit. However, they are different colors.

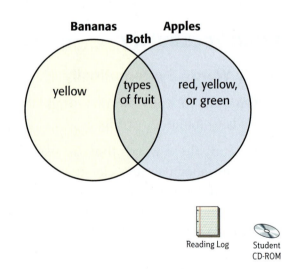

1. Make a diagram like this one in your Reading Log. In place of "Bananas" and "Apples" write the titles of the selections.
2. Compare and contrast the events of each selection.

Reading Log   Student CD-ROM

The California Gold Rush

an excerpt from an informational book
by Pam Zollman

Dame Shirley and the Gold Rush

an excerpt from a historical novel
by Jim Rawls

Audio
CD 2, Tr. 5

The California Gold Rush
an excerpt from an informational book by Pam Zollman

1   The year 1849 changed North America's history. In that year the first of about 300,000 people from all over the world began to hurry to California to look for gold. The rush included so many people that it was called the Gold Rush. The newspapers called the Gold Rush people forty-niners because that year was so important to the growth of California. No matter whether they came in 1849 or in the following years, all the Gold Rush people were called forty-niners.

Compare and Contrast

How are the houses of the forty-niners similar to and different from houses today?

2   Most of the forty-niners were men in a hurry to get to the gold fields, the places where gold might be found. They didn't make time to plan how they'd live once they arrived. Most knew little or nothing about looking for gold. Some of the **prospectors** didn't take time to build houses or cabins. Instead they built **lean-tos** or bush houses, by piling bushes and limbs together to form a shelter. Some used tents or lived in their covered wagon. Others built **shacks** from the wood in the wagons. Some even slept in holes in the ground.

---

prospectors   people who look for gold

lean-tos   shelters with only roofs that are made of tree branches

shacks   small houses that are roughly built

Compare and Contrast

How is the work of the forty-niners similar to and different from work that you do?

3   The forty-niners found that **mining** for gold was hard work. Their day began at **dawn** with a breakfast of coffee and hard biscuits. They then spent 10 to 12 hours looking for gold. The sun burned their neck and back. Once in a while, a lucky **miner** might find a gold **nugget** in a stream, river, or **gully.** Or he might find a handful of gold dust in a **crevice** between rocks. For most of the miners, though, looking for gold meant **backbreaking** work that required them to separate gold dust and flakes from **tons** of sand and gravel. In the western United States, $1 a day was good pay for a day's work. The average prospector might earn $15 per day in California, but he might earn nothing. And he might earn nothing for days.

---

mining   looking for things found underneath the earth

dawn   early in the morning

miner   a person who looks for things underneath the earth

nugget   a small piece of something

gully   a deep, long hole made in the ground after heavy rain

crevice   a small space between two things

backbreaking   something that is very hard to do

tons   measurement of weight; one ton = 2,000 lbs.

About the Author   Pam Zollman

Pam Zollman has been writing for children for years. Her stories have been printed in several children's magazines. Zollman teaches writing about children's stories at colleges.

➤ What question would you like to ask Pam Zollman about this selection?

Dame Shirley and the Gold Rush

an excerpt from a historical novel by Jim Rawls

A Trip to the Mines

1 Dame Shirley rubbed the sleep from her eyes and pulled the **coarse** woolen blanket up around her shoulders. The early morning air was cool and still. She lay quietly, listening to the sounds of daybreak drifting through the cabin window. Outside, a mule **brayed,** and a screeching rooster **saluted** the rising sun.

2 It was early September 1851. Dame Shirley and her husband, Dr. Fayette Clappe, had spent the night at a ranch near Marysville, California. Today they were to begin their ride north along the Feather River to the gold mining camp of Rich Bar.

3 The couple had been **lured** to California by the Gold Rush. They were not alone. Thousands of others had come for the same reason.

4 Dame Shirley thought about how far they had come from their home in New England. At the time, no highways or railroads **linked** California with the rest of the United States. So Dame Shirley and Fayette had to sail all the way around South America to reach San Francisco—a trip of about seventeen thousand miles!

> **Compare and Contrast**
>
> How are the characters similar and different in the two stories?

---

coarse   rough
brayed   made a loud sound
saluted   greeted

lured   attracted
linked   brought together

Compare and Contrast

How is traveling for Dame Shirley and Fayette similar to and different from the way that you travel?

5   From there, they rode a **stagecoach** north to mining country. The stage's wooden wheels had bounced and jumped over a road that was more trail than highway. It was like being trapped for several days in a small wooden box that someone was shaking. The ride was a bit longer than one hundred miles, but seemed like a thousand.

6   This morning, though, Dame Shirley and Fayette were rested and ready to continue their travels. They were going to Rich Bar to find work for Fayette. Dame Shirley and Fayette knew that Rich Bar had a population of several thousand miners. They also knew that it had just one doctor. Fayette was certain he would have plenty of opportunities to practice medicine there.

7   Friends in San Francisco had warned Dame Shirley not to go to the mines. One woman had **predicted** that she would never make it to Rich Bar alive. Another had said that Dame Shirley was crazy to think of living in a mining camp made up almost entirely of men. Even Fayette had **advised** her to remain in San Francisco. Everyone said that going to the mines was too dangerous for a woman.

---

stagecoach   a covered, four-wheel wagon
predicted   stated something will happen in the future

advised   recommended or suggested

8   But Dame Shirley would have none of it. All her life she had dreamed of travel and adventure. She once said that she was a "**thistle-seed**," ready to blow wherever the wind might take her. She felt a **restlessness** in her **soul.** She had the spirit of a **nomad.** And having come so far already, she meant to experience life in the mines, not merely to hear about it from her husband or the newspapers.

9   Dame Shirley nudged her mule again with her foot. Then she felt a strange **sensation. Her saddle** was slipping! Suddenly, she and the saddle were a mini-**avalanche** sliding sideways off the mule. Before she knew it, she was lying in the road, a cloud of dust mushrooming around her. Her saddle swung upside down beneath her mule. Dust filled her eyes, nose, and ears. Her fine riding outfit was coated with dust.

10   A look of horror filled Fayette's face. He quickly **dismounted** and rushed to help Dame Shirley to her feet. Shirley, though, didn't need any help. She was startled, but unhurt. Getting up, she looked at Fayette. A grin spread across her face. She began to laugh.

Compare and Contrast

How did Dame Shirley look before she got up from the ground? How did she look after she got up?

---

thistle-seed   a part of a weed-like plant
restlessness   unable to stay in one place
soul   a part of a person's thoughts and feelings
nomad   a person who moves from home to home

sensation   a feeling
saddle   a seat strapped to a horse
avalanche   something sliding down suddenly
dismounted   got off

11   When he went to fix her saddle, Fayette discovered that it was far too large for her mule. He could fix it so it might hold for a bit, but he wasn't sure how **reliable** it would be. He suggested they turn back instead. At the very least, he said, she should return to the ranch and put on some clean clothes and make a fresh start.

12   Dame Shirley said no to both suggestions. She surveyed her appearance. Indeed, she was a sight. She was covered in dust, from tip to toe. But so what? This was California. This was mining country. Who on Earth was she going to run into here? Certainly not anyone who would turn up his nose at a little dust. Something about the idea of her great adventure beginning with a little **comedy** pleased her. She climbed back on her mule and rode **merrily** on.

13   Finally, at about midnight, they reached Marysville. There they spent the night after dining on a feast of hot **oysters,** toast, tomatoes, and coffee. It was their first meal since breakfast.

Compare and Contrast

Which events are the same in the two stories? Which are different?

---

reliable   something that one can depend on
comedy   something that is funny

merrily   happily
oysters   sea animals with a hard shell

About the Author

Jim Rawls (born 1945)

Jim Rawls lives in California. He likes to learn about the history of California. Rawls thinks many people's hopes and dreams have happened or been challenged in California. He has written many books and stories on the history of California.

► Why do you think Jim Rawls wrote this text? What challenges do you think he faced to write historical fiction?

Beyond the Reading

Reading Comprehension

Question-Answer Relationships (QAR)

"Right There" Questions

1. **Recall Facts** In "The California Gold Rush," what year changed U.S. history?

2. **Recall Facts** In "The California Gold Rush," what did the miners earn?

3. **Recall Facts** In "Dame Shirley and the Gold Rush," what year did Shirley and Fayette set out for the mining camp?

4. **Recall Facts** In "Dame Shirley and the Gold Rush," what city were they traveling to? How did they make the trip?

"Think and Search" Questions

5. **Analyze Style, Elements, and Media** View the art and photos in these readings. How do the style and elements extend (add to) the texts? What ideas do you gain?

6. **Explain** In "Dame Shirley and the Gold Rush," why was the couple traveling to the mining town?

7. **Analyze Character Traits** What kind of person was Dame Shirley?

"Author and You" Question

8. **Connect Main Ideas** Do you agree with the sentence, "Life in a mining camp was hard"? Why do you think this?

"On Your Own" Questions

9. **Compare with Your Own Experience** Have you made a difficult journey in your life?

10. **Speculate** If you lived in 1861, would you join the Gold Rush? Why or why not?

Activity Book
p. 114

Student
CD-ROM

Build Reading Fluency

Read Silently

Reading silently is good practice. It helps you learn to read faster. An effective reader reads silently for increasing lengths of time.

1. Listen to the audio recording of paragraphs 1–3 on page 210.

2. Listen to the chunks of words as you follow along.

3. Reread paragraphs 1–3 silently two times.

4. Your teacher will time your second reading.

5. Raise your hand when you are done.

Listen, Speak, Interact

Present the Story of a Journey

Have you ever taken a journey? Think about your trip and tell the class about it.

1. Record notes on note cards about the details of your journey. Use these questions to help you.
   a. Where did you go?
   b. How long did it take?
   c. How did you feel before your journey? During your journey? At the end?
   d. Would you want to make this journey again? Why or why not?
2. Make visuals for your presentation.
   a. Make a map showing important places and your route.
   b. Make a timeline showing important dates.
3. Practice your presentation with a partner.
   a. Do not read your note cards. Use your visuals.
   b. Ask your partner for feedback on your presentation.
   c. Revise your presentation.
4. Give your presentation for the class.
   a. Be dramatic. Use gestures to help make your points.
   b. Pay attention to your voice. Use effective rate, volume, pitch, and tone.

Elements of Literature

Analyze Character Traits and Motivation

Authors can give the reader a lot of information about the characters in a story.

Traits are what a character is like. For example, a character can be honest.

Motivation tells us why a character does something. For example, Dame Shirley wanted adventure.

1. Work with a partner. Reread paragraphs 7–12 of "Dame Shirley and the Gold Rush," on pages 211–212.
2. Answer the following questions in your Reading Log.
   a. Why did friends warn Dame Shirley not to go to California?
   b. What words would you use to describe Dame Shirley's character traits?
   c. What is Dame Shirley's motivation for going to Rich Bar?
3. Compare and contrast your answers with other students'.

Reading Log   Activity Book
                      p. 115

Student
CD-ROM

Word Study

Learn Words from Context and Experience

When you don't understand a word in a reading, try to understand it by using the context and your experience. Follow the steps in this example.

Word you don't know: **shelter**

1. Read the sentence that has the word in it.

   Instead they built lean-tos . . . to form a **shelter.**

2. Read the sentence that comes before this one. Look for context clues.

   Some of the prospectors didn't take time to build houses or cabins.

3. Read the sentence that follows. Look for context clues.

   Some used tents or lived in their covered wagon.

4. In the sentence that comes before, the author describes where the prospectors lived.

5. In the sentence that follows, the author gives more places where the prospectors lived.

6. From your experience, you know that houses, cabins, and tents protect people from bad weather.

7. From the context and your experience, you can guess that *shelter* means a place to live or a place that protects people.

Activity Book   Student
p. 116   CD-ROM

Grammar Focus

Use Adverbs

An **adverb** describes a verb or an adjective. It often tells how something is done. An adverb is often formed by adding *-ly* to an adjective.

She spoke soft**ly.**

"Softly" tells how she spoke.

If an adjective ends in *-y,* you change the *-y* to *-i* before adding *-ly.*

Adverbs can help make your writing more interesting and precise.

1. Reread paragraphs 1 and 10 in "Dame Shirley and the Gold Rush."
2. Identify the adverbs in each paragraph.
3. Write two sentences of your own. Use an *-ly* adverb in each one.

Activity Book   Student   Student
pp. 117–118   Handbook   CD-ROM

From Reading to Writing

Compare and Contrast Two Reading Selections

The two readings in this chapter are similar in some ways and different in others. Write three paragraphs to compare and contrast the two readings.

1. Create a Venn Diagram like this one.
   a. List the things that are different about the readings in each large circle.
   b. List the things that are the same in the space where the circles overlap.
2. Write your paragraphs using the information in the diagram.
   a. In the first paragraph, state your main idea.
   b. In the second paragraph, give reasons and examples of how the readings are the same and different.
   c. In the third paragraph, write a summary of your ideas.

3. Write a final draft.
   a. Use resources to check spelling.
   b. Use a variety of sentence types. Combine short sentences into compound or complex sentences.
   c. Use adverbs to make your writing interesting and more precise.
   d. If possible, prepare your final draft on a computer.

Activity Book
p. 119

Student Handbook

Across Content Areas

Learn About Natural Resources

Earth is full of natural resources. Research the natural resources that are in the area where you live.

1. Take notes from at least two resources (see page 203) to identify the natural resources in your area.

2. What other questions come to mind? Research these questions.
3. Present your research to your class.

Activity Book
p. 120

Apply and Expand

Listening and Speaking Workshop

Exposition: Give a Presentation About a Place

Topic

In this unit, you read about journeys that people took. Give a presentation about a place that you would like to take a journey to.

Step 1: Choose a topic.

1. Brainstorm some places that you think are interesting.
2. Choose one. It can be:
   a. a city or town you know
   b. a historic site
   c. a place you have read about
   d. somewhere far away

Step 2: Research the place.

Use the resources in your school library, or use the Internet. Use the name of your place as a keyword for an Internet search.

Step 3: Take notes about the place.

1. Write answers to these questions on note cards. Use one note card for each idea. Add other questions you think of.
   a. What is the name of the place?
   b. Where is it?
   c. How do you know about it?
   d. What does it look like?
   e. Did something important happen there? What was it?
   f. What can you do there?

2. If something important happened in the place, organize your notes about the events in a timeline.
3. Identify any special language or sayings from the region or culture of your place. How do the language or the sayings reflect the region or culture?

Step 4: Prepare visual aids.

A visual aid is something that readers see instead of read.

1. Use a map to show the location.
2. Show pictures of the place. Use pictures from the Internet or from a book, pictures you draw, or photographs and postcards.
3. Bring an item from the place if you have one.

Step 5: Practice your presentation.

1. Tell a partner about your place. Remember to clarify and support your ideas with evidence, elaborations, and examples.
2. Your partner should fill out the Active Listening Checklist. You should fill out the Speaking Checklist. Add an evaluation point based on what you want to improve.
3. Revise your presentation. Use what you learned from the checklists.

✓ **Speaking Checklist**

1. Did I speak slowly and clearly?

2. Did I explain the topic clearly?

3. Was my partner able to see my visual aid?

✓ **Active Listening Checklist**

1. I liked this presentation because _____ .

2. I learned _____ .

3. I would like to know more about _____ .

Step 6: Give your presentation.

Give your presentation to the class.

1. If possible, use presentation software.
2. You may want to record your presentation on video or audio to share with your family.

Student Handbook

Viewing Workshop

View and Think

Compare and Contrast Cultures

A culture is the way a certain group of people lives.

1. Find a video that shows life in another region or culture. Ask your librarian or teacher for help.
2. Watch the video.
   a. Where is the culture? What is the place like?
   b. How do the people live? What do the people do?
   c. What language do the people speak? How does the language reflect the region or culture?
3. Compare and contrast this culture or place to where and how you live. How is it similar? How is it different?

4. Did the video change your opinions or feelings in any way? How?
5. Think about what you learned.
   a. How did the language in the video help you learn?
   b. What did you learn from the video that you would not have learned from a book?
   c. How did the video's presentation and organization help you learn?

Further Viewing

Watch the *Visions* CNN Video for Unit 3. Do the Video Worksheet.

CNN Video

Writer's Workshop

Exposition: Write a Research Report

Writing Prompt

In this unit, you learned about a journey people made to California in the 1800s. Write a research report about a famous place people made a journey to in the history of the United States.

Step 1: Ask questions.

1. Think of a place to write about. Brainstorm with your class. Some ideas include Plymouth, Massachusetts, Texas, or Florida.
2. Think of questions you have about this place. Possible questions are:
   a. Where is the place?
   b. What time period was it in?
   c. Was it important? Why?
   d. What important things happened there during this time?
   e. How has life in this place changed?
   f. Add your own questions.

Step 2: Research answers to your questions.

1. Use multiple resources in your school library to find answers.
2. Interview an expert, such as a teacher, for more answers.
3. As you research, use tables of contents and headings. These features will help you find important information.
4. Some of your questions may change. Revise or add questions if needed.

Step 3: Record and organize information.

1. Use note cards to record information for your report.
2. Write the information in your own words. Do not copy word-for-word.
3. Use quotation marks (" . . . ") if you use someone else's words. You must copy the exact words if you do this.
   a. Write the name of the person who said the words.
   b. Write the source from which you copied the words.
4. Organize your information in an outline or a timeline. Refer to your Student Handbook.

Step 4: Write a draft.

Write five paragraphs. Use the information you organized in Step 2 to develop your paragraphs. Use a computer, if possible.

1. Your first paragraph will be the introduction.
   a. Write one sentence that is a thesis statement. This sentence tells what your report is about.
   b. Tell why your place was important.
2. Your middle paragraphs will be the body.
   a. Write information that explains what happened there.
   b. Include facts and examples.

3. Your fifth paragraph will be the conclusion.
   a. Retell your thesis statement in different words.
   b. Add one or two sentences that tell what the place means to people today.
4. Include a section at the end of your report where you list the sources you used. Include books, encyclopedias, and Web sites. The title of this section is "Bibliography." Refer to your Student Handbook for correct format.

Step 5: Revise your draft.

1. Exchange reports with a partner.
2. Use the Peer Editing Checklist in your Student Handbook to tell your partner what you like about the report. Tell how to make it better.
3. Use your partner's evaluation to revise your report.
4. Add text to clarify and elaborate. Delete text if you repeat things.
5. Combine and rearrange sentences to make your writing more logical and coherent. Be sure one idea leads to the next.
6. Blend paragraphs to make the report easier to read.
7. Be sure all ideas in your report are supported with examples.

Step 6: Edit and proofread your report.

1. Proofread your revised report. Look for correct spelling, grammar, punctuation, capitalization, and paragraph indentation.
2. Use the Editor's Checklist in your Student Handbook.
3. Proofread your partner's report. Point out any errors you find.

Step 7: Publish.

1. Write the final draft of your report.
2. If you write your report by hand, use your best handwriting. If you use a computer, use the spell check and grammar check.
3. Include a picture of the place. This picture can be from the Internet or you can draw a picture.
4. Bind everyone's reports together in a book. Create a Table of Contents. Ask your teacher to help you.
5. Choose one or two students to make the cover for the book. The title of the book will be "Journeys."
6. Read your classmates' reports. Evaluate them. What are their strengths and their weaknesses?
7. Use your classmates' writing as models for your future writing.
8. Place the book in a place where a specific audience can enjoy it.

Student Handbook

Projects

These projects will help you expand what you learned about journeys. Work alone or with a partner. Ask your teacher or librarian if you need help.

Project 1: Research an Explorer

Explorers journey to different places. They go there to find out more about our world. Research information about a famous explorer.

1. Choose an explorer you would like to learn more about. Here are some ideas to help you brainstorm:
   a. Choose an explorer you have read about in social studies.
   b. Use the Internet. Do a keyword search for *famous explorers*.
2. Use the library to research this explorer. Take notes about important information. Be sure to cover these things:
   a. the dates the explorer lived
   b. where the explorer came from
   c. the place he or she explored
   d. why the exploration was important
3. Draw a map of where the journey took place.
4. Tell a small group what you learned. Use your map as a visual.
5. If possible, use presentation software to present your research.

Project 2: Plan a Time Capsule

A time capsule contains things from a certain time. People put things in a time capsule to show how they live. The time capsule is then saved for people to open at some time in the future.

1. Suppose that your school is making a time capsule. One hundred years from now students from your school will open the capsule.
2. What would you want students from the future to know about your life? Some ideas are: newspapers or magazines, clothes, CDs, photographs.
3. On a note card, write a description of each item.

> *Idea for Time Capsule*
> Newspaper article : July 28, 2002
> Event: Lance Armstrong wins his
> fourth Tour de France.

4. Ask your teacher for an envelope. Put your note cards in the envelope.
   a. Write "Time Capsule" and your name on the envelope.
   b. Exchange envelopes with your classmates. Look inside their time capsules. What things did they write?

Further Reading

The following books discuss the theme of journeys. Choose one or more of them. Write your thoughts and feelings about what you read in your Reading Log. Take notes about your answers to these questions:

1. How are the journeys you read about similar to experiences you have had?
2. What did the characters learn from their journeys?

The Voyage of the Lucky Dragon
by Jack Bennett, Prentice Hall, 1985. A Vietnamese boy tells the story of his family's escape from Vietnam. First they go to Indonesia, then Singapore, and finally Australia.

The Time Bike
by Jane Langton, HarperCollins, 2002. Eddy receives a gift from his uncle. At first the bike seems like an ordinary bike. But soon Eddy discovers that it can travel through time.

Dame Shirley and the Gold Rush
by Jim Rawls, Steck Vaughn, 1992. This book is based on the letters of a woman known as Dame Shirley. Her letters were published in *San Francisco Magazine* in 1854 and 1855. The letters are combined into a story about the California gold rush.

The International Space Station: A Journey into Space
by Wolfgang Engelhardt, Tessloff Publishing, 1998. This book talks about the International Space Station. Many nations, including the United States, Japan, Russia, the European Space Administration, and Canada, are working together to research life in space.

Home: A Journey Through America
by Thomas Locker, Voyager Books, 2000. This book is a collection of poems and stories written about various parts of the U.S. landscape. Included in this book are works by Carl Sandburg, Robert Frost, Henry David Thoreau, and Joseph Bruchac.

A Journey: The Autobiography of Apolo Anton Ohno
by Apolo Anton Ohno, Simon & Schuster Children's, 2002. Apolo Anton Ohno tells the story of his life as a skater and how he became a gold medalist at the 2002 Olympic Games.

Journey to the Center of the Earth
by Jules Verne, Baronet Books, 1983. A team of explorers journey into a crater in Iceland. This crater leads them to the center of the earth, where amazing and dangerous things happen to them.

Companion
Web site

Reading Log

Heinle
Reading Library
20,000 Leagues
Under the Sea

UNIT 4

Cycles

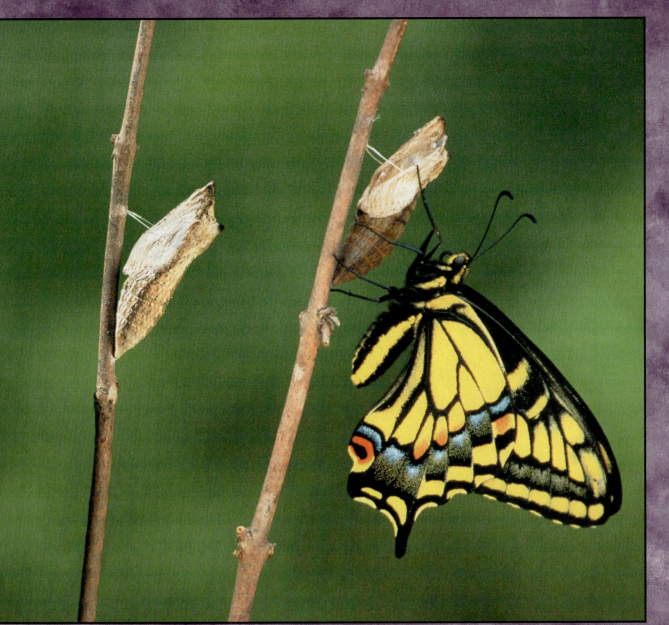

Stages of Butterfly Metamorphosis, photo, Ralph A. Clevenger.

View the Picture

1. What does this picture show? How does the picture show a cycle?

2. What other cycles do you know about?

In this unit, you will read a poem, a myth, an autobiographical short story, and an excerpt from an informational book. You will also write in these forms.

Water Dance

a poem
by Thomas Locker

Objectives

Reading Describe mental images as you read a poem.

Listening and Speaking Respond to mood.

Grammar Use comparative adjectives.

Writing Write a poem.

Content Math: Calculate averages.

Use Prior Knowledge

Talk About Uses of Water

Water is part of your everyday life. How do you use water?

1. Think about all the ways that you use water. List these ways on a piece of paper.

How I Use Water
1. I brush my teeth.
2. I water my plants.

2. Share your list with a partner.
3. Based on your lists, do you think water is important? Why or why not? Talk about your answer with your partner.
4. Have a class discussion about the use of water in your community.
   a. Where does the water come from?
   b. Do you think people in your community use too much water?
   c. How can you save water?

Build Background

The Water Cycle

Water moves in a cycle on Earth. First, the sun warms Earth. The water on the surface of Earth evaporates (turns to gas) as it warms. It forms clouds in the sky and falls back to Earth as rain or snow. Then the cycle begins again.

Content Connection

The amount of water on Earth never changes. The water just changes from one form to another. Earth is more than 70% water.

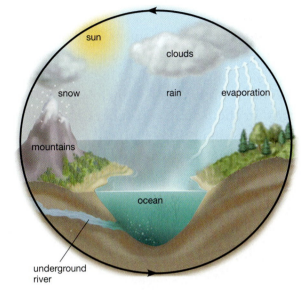

Build Vocabulary

Learn Vivid Verbs

A **verb** is a part of speech. Some other parts of speech are nouns, adjectives, and adverbs. If you choose these words carefully in your writing, you can make it vivid (interesting) and precise (exact). Compare the verbs in these sentences:

ordinary verb Kostas <u>ran</u> to school because he was late.

vivid verb Kostas <u>sprinted</u> to school because he was late.

Ran means "moved very fast." *Sprinted* means "ran very fast." *Sprinted* helps you form a clearer picture than *ran*. Kostas is sprinting because he is late.

Write the following sentences in your Personal Dictionary. The underlined words are ordinary verbs. Replace each one with a vivid verb from the box.

> trembles   leap   cascades

1. Sometimes the water <u>falls</u> down over the moss-covered rocks.
2. I <u>jump</u> from a stone cliff.
3. The earth <u>shakes</u> with my thunder.

Personal Dictionary   The Heinle Newbury House Dictionary   Activity Book *p. 121*   Student CD-ROM

Text Structure

Poem

"Water Dance" is a **poem.** The writer of a poem is a poet. In a poem, the poet uses vivid language to describe an object, person, or event. Look at the chart on the right for the features of a poem.

Think about who or what the speaker is in "Water Dance."

Poem	
Stanzas	The poem has a group of lines called stanzas.
Vivid Verbs	The words help you picture exactly what is happening.
Sense Words	These words describe how things sound, smell, taste, look, or feel.
A Speaker	The speaker is the voice that is speaking in the poem. The speaker is not always the poet. Sometimes the speaker is not even a person.

Student
CD-ROM

Reading Strategy

Describe Mental Images

Many words in "Water Dance" help you form **mental images** (pictures in your mind). Describing these mental images will help you understand the poem.

> The tall, green trees swayed softly in the gentle, warm wind.

The underlined words help you form mental images. They help you picture how the trees look and feel.

1. Read stanzas 1 to 3 of "Water Dance."
2. Draw pictures of your mental images from stanza 3. Then list the words from the stanza that helped you draw your pictures.

3. Share your drawings with a partner. Did you form the same mental images?
4. Pause after reading each stanza of "Water Dance." In your Reading Log, describe the mental images you form.

Before you read the poem, think about your purpose in reading it. Will you read it for enjoyment or to understand something? As you read, you may want to adjust (change) your purpose so that you can appreciate the writer's craft.

Reading Log

Student
CD-ROM

Water
Dance

a poem
by Thomas Locker

1 SOME PEOPLE SAY that I am one thing.
Others say that I am many.
Ever since the world began
I have been moving in an endless circle.
Sometimes I fall from the sky.

2 *I am the rain.*

Describe Mental Images

What mental images do you form from this stanza?

3 Sometimes I cascade.
I **tumble**
down,
down,
over the **moss**-covered rocks,
through the forest shadows.

4 *I am the mountain **stream**.*

5 At the foot of the mountains,
I leap from a stone cliff.
Spiraling.
Plunging.

6 *I am the **waterfall**.*

7 In the shadows of the mountain,
I am still and deep.
I fill
and **overflow.**

8 *I am the lake.*

---

tumble roll

moss a short, soft plant that grows on the ground and on trees

stream a flowing body of water, smaller than a river

spiraling twisting up or down

plunging diving or falling fast and far

waterfall water falling from a high place

overflow flow over the edges of something

9   I wind through broad, golden valleys
    joined by streams,
    joined by **creeks.**
    I grow ever wider,
    broader and deeper.

10 *I am the river.*

Describe Mental Images

What mental images do you form when you read "Cool silver moonlight sparkles and dances"?

11 I pass through a gateway
    of high stone **palisades,**
    leaving the land behind.
    Cool silver moonlight
    sparkles and dances
    on my waves.

12 *I am the sea.*

13 **Drawn** upward
    by warm sunlight,
    in white-silver **veils**
    I rise into the air.
    I disappear.

14 *I am the **mist.***

---

creeks   small streams
palisades   rows of cliffs
sparkles   gives off bits of light
drawn   pulled toward something

veils   pieces of cloth that cover the face
mist   a fog, very fine drops of water forming a cloud near the ground

15 In thousands of shapes I reappear
high above the earth in the blue sky.
I float.
I drift.

16 *I am the clouds.*

17 Carried by winds
from distant seas
I move,
growing heavier,
growing darker,
returning.

18 *I am the **storm front.***

19 At the wall of the mountains,
I rise up
as **gleaming** power-filled towers
in the darkened sky.

20 *I am the **thunderhead.***

Describe Mental Images

Do you think the words in this stanza describe a storm well? Why or why not?

21 I blind the sky with lightning.
The earth **trembles** with my thunder.
I **rage.**
I **drench** the mountainside.

22 *I am the storm.*

---

storm front a mass of air that brings a storm
gleaming shining brightly
thunderhead a part of a large cloud; often appears
   before a thunderstorm

trembles shakes
rage show uncontrolled anger
drench make completely wet

23 Storms come.
    Storms pass.
    I am **countless droplets** of rain
    left floating in the silent air.
    I reflect all the colors of sunlight.

24 *I am the rainbow.*

Describe Mental Images

What mental image do you form after you read the words "I am the rainbow"?

25 I am one thing.
    I am many things.

26 *I am water.*

27 This is my dance through our world.

---

countless too many to be counted

droplets small drops

About the Author

Thomas Locker (born 1937)

Thomas Locker is both a writer and a painter. Locker's paintings make his stories and poems very special. At first, Locker only painted pictures. Then he realized that his paintings could help him tell his stories. Locker has painted pictures for about 30 books. He also wrote several of these books.

➤ The selection shows Thomas Locker's paintings. Describe how these paintings help you understand the poem better. How does Locker's choice of style and media extend the meaning of the poem?

Beyond the Reading

Reading Comprehension

Question-Answer Relationships (QAR)

"Right There" Question

1. **Recall Facts** How long has the speaker been moving in an endless circle?

"Think and Search" Questions

2. **Make Inferences** Who or what is the speaker in the poem?
3. **Identify** What different things does the speaker ("I") become? (Hint: Look at the *italic* type.)
4. **Identify Main Ideas** What main idea does this poem describe?
5. **Identify Cause and Effect** Why does Earth tremble?

"Author and You" Questions

6. **Understand Text Features** The poet uses *italic* type many times. Why do you think he does this? How does it help you understand the poem?
7. **Describe Mood** What is the mood (feeling you get) in stanza 21? Is it happy? Scary?

8. **Analyze Point of View** Why did the author write the poem in the first person ("I") instead of in the third person ("it")?

"On Your Own" Questions

9. **Speculate** How do you think the poet wants you to feel about water?
10. **Analyze Inductive Organization** In Unit 3, Chapter 4, the author used the deductive method to explain his information—he stated his main idea then supported it with details and examples. In this poem, the poet uses the inductive method. He states his details, which lead us to his main idea. Find examples of this type of organization and presentation in the poem.

Activity Book
p. 122

Student
CD-ROM

Build Reading Fluency

Read Aloud to Engage Listeners

Reading aloud helps increase your fluency and expression. Learning to read with expression makes others want to listen to you.

1. Listen to the audio recording of "Water Dance."

2. Turn to page 230 and follow along.
3. Listen to the phrasing and expression.
4. With a partner, read aloud paragraphs 1–7 three times.
5. Select your favorite two paragraphs.
6. Read them in front of the class with expression.

Listen, Speak, Interact

Respond to Mood

"Water Dance" uses vivid words to describe how water moves around Earth. The poet uses these words to create different moods—feelings that a reader gets.

1. Work with a partner. Take turns reading aloud the stanzas. Adapt your spoken language to the audience, purpose, and occasion.

2. Read the poem to enjoy and appreciate it.
3. As your partner reads, list words that describe the different moods you feel.
4. Talk about your lists. Which stanzas made you feel a certain way?
5. Did you get any insights (new truth or knowledge) from the poem? Share your insights with your partner.

Elements of Literature

Use Figurative Language

Poets often use **figurative language.** One kind of figurative speech is **personification**—when a writer gives human characteristics to a thing. For example:

The sun smiles at us.

The sun is not really smiling. Personification makes the sun into a human being who is smiling. This sentence tells us that the sun is shining brightly. It also gives us the idea that the sun is a friendly thing.

1. Read the following examples of personification from "Water Dance."

a. Cool silver moonlight sparkles and dances on my waves.
b. I blind the sky with lightning.

2. What things are given human characteristics? What are the characteristics? How do they affect meaning?
3. Check with a partner to see if your answers are the same.
4. Write your own sentence with an example of personification.

Activity Book
p. 123

Student
CD-ROM

Word Study

Distinguish Denotative and Connotative Meanings

Words can have two kinds of meanings. A **denotative meaning** is what you find in a dictionary. A **connotative meaning** is the feelings that we have about the word.

Reread these lines from the poem:

Cool silver moonlight <u>sparkles</u> and dances on my waves.

The denotative meaning of *sparkle* is "give off bits of light." But our feeling about the word is that beautiful, valuable things sparkle, like diamonds. This is the connotative meaning of *sparkle*.

1. Copy this chart in your Personal Dictionary.

Word	Meanings
tremble	_____ be afraid _____ shake
drench	_____ to make wet _____ to soak and make uncomfortable

2. Reread stanza 21. Pay close attention to the words *trembles* and *drench*. Then write D before the denotative meaning of each word, and C before the connotative meaning.

Personal Dictionary   The Heinle Newbury House Dictionary   Activity Book p. 124   Student CD-ROM

Grammar Focus

Use Comparative Adjectives

In Unit 3, Chapter 4, you learned to add *-er* to an adjective to make its comparative form.

Sometimes the adjective changes its spelling when you add *-er*.

1. Study this chart to see the changes.

Adjective	Comparative Form
wide	wider
blue	bluer
busy	busier
big	bigger

2. Can you make up the rules?

3. Find a comparative adjective in stanza 17 that follows one of these patterns.

4. On a piece of paper, write four sentences. Use a different comparative adjective from the chart in each sentence. Write your sentences like this:

_____ is _____er than _____ .

Activity Book pp. 125–126   Student Handbook   Student CD-ROM

From Reading to Writing

Write a Poem

Write a three-stanza poem about something that you like.

1. Brainstorm things you like, for example, snow, your favorite relative, a pet.
2. Use figurative language such as personification to help readers form mental images. For example, your dog might be very funny. You could write, "My dog is a clown."
3. Use comparative adjectives. Compare your favorite thing to three different things. For example, "My fish is bluer than the sky."

4. Present your poem to the class.
5. Make a class collection of the poems. As a class, evaluate the poems for their strengths and weaknesses.
6. Use your classmates' poems as models for your own writing. Determine how they can help you set your goals as a writer.

Activity Book
p. 127

Student Handbook

Across Content Areas

Calculate Averages

If a city has 8 inches of **precipitation** (rain, snow, or sleet) in one year and 10 inches the next year, then the **average precipitation** for the two years is 9 inches. Calculate an average like this:

Inches the first year	8
Inches the second year	10
Total inches for two years	18

Divide the total inches by the total number of years: $18 \div 2 = 9$

The average yearly precipitation is 9 inches.

This chart shows the average amount of precipitation that falls in four cities in Arizona in a year.

City	Average Yearly Precipitation
Phoenix	7.2 inches
Tucson	12.0 inches
Winslow	8.0 inches
Yuma	3.2 inches

Copy and complete this chart to find the average yearly precipitation for the four Arizona cities together.

(A) Amount of precipitation for all cities	
(B) Number of cities	4
Average: Divide (A) by (B)	

Activity Book
p. 128

Persephone and the Seasons

a myth
by Heather Amery

Objectives

Reading Use chronology to locate and recall information as you read a myth.

Listening and Speaking Act out a story.

Grammar Write using irregular past tense verbs.

Writing Summarize and paraphrase to inform.

Content Language Arts: Distinguish the meanings of *myth*.

Use Prior Knowledge

Share Experiences with Seasons

A season is a period of time that has a certain type of weather. Some parts of the world have four seasons: spring, summer, autumn (fall), and winter. Other parts of the world have two seasons: the rainy season and the dry season.

1. Make a chart like the one here.

2. Think about a place that you know about. List information about the seasons in this place.

3. Put a star (★) next to your favorite season. Put an *X* next to your least favorite season. Why did you choose these seasons? Explain your answers to a partner.

Seasons in _____				
Season	When	Weather (rain, snow, sun)	Temperature (hot, cold, warm, cool)	Things People Do
spring	April, May, June	sunny rainy	warm	lie in the sun plant gardens

Build Background

Hemispheres and the Seasons

Not all parts of the world have the same season at the same time. Why?

Earth is divided into two parts called hemispheres. As Earth moves around the sun, one hemisphere is turning toward it. The other hemisphere is turning away from it. The hemisphere pointing toward the sun is warmer. It is summer there. The hemisphere pointing away from the sun is cooler. It is winter there.

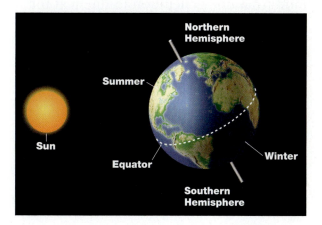

Content Connection

SOCIAL STUDIES

The **equator** is the imaginary circular line that divides Earth into the two hemispheres.

Build Vocabulary

Use a Dictionary to Find Definitions, Pronunciations, and Derivations

Read this dictionary entry.

> se•ri•ous /'sɪriəs/ *adj*. **1** thoughtful and quiet, humorless [from Latin *sērius*]

This entry gives you the pronunciation of the word, its part of speech (*adj.* = adjective), its meaning, and its derivation (where it came from).

1. Copy this chart.
2. Look up these words in a large dictionary and fill in the chart.
3. With your teacher's help, pronounce the words.

Word	Meaning	Derivation
serious	thoughtful and quiet, humorless	Latin *sērius*
chariot		
haggard		

Personal Dictionary   The Heinle Newbury House Dictionary   Activity Book *p. 129*   Student CD-ROM

Text Structure

Myth

"Persephone and the Seasons" is a **myth** from ancient Greece. A myth is a made-up story. It is an oral tradition—it was told out loud from one generation to the next for thousands of years. Look for the features of a myth as you read the selection.

As you read, notice how the myth explains an event in nature. Which event does it explain?

	Myth
Characters	Characters may have special powers that people in real life do not.
Events	Many events could never happen in real life.
Explanation	Many myths give a made-up explanation of events in nature.

Student
CD-ROM

Reading Strategy

Use Chronology to Locate and Recall Information

Chronology is the order in which events happen. *Chronology* comes from the Greek root word *khronos,* which means *time.* Knowing the chronology of events can help you locate information in a text. It can also help you recall what you read.

1. Make a timeline in your Reading Log. As you read, take notes on the important events on a timeline like this.

2. After you read, use the timeline to help you locate and recall information.

Reading Log   Student
                  CD-ROM

Persephone and the Seasons

Demeter
left for
the day.

Pluto took
Persephone
away.

PERSEPHONE AND THE SEASONS

a myth by Heather Amery

1   One bright, sunny morning, the **goddess** Demeter said goodbye to her daughter Persephone. "I'll be back for supper," she called. Demeter was the goddess of all the plants in the world. She made sure the corn grew tall in the fields and fruit **ripened** on the trees. The weather was always fine and there were **harvests** all year.

2   After her mother had gone, Persephone went out to meet her friends and pick flowers with them. Searching for the very best lilies, she wandered away and was soon on her own.

3   Suddenly, she heard a noise and looked up. She saw a **chariot** pulled by four black horses, driven by Pluto, god of the **Underworld.** Pluto had fallen in love with Persephone, but knew Demeter would never allow him to marry her daughter.

4   Before Persephone could scream, Pluto dragged her into the chariot and raced away. As they **thundered** across the ground, a huge **cleft** opened. Pluto drove straight down it and the ground closed up behind them. He and Persephone had disappeared into the Underworld.

5   When Demeter came back that evening, she called to Persephone but there was no **reply.** The house was empty. When it grew dark, Demeter began to worry. Where could

Use Chronology to Locate and Recall Information

Had Demeter come home when Pluto took Persephone?

Audio
CD 2, Tr. 8

---

goddess   a female being or spirit with special powers; people in ancient Greece believed in the goddess Demeter

ripened   became ready to use or eat

harvests   times when people gather crops

chariot   a two-wheeled vehicle pulled by horses; used in ancient times

Underworld   in ancient Greek myths, the place where people go when they die

thundered   sounded like thunder

cleft   a crack or split

reply   an answer

Persephone be? At midnight, she lit a flaming torch and set out to look for her. All night she searched, calling, "Persephone, Persephone, where are you?" But there was no answer. For nine days and nine nights, Demeter searched, not stopping to sleep or even to eat.

Use Chronology to Locate and Recall Information

What happened after Demeter stopped looking after the crops?

6   Dressed in black instead of her usual bright clothes, Demeter **wandered** all over the country as a haggard, old woman. Because she no longer looked after the crops, the corn **rotted** in the fields, no fruit ripened on the trees and the grass turned brown. There was nothing for the sheep and goats to eat and all the people grew short of food. Soon they were near to **starving.**

7   Zeus called a meeting of all the gods and goddesses. "This is very serious," he said in the voice that rolled like thunder. "Unless we can **persuade** Demeter to take care of the Earth again, all the people will die."

8   "Pluto must let Persephone leave the Underworld," said a goddess. "Only then will Demeter save the Earth."

9   Zeus called for Hermes, the messenger of the gods. "Go to Pluto and ask him, very politely, to return Persephone to her mother," he said. Hermes flew off at once. Only the gods and goddesses could go into the Underworld, the home of all the people who had died, and come out again.

---

wandered went from place to place
rotted became too old to eat

starving dying from not having enough food
persuade lead a person or group to believe or do something by arguing or reasoning with them

10   "I will never let Persephone go," growled Pluto. "I love her and I want to marry her." "Please, Pluto," begged Hermes, "please be **reasonable.** You know Persephone doesn't love you and won't marry you."

11   "Very well," **roared** Pluto, very angry. "I'll let her go if she hasn't eaten any food while she's been here. You know the rule. If she has eaten anything in the Underworld, she must stay here forever."

12   "That's easy," said Hermes. "Let's ask her." Persephone cried, in answer to the question, "I couldn't eat anything here. I've never touched even the smallest crumb of food."

13   A **misty** ghost of a gardener was listening. "Oh yes you did," he **croaked.** "I saw you. You picked a ripe **pomegranate** and ate it."

14   "No, no," cried Persephone, "I didn't eat it all. I was so thirsty, I just swallowed a few of the seeds." "That's enough," shouted Pluto.

15   "Please, Pluto," begged Hermes, "let her go for a little while. A few seeds aren't much." "Oh, all right," growled

Use Chronology to Locate and Recall Information

When did Persephone eat something?

---

reasonable   referring to the right thing to do
roared   shouted very loudly and angrily
misty   not easy to see, as if covered by a cloud

croaked   made a deep sound like a frog
pomegranate   a fruit with many juicy red seeds

Pluto. "Persephone may go back to the Earth for half of each year but must spend the other months here with me, in the Underworld."

16   Holding Persephone's hand, Hermes flew with her out of the Underworld to Demeter. "Oh, my darling daughter," cried Demeter, hugging Persephone. "You have come back to me at last." "Yes," **sobbed** Persephone, "but I must go back to the Underworld for part of every year."

17   Demeter knew she had to accept this. At once, she looked young again. She put on her brightest clothes and began work, making new **shoots** of corn and grass grow and leaves open on the trees. It was spring all over the Earth.

18   All through the summer Demeter was happy and busy, watching the fine harvests of corn and fruit. But when Persephone had to go back to the Underworld, she was sad and it became autumn. The leaves on the trees turned brown, the grass stopped growing and the weather turned cold. It was winter until Persephone returned. Then Demeter was happy and it was spring again.

> **Use Chronology to Locate and Recall Information**
>
> What happened after Demeter began to work again?

---

sobbed   cried

shoots   small, young plant growth

About the Author   Heather Amery

Heather Amery lives in England. She has written more than 100 books for young people. Amery has many hobbies. She enjoys riding her bicycle, sailing, and swimming. She also likes to visit new places. Of course, Amery loves to read. It is a part of her everyday life.

➤ Heather Amery wrote her own version of this famous myth. What strategies do you think she used in researching and writing this story? What question would you ask Heather Amery about this text?

Beyond the Reading

Reading Comprehension

Question-Answer Relationships (QAR)

"Right There" Questions

1. **Recall Facts** What is Persephone doing when Pluto takes her away?
2. **Recall Facts** What is Demeter the goddess of?
3. **Recall Facts** Who brings Persephone back to Demeter?

"Think and Search" Questions

4. **Identify Cause and Effect** Why does Pluto take Persephone?
5. **Find Supporting Arguments** Hermes and Pluto argue over letting Persephone go. What reasons does Hermes give for why Pluto should let her go?
6. **Analyze Change** How does Earth change when Persephone is in the Underworld?

"Author and You" Questions

7. **Resolve a Problem** How do the characters resolve the problem? Is it a good solution? Why?
8. **Make Inferences** How does Demeter feel about Persephone? How can you tell?
9. **Analyze Characters** How do you think Persephone feels when she must go back to the Underworld every year? Why do you think so?

"On Your Own" Question

10. **Make Connections Across Cultures** Do you know of a myth, a legend, or another oral tradition from another culture or region? Compare and contrast it to this myth.

Activity Book
p. 130

Student
CD-ROM

Build Reading Fluency

Read Silently and Aloud

Reading silently for practice then reading aloud helps you read with expression.

1. Listen to the audio recording of "Persephone and the Seasons."
2. Follow along on page 242.
3. Read silently paragraphs 1–3 three times.
4. With a partner read aloud.
5. Your partner will time you.

Listen, Speak, Interact

Act Out a Story

Present a dramatic interpretation of "Persephone and the Seasons" to the class.

1. In groups, choose a character that each person will be: Persephone, Demeter, Pluto, Zeus, and the Gardener.
2. Go through the story and identify all of the dialogue (the words with "quotation marks" around them).
3. Practice the dialogue. Each person reads his or her words in the story.
4. Act out the places where there is no dialogue.
5. Evaluate yourself: Are you speaking clearly and slowly? Are you speaking loudly enough and with the right pitch and tone? Will your audience believe you?
6. Use good pronunciation and intonation.
7. After you practice, perform your story for your class or another class.
8. Ask your audience if they understood your verbal words and your nonverbal messages. Did they believe your role?

Elements of Literature

Recognize Foreshadowing

In **foreshadowing,** an author gives clues about something that will happen later in a story. Look at this example:

> It was a dark day. The clouds were heavy and black. Sam turned on the television and saw the serious face of the weather announcer.

This paragraph uses foreshadowing. It gives us the feeling that something bad will probably happen later.

Sometimes we notice foreshadowing more easily when we reread a story. That is because when we reread, we already know how the story ends.

1. Reread this sentence from paragraph 2 of "Persephone and the Seasons."

   > Searching for the very best lilies, she wandered away and was soon on her own.

2. Work with a small group. Talk about these questions:
   a. The author says that Persephone is alone. Does this tell you that something bad will happen?
   b. Why do you think so?

Activity Book
p. 131

Student
CD-ROM

Word Study

Recognize Contractions

Negative sentences usually use the word *not*. In speech and in informal writing, we often contract *not* with a verb. We shorten it to *n't*.

You know Persephone <u>doesn't</u> love you.

Here are some more examples:

Full Form	Contracted Form
is not	isn't
do not	don't
cannot	can't
will not	won't

1. Find three contracted forms of *not* in paragraphs 12, 14, and 15 of the reading.
2. Rewrite the following sentences, contracting *not* with its verb.
   a. Persephone did not like life in the Underworld.
   b. Demeter could not find Persephone.
   c. Pluto would not let her go.

Activity Book   Student
p. 132   CD-ROM

Grammar Focus

Write Using Irregular Past Tense Verbs

Use the past tense to talk about actions that happened in the past. The past tense form of regular verbs is the verb plus the ending *-ed* added to the verb.

As they <u>thundered</u> across the ground, a huge cleft <u>opened</u>.

Irregular past tense verbs are formed in different ways.

Persephone <u>went</u> out to meet her friends.

Went is the past tense form of *go*. You have to memorize the past tense forms of irregular verbs.

Simple Form	Past Tense Form
make	made
hear	heard
know	knew
see	saw

Refer to the list of irregular verbs in your Student Handbook.

1. Reread paragraph 3 of the reading. List three irregular past tense verbs.
2. Write two sentences with irregular past tense verbs.

Activity Book   Student   Student
pp. 133–134   Handbook   CD-ROM

From Reading to Writing

Summarize and Paraphrase to Inform

Imagine that you have a friend who lives far away. This friend is interested in oral traditions, so you want to tell him or her about the Persephone myth. You decide to summarize the story (give its main ideas) and paraphrase some of the dialogue (restate it in your own words).

1. Review the timeline of the story that you made in the Reading Strategy section. Make sure that you included all of the main events.
2. Write a summary. It should tell the story using only the main events. Use regular and irregular past tense verbs correctly.

3. Choose some dialogue in the story that you want to include.
4. Reread the dialogue carefully. Then close your book and paraphrase it. Put this paraphrase in your summary.
5. You want your friend to have your summary right away. Should you put it in a letter or in an e-mail message?

Activity Book
p. 135

Student
Handbook

Across Content Areas

Distinguish the Meanings of *Myth*

Listed below are two definitions of the word *myth*.

> **myth** /mɪθ/ *n.* **1** stories from ancient cultures about history, gods, and heroes: *Students learn about the myths of ancient Greece and Rome.* **2** an untrue or unproved story: *His stories about his great successes in sports are myths.*

Read the following sentences. On a piece of paper, match each sentence with the correct definition. Write *Definition 1* or *Definition 2*.

1. I read a myth about the hero Hercules.
2. Monica's stories about her old school are all myths.
3. Many other cultures tell myths about why the seasons change.
4. We heard that John reads 15 books a day. But we think that this is a myth.

Activity Book
p. 136

CHAPTER 3

The Circuit

an autobiographical
short story
by Francisco Jiménez

Objectives

Reading Compare text to your own knowledge and experience as you read an autobiographical short story.

Listening and Speaking Present an experience.

Grammar Identify dependent clauses.

Writing Write a letter to an author.

Content Language Arts: Understand the influence of other languages and cultures on English.

Use Prior Knowledge

Talk About Moving

When people leave one home and go to live in another, we say they have moved.

Have you ever moved? Think about what it would feel like to move to a new home. What questions would you have?

1. Write your questions in a chart.
2. Share your questions with a partner. Are any of your questions the same?
3. Which question is the most important one for you? Why? Compare with your partner.
4. State the main idea and supporting details of what your partner said.

5. Share your thoughts about moving with the class.

Questions About Moving		
The New Neighborhood	The New School	New Friends
Will the people be friendly?	Will the teachers be nice?	How will I make friends?

Build Background

Farming in the United States

Most farms in the United States today are very large. Machines do a lot of the work, but they cannot pick some crops.

Some farmers pay migrant workers to pick crops by hand. These workers move from one farm to another.

Content Connection

California produces more food than any other state in the United States.

Build Vocabulary

Study Word Origins and Guess Meaning

There are many Spanish words in the selection you will read. You can guess the meaning of these words by using **context clues** and **language structure.** Context clues are words or sentences that are around a word. Language structure is how the word is used in the sentence.

Some English words come from Spanish, for example, *patio, plaza,* and *rodeo.* How do you think they become English words?

1. Copy this chart in your Personal Dictionary.
2. Look at the definitions at the bottom of the chart. Match the underlined words to their definitions.

Use Context Clues and Language Structure

Everything was packed. Papá said wearily, "<u>Es todo</u>."	*that's everything*
Mamá liked the pot. "<u>Mi olla</u>," she used to say proudly.	
"Do you like music?" he asked me. "Yes, I like <u>corridos</u>," I answered.	
that's everything *style of music* *my stewpot*	

Personal Dictionary

Activity Book
p. 137

Student CD-ROM

Text Structure

Autobiographical Short Story

"The Circuit" is an **autobiographical short story.** An autobiographical short story is a story that an author writes about his or her own life. Look for the features of an autobiographical short story as you read the selection.

Autobiographical Short Story	
Setting	The real time and place are from the author's life.
Characters	The main character is the author; other characters are people from the author's life.
Events	The action happens in a few pages.
First Person Point of View	The author tells the story—he is the narrator. He uses the pronouns *I, me, we,* and *us* to tell the story.

Student
CD-ROM

Reading Strategy

Compare Text to Your Own Knowledge and Experience

When you read, what you know and some of your experiences may be similar to those in the reading selection. To understand the reading, you should compare your knowledge and experiences to characters and events in the story.

1. Read this paragraph from the selection.

   Two hours later, around eight o'clock, I stood by the side of the road waiting for school bus number twenty. When it arrived I climbed in. Everyone was busy either talking or yelling. I sat in an empty seat in the back.

2. Answer these questions to help you compare your experiences to the character's experiences.

   a. How do you get to school? Do you walk? Do you take the bus?

   b. The character doesn't know anyone on the bus. Have you ever been in a situation where you didn't know anyone? How did you feel? What did you do?

Compare your knowledge and experiences as you read "The Circuit."

Student
CD-ROM

The Circuit

an autobiographical short story by Francisco Jiménez

Audio
CD 2, Tr. 9

Compare Text to Your Own Knowledge and Experience

Compare your experience and feelings with those of the author.

1   Yes, it was that time of year. When I opened the front door to the **shack,** I stopped. Everything we owned was neatly packed in cardboard boxes. Suddenly I felt even more the weight of hours, days, weeks, and months of work. I sat down on a box. The thought of having to move to Fresno and knowing what was in store for me there brought tears to my eyes.

2   That night I could not sleep. I lay in bed thinking about how much I hated this move.

3   A little before five o'clock in the morning, Papá woke everyone up. A few minutes later, the yelling and screaming of my little brothers and sister, for whom the move was a great adventure, broke the silence of dawn. Shortly, the barking of the dogs **accompanied** them.

4   While we packed the breakfast dishes, Papá went outside to start the "*Carcanchita.*" That was the name Papá gave his old black Plymouth. . . . Papá parked the car out in front and left the motor running. . . .

shack   a small house or shed, usually of wood and not well built

accompanied   went with someone

5   Everything was packed except Mamá's pot. It was an old large **galvanized** pot she had picked up at an army **surplus** store in Santa Maria. The pot had many **dents** and **nicks,** and the more dents and nicks it **acquired** the more Mamá liked it. "*Mi olla,*" she used to say proudly.

6   I held the front door open as Mamá carefully carried out her pot by both handles, making sure not to spill the cooked beans. When she got to the car, Papá reached out to help her with it. Roberto opened the rear car door and Papá gently placed it on the floor behind the front seat. All of us then climbed in. Papá sighed, wiped the sweat from his forehead with his sleeve, and said **wearily,** "*Es todo.*"

7   As we drove away, I felt a lump in my throat. I turned around and looked at our little shack for the last time.

8   At sunset we drove into a **labor camp** near Fresno. Since Papá did not speak English, Mamá asked the camp **foreman** if he needed any more workers. "We don't need no more," said the foreman, scratching his head. "Check with Sullivan down the road. Can't miss him. He lives in a big white house with a fence around it."

Compare Text to Your Own Knowledge and Experience

What does it feel like to ask for help from someone you do not know?

---

galvanized metal covered with zinc
surplus extra, leftover
dents holes made by a hit
nicks small cuts or marks

acquired got
wearily in a tired way
labor camp a place where many workers live
foreman a boss of a group of workers

9   When we got there, Mamá walked up to the house. She
went through a white gate, past a row of rose bushes, up
the stairs to the house. She rang the doorbell. The porch
light went on and a tall **husky** man came out. They
exchanged a few words. After the man went in, Mamá
clasped her hands and hurried back to the car. "We have
work! Mr. Sullivan said we can stay there the whole season,"
she said, **gasping** and pointing to an old garage near the
stables. . . .

10   It was Monday, the first week of November. The grape
season was over and I could now go to school. I woke up
early that morning and lay in bed, looking at the stars and
savoring the thought of not going to work and of starting
sixth grade for the first time that year. . . .

11   Two hours later, around eight o'clock, I stood by the
side of the road waiting for school bus number twenty.
When it arrived I climbed in. Everyone was busy either
talking or yelling. I sat in an empty seat in the back.

**Compare Text
to Your Own
Knowledge and
Experience**

Have you had to go
to a new school in
the middle of the
year? How was the
experience? If not,
imagine what it
would be like.

---

husky   strong and solid
exchanged   gave and received words and ideas

gasping   breathing in quickly, usually from surprise
     or shock
savoring   appreciating and enjoying an experience

Compare Text to Your Own Knowledge and Experience

Have you ever had trouble understanding another language? What did you do?

12   When the bus stopped in front of the school, I felt very **nervous.** I looked out the bus window and saw boys and girls carrying books under their arms. I put my hands in my pant pockets and walked to the principal's office. When I entered, I heard a woman's voice say: "May I help you?" I was **startled.** I had not heard English for months. For a few seconds I remained **speechless.** I looked at the lady who waited for an answer. My first **instinct** was to answer her in Spanish, but I held back. Finally, after struggling for English words, I managed to tell her that I wanted to **enroll** in the sixth grade. After answering many questions, I was led to the classroom.

13   Mr. Lema, the sixth grade teacher, greeted me and **assigned** me a desk. He then introduced me to the class. I was so nervous and scared at that moment when everyone's eyes were on me that I wished I were with Papá and Roberto picking cotton. After **taking roll,** Mr. Lema gave the class the assignment for the first hour. "The first thing we have to do this morning is finish reading the story we began yesterday," he said enthusiastically. He walked up to me, handed me an English book, and asked me to read. "We are on page 125," he said politely. When I heard this, I felt my blood rush to my head; I felt **dizzy.** "Would you like to read?" he asked hesitantly. I opened the book to page 125. My mouth was dry. My eyes began to water. I could not begin. "You can read later," Mr. Lema said understandingly.

---

nervous   worried about a future event

startled   surprised, sometimes enough to jump

speechless   not able to speak, sometimes from surprise or sadness

instinct   a natural behavior

enroll   join officially

assigned   gave a spot

taking roll   calling out the names of students and writing down if they are present

dizzy   light-headed, faint

14   During **recess** I went into the **rest room** and opened my English book to page 125. I began to read in a low voice, pretending I was in class. There were many words I did not know. I closed the book and headed back to the classroom.

15   Mr. Lema was sitting at his desk correcting papers. When I entered he looked up at me and smiled. I felt better. I walked up to him and asked if he could help me with the new words. "Gladly," he said.

16   The rest of the month I spent my lunch hours working on English with Mr. Lema, my best friend at school.

17   One Friday during lunch hour Mr. Lema asked me to take a walk with him to the music room. "Do you like music?" he asked me as we entered the building. "Yes, I like *corridos*," I answered. He then picked up a **trumpet,** blew on it, and handed it to me. The sound gave me **goose bumps.** I knew that sound. I had heard it in many *corridos*. "How would you like to learn how to play it?" he asked. He must have read my face because before I could answer, he added: "I'll teach you how to play it during our lunch hours."

Compare Text to Your Own Knowledge and Experience

Compare Mr. Lema to teachers you have had.

---

recess   a short stop or break in classes
rest room   a washroom, bathroom
trumpet   a brass musical instrument

goose bumps   small raised bumps on the skin caused by cold, fear, disgust, or excitement

Compare Text to Your Own Knowledge and Experience

Have you ever been in a situation like this? How did you feel? How do you think the author felt?

That day I could **hardly** wait to tell Papá and Mamá the great news. As I got off the bus, my little brothers and sister ran up to meet me. They were yelling and screaming. I thought they were happy to see me, but when I opened the door to our shack, I saw that everything we owned was neatly packed in cardboard boxes.

hardly   barely, almost no

About the Author

Francisco Jiménez (born 1943)

Francisco Jiménez was born in Mexico. He came to California as a young boy. "The Circuit" tells about his life as a young boy. Jiménez's family moved a lot. This made school hard for Jiménez. However, he loved to learn. Finally, Jiménez's family was able to stay in one place. Jiménez finished school. He became a teacher. Jiménez writes stories about his experiences to share with other people.

► What challenges did the author face in becoming a writer? What strategies do you think he used to write this story?

Beyond the Reading

Reading Comprehension

Question-Answer Relationships (QAR)

"Right There" Questions

1. **Recall Facts** What does the author's family do to earn money?
2. **Recall Facts** What does Mr. Lema help the author learn? What does he offer to teach the author?

"Think and Search" Questions

3. **Make Inferences** Why does the author start school in November?
4. **Make Inferences** Why does he say that he is "starting sixth grade for the first time that year"? (Paragraph 10)
5. **Analyze Characters** Why does the author hesitate to read? What does Mr. Lema conclude about the author?
6. **Make Inferences** Why are there packed boxes in the shack at the end of the reading? Explain what is happening and why.

"Author and You" Questions

7. **Analyze Cause and Effect** Why was the author's first instinct to answer in Spanish when the woman at school spoke to him?
8. **Recognize Style** In paragraphs 1 and 18, the author writes, "everything we owned was neatly packed in cardboard boxes." Why does he repeat these words?

"On Your Own" Questions

9. **Evaluate** How would you describe the author? Why do you think this?
10. **Speculate** What is the cycle of the author's life? Will it change?

Activity Book
p. 138

Student
CD-ROM

Build Reading Fluency

Rapid Word Recognition

Rapidly recognizing words helps increase your reading rate. It is an important characteristic of effective readers.

1. With a partner, review the words in the box.
2. Read the words aloud for one minute. Your teacher will time you.

3. Count how many words you read in one minute.

front	whom	thought	weight	thought	front
shack	weight	whom	thought	weight	thought
weight	brought	shack	front	brought	shack
thought	shack	weight	shack	front	brought
brought	whom	front	brought	whom	weight

Listen, Speak, Interact

Present an Experience

Work with two classmates. Each of you will present an experience you have had. For example, you can talk about moving to a new home, changing schools, or a good experience with a teacher.

1. Tell your classmates:
   a. Who was involved?
   b. What happened?
   c. When did it happen?
   d. Where did it happen?
   e. Why did it happen?
   f. How did you feel? Why?
2. As you listen to your classmates, take notes on their main ideas and supporting evidence. Ask for clarification as needed.

3. Write summaries of your classmates' experiences on a piece of paper.
4. Let your partners read your summaries. Ask them to tell you if you understood their main ideas and supporting evidence.
5. Compare your understanding of a classmate's story with your other classmate's understanding.
6. What are your classmates' points of view (perspectives) on their experiences?
7. How are the group's experiences similar and different?
8. How are the group's experiences similar to and different from those of Francisco Jiménez?

Elements of Literature

Identify Language Use to Show Characterization

One way to understand characters is to pay attention to the kind of language they use.

1. Listen to or read paragraph 5 aloud. Mamá says "Mi olla." What does this tell you about her culture and region? What does it tell you about the author's feelings about his language and culture?

2. Listen to or read paragraph 15 aloud. Mr. Lema says "Gladly." This word is usually formal. What does this language use tell you about Mr. Lema's experience and culture?

Activity Book
p. 139

Student
CD-ROM

Word Study

Apply Letter-Sound Correspondences

The letter *s* in English is often pronounced like the first letter of the word *see*. However, when *s* is combined with *h*, the sound is like the first sound in the word *shoe*.

Listen as your teacher pronounces *see* and *shoe*. Can you hear the difference between the first sounds? Pronounce the two words after your teacher.

Listen as your teacher reads the following sentences from "The Circuit." Then practice reading the sentences aloud with a partner.

1. My fir_s_t in_s_tinct was to an_s_wer her in _S_pani_sh_, but I held back.
2. Finally, after _s_truggling for Engli_sh_ words, I managed to tell her that I wanted to enroll in the _s_ixth grade.

In a dictionary, look at the pronunciation of the word *Spanish*. Which symbol represents the letter *s*? Which symbol represents the letters *sh*?

The Heinle
Newbury House
Dictionary

Activity Book
p. 140

Student
CD-ROM

Grammar Focus

Identify Dependent Clauses

A **dependent** clause contains a subject and a verb, but it cannot stand alone. It *depends* on the rest of the sentence.

When a dependent clause is at the beginning of a sentence, it must be followed by a comma.

Some dependent clauses tell you when something happens. They start with words like *when, as, while, before, after,* or *until.* Look at this example:

When she got to the car, Papá reached out to help her with it.

1. Find the sentences with dependent clauses in paragraphs 4, 7, 9, and 11 of the reading.
2. Underline the dependent clauses. Put an S over the subject of the sentence and a V over the verb. Circle the word at the beginning of the clause that tells when something happened.

Activity Book
pp. 141–142

Student
Handbook

Student
CD-ROM

From Reading to Writing

Write a Letter to an Author

Write a letter to Francisco Jiménez.

1. Work with a partner. Copy the letter parts to the right. Also refer to your Student Handbook.

2. Fill in the blanks with your own words. Tell the author what you think about the story. Ask him a question.

3. Organize and revise your letter with your partner. Use a dictionary or a thesaurus to choose vivid words.

4. Use your best handwriting or a computer. Be sure to check your spelling and punctuation.

5. Capitalize and punctuate so that your meaning is clear.

> (Your Address)
> _____
> (Date)
>
> Mr. Francisco Jiménez
> c/o Publisher
> Heinle/Thomson
> 25 Thomson Place
> Boston, MA 02210
> Dear Mr. Jiménez,
>   I read your story, "The Circuit."
> I think it is _____. I liked
> your story because _____.
> I want to know _____.
>
> Sincerely,
> _____

The Heinle Newbury House Dictionary

Student Handbook

Activity Book
p. 143

Across Content Areas

LANGUAGE ARTS

Understand the Influence of Other Languages and Cultures on English

English has borrowed many words from French. For example, the work *circuit* comes from old French. There are not many words in English that have the letters *u* and *i* together. We can see that French has influenced English spelling. Other examples are *gui̱de*, *flui̱d*, and *disgui̱se*.

In the year 1066, people from France invaded England and ruled it for many years. Their language and culture influenced English spellings.

1. Look up these words with *ui* in a large dictionary and check the derivations. Are they of French or English origin?

juice/quick/nuisance/ruin/squirt

2. Can you make a generalization about English words spelled with *ui*?

Activity Book
p. 144

CHAPTER 4

The Elements of Life

an excerpt from an informational book by Paul Bennett

Objectives

Reading Find the main idea and supporting details as you read an excerpt from an informational book.

Listening and Speaking Listen and take notes.

Grammar Recognize the active and passive voices.

Writing Write about a process and create a diagram.

Content Science: Understand symbols for elements.

Use Prior Knowledge

Talk About Living and Nonliving Things

Some things are living. People, cats, and bean plants are living things. Other things are nonliving, such as chairs, water, and rocks. What are the characteristics of living things and nonliving things?

1. Copy this chart on a piece of paper.
2. With a partner, discuss each of the characteristics in the chart. Does each characteristic apply to living things, nonliving things, or both? Check "Yes" or "No."
3. If you are unsure, use resources such as an expert, a science teacher, a dictionary, the Internet, or an encyclopedia to find out.

Characteristics	Living Things		Nonliving Things	
	Yes	No	Yes	No
can move around on its own	X			X
can reproduce itself	X			X
made of chemical elements	X		X	

Build Background

Elements

Both living and nonliving things are made of elements. Elements are simple materials. Chemists are scientists who study the elements. They have so far discovered 109 different ones.

Some elements are very rare (uncommon). Others are almost everywhere. For example, the oxygen in the air is an element.

Some elements are very valuable. You may have a ring or a bracelet made of gold or silver. These are elements.

Elements combine to make other things. For example, water is made up of oxygen and hydrogen. The elements sodium and chloride combine to make ordinary table salt.

Content Connection

Scientists have created a chart called the **Periodic Table of Elements.** It organizes all of the elements that scientists know about.

Build Vocabulary

Learn Science Terms

"The Elements of Life" has **science terms** (words related to science). You can learn new science terms in different ways.

1. **Definitions** Sometimes the author tells the meaning of a word. Check the words around it for clues.
2. **Glossaries** Often a textbook has a list of important words and their meanings. This list is a **glossary.** In this book, words are glossed at the bottom of each page.
3. **Dictionaries** If you still do not understand a word, you can find its meaning in a dictionary. A dictionary also gives the pronunciation.
4. **Graphics** Photos and drawings are used to explain scientific words and ideas. As you read, study the graphic features to locate and organize information.

The Heinle Newbury House Dictionary

Activity Book p. 145

Student CD-ROM

Text Structure

Informational Text

You learned that an **informational text** gives facts about a topic. "The Elements of Life" is an informational text. The chart shows some features of an informational text. Look for these features as you read the selection.

Informational Text	
Examples	gives information that supports facts
Definitions	includes meanings of special words or ideas
Process	tells how something happens and in what chronological order
Problem	tells a problem related to the topic

Student
CD-ROM

Reading Strategy

Find the Main Idea and Supporting Details

The **main idea** is the most important idea in a paragraph or larger piece of writing. **Supporting details** are facts or explanations that show how the main idea is true.

Read the following paragraph.

> Oxygen is a very important element. Almost half of the earth's crust is made up of oxygen. The human body also has a lot of oxygen. We breathe oxygen. We need oxygen to live.

1. What is the main idea in this paragraph?
2. What details support the main idea?

As you read the selection, look for the main ideas and supporting details.

Student
CD-ROM

The Elements of Life

an excerpt from an informational book
by Paul Bennett

1   In ancient times it was thought that everything could be broken down into four elements: earth, air, fire, and water. These broad **categories** seemed to account for the makeup of things until about three hundred years ago when scientists began to doubt such a simple **theory.**

2   Elements are the basic substances from which all things are made. Today we know of 109 elements. About ninety of these occur naturally on earth—the rest are made in **nuclear reactors.**

3   Some of the elements, such as gold and silver, are metals. They have been made into jewelry since early times. The element iron, too, is a metal, and has been used to make weapons and tools for over three thousand years.

> **Find the Main Idea and Supporting Details**
>
> What is the main idea of this paragraph? What are two supporting details?

Audio
CD 2, Tr. 10

Silver

Gold

Iron

---

categories groups or types of things
theory an idea or argument that something is true

nuclear reactors machines used to make and contain nuclear reactions

4   We have many elements in our bodies—about 25 of them. Oxygen and hydrogen account for most, since these elements join together to form water, and our bodies are made up of 60 to 80 percent water.

Find the Main Idea and Supporting Details

What is the main idea in this paragraph? What are the supporting details?

5   Water is a compound—a combination of elements. So is the paper on which these words are printed. Paper is made of a material called **cellulose,** which comes from trees and consists of the elements carbon, hydrogen, and oxygen.

6   Elements and compounds are needed by all living things in order to stay alive. Living **organisms** obtain these **raw materials** or resources from their surroundings. But only limited amounts of these **vital** elements can be found on Earth, and so if they could be used only once, they would run out, and animals and plants would die. But in nature the elements are **recycled,** so they can be used over and over again.

The elements in these trees can still be found in a piece of paper.

cellulose   a basic substance in nearly all plant cells
organisms   living creatures
raw materials   things in a natural state, not manufactured

vital   most important, absolutely necessary
recycled   processed to be used again

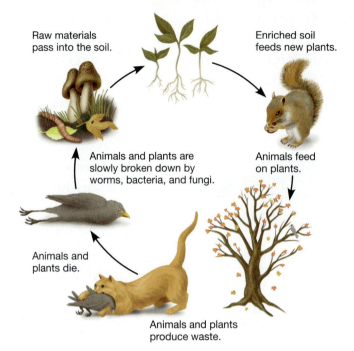

Raw materials pass into the soil.

Enriched soil feeds new plants.

Animals and plants are slowly broken down by worms, bacteria, and fungi.

Animals feed on plants.

Animals and plants die.

Animals and plants produce waste.

7   For example, when animals and plants die in a **woodland,** they are slowly broken down by worms, **bacteria,** and **fungi.** As animals and plants **rot** away, the substances from which they are made pass into the soil. The **enriched** soil feeds new plants and, in turn, animals will feed on the plants. The animals and plants produce waste, which is also broken down and taken back into the soil.

Find the Main Idea and Supporting Details

What is the main idea of this paragraph? What are the supporting details?

8   The process of death, **decay,** new life, and growth is never ending. In this way, the elements and compounds that are **essential** to life are recycled.

---

woodland   a forested area
bacteria   tiny living things
fungi   organisms that feed on living or dead plants or animals and cannot survive apart from them

rot   break down, usually after death
enriched   added good things to
decay   rot
essential   necessary, required

However, the activities of people have upset this **delicate natural balance.** Vital resources such as water and the elements carbon, nitrogen, sulfur, and phosphorus are no longer in balance. As a result, a large number of animal and plant **species** are in danger.

By understanding the earth's recycling systems and how people affect them, we can help **reduce** the **harmful** effects of human activity.

> ### Find the Main Idea and Supporting Details
>
> What is one supporting detail in this paragraph? What is the main idea?

---

delicate   easily broken or hurt
natural   formed by nature
balance   in equal strength

species   groups of living things
reduce   make smaller in size or weight
harmful   causing hurt or damage

About the Author

Paul Bennett

Paul Bennett likes to answer questions about science. He has written about 20 books about science. For example, he has written about why some animals hibernate (sleep for the winter), and he has written about electricity and telephones.

► What science question would you like to ask the author?

Beyond the Reading

Reading Comprehension

Question-Answer Relationships (QAR)

"Right There" Questions

1. **Recall Facts** What is an element? Give an example.
2. **Recall Facts** How many elements do scientists know about?

"Think and Search" Questions

3. **Give Reasons** Why are oxygen and hydrogen the most common elements in our bodies?
4. **Identify Steps in a Process** How are elements recycled?
5. **Identify Cause and Effect** What has happened to nature's balance because of people?

"Author and You" Question

6. **Understand Author's Perspective** How do you think the author feels about nature? What does he think people should do for nature? Show text evidence for your answers.

"On Your Own" Questions

7. **Speculate** What could happen to Earth if nature's balance is not protected?
8. **Connect Your Experiences** What are some ways that you can protect nature's balance?

Activity Book
p. 146

Student
CD-ROM

Build Reading Fluency

Adjust Your Reading Rate to Scan

When you scan for information you adjust your reading rate to read fast. Work with a partner. Read aloud key words in the reading selection as you scan for the answers. Write your answers on a piece of paper.

1. What are the names of three metals?
2. What two elements mainly make up our bodies?
3. What are needed by all living things?
4. What three things break down dead plants and animals?

Listen, Speak, Interact

Listen and Take Notes

Listen as your teacher reads or plays the audio recording of "The Elements of Life."

1. Before you listen, determine a purpose for your listening. Will you learn new information? Will you solve problems? Will you be entertained?
2. As you listen, take notes on the main ideas and supporting details.
3. Use the main ideas and supporting details to write an outline of the selection.
4. Use your outline to summarize the selection orally to a partner.

5. Listen to your partner's summary.
   a. Interpret your partner's verbal and nonverbal messages. Do they support your partner's purposes and perspectives?
   b. Is your partner using facts or opinions?
   c. Do you believe your partner?
   d. Do you understand the presentation? Ask questions if you do not understand something.
   e. Was your partner's information clear?
   f. What was your partner's perspective?

Elements of Literature

Use a Diagram

"The Elements of Life" includes a **diagram.** The diagram shows how elements are recycled. It has drawings and **labels** (words that explain the drawings).

1. Look at the diagram on page 270.
2. Each label explains a **step** (an action). The arrows show the **sequence** (order) in which the steps happen.

3. On a piece of paper, write the steps that the diagram shows. Number the steps in order. Start with "Animals and plants die."

Activity Book
p. 147

Student
CD-ROM

Word Study

Study Word Origins and Roots

Some English words have the same word origin. *Recycled* comes from the Greek root word *kyklos*. This Greek word means "wheel or circle."

The words in the box below also come from the root word *kyklos*. Match each word with the correct definition. Use a dictionary to look up any words you do not know.

cycle	motorcycle	cyclone
bicycle	encyclopedia	

Definitions

1. a vehicle with two wheels that is run by pedaling
2. a reference source
3. a process that begins and ends with the same thing
4. a vehicle with two wheels that is run by a machine
5. a violent storm in which winds move in a circle

The Heinle Newbury House Dictionary   Activity Book *p. 148*   Student CD-ROM

Grammar Focus

Recognize the Active and Passive Voices

Sentences in the **active voice** have subjects that do an action. Look at this example:

<u>Nuclear reactors</u> <u>make</u> the rest.
subject ⇒ **action**

Sentences in the **passive voice** have subjects that receive an action. They include the verbs *was, were, am, are, is, be,* or *been.* These verbs are added to **past participles** (a form of a verb). Look at this example:

<u>The rest</u> <u>are made</u> in nuclear reactors.
subject ⇐ **action**

1. Copy the following sentences on a piece of paper.

a. Elements are needed by all living things.
b. The enriched soil feeds new plants.
c. Living organisms obtain resources from their environments.
d. They are broken down by worms, bacteria, and fungi.

2. Write *A* for *active* and *P* for *passive* for each sentence.

3. If the sentence is active, rewrite it in the passive voice. If it is passive, rewrite it in the active voice.

Activity Book *pp. 149–150*   Student Handbook   Student CD-ROM

From Reading to Writing

Write About a Process and Create a Diagram

Choose a process you know about. This process might be something you know how to do. Write and illustrate a paragraph that tells the steps in the process.

1. Tell what the process is about in the first sentence.
2. Write the steps that are part of the process in order.
3. Use transition words such as *first, next, then, finally.*
4. Create a diagram to show the process. If possible, create your diagram on the computer.
5. Read your paragraph to a partner. Find out if your partner understands the process. Make changes if you need to clarify your meaning.

> **How to Fry an Egg**
>
> Frying an egg is a little tricky, but you can do it if you practice. First, put a little oil in a non-stick pan and turn on the heat. When the oil is medium-hot, crack the egg and let the inside drop gently into the oil. Let it cook until the white part is almost set. Then use a spatula to turn the egg over. Then let the egg finish cooking. Finally, take it out and enjoy it!

Activity Book
p. 151

Student
Handbook

Across Content Areas

SCIENCE

Understand Symbols for Elements

Chemists have given each element a name and a symbol to stand for it. The chart gives a few of them.

Element	Symbol
carbon	C
oxygen	O
hydrogen	H
sodium	Na
chlorine	Cl

Scientists use these symbols to describe chemical compounds. For example, H_2O is water. It is made of two atoms of hydrogen and one atom of oxygen. (An *atom* is the smallest possible amount of an element.)

Complete these sentences.

1. NaCl is table salt. It is made up of sodium and _____ .
2. CO_2 is a gas. It has _____ atom of carbon and _____ atoms of oxygen.

Activity Book
p. 152

Listening and Speaking Workshop

Give an Oral Presentation

> **Topic**
>
> With a partner, choose a cycle from the unit. You and your partner will make a ten-minute presentation to your class about this cycle.

Step 1: Identify the cycle.

With your partner, list the steps that are part of the cycle.

Step 2: Prepare a visual.

1. Organize the steps in order in a circle form like this one.
2. Use presentation software or use a piece of posterboard.

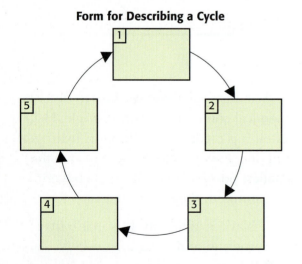

Form for Describing a Cycle

Step 3: Make an outline.

1. On note cards, write a few sentences that summarize the steps of the cycle.

2. Support your steps with examples. Write on the note cards.
3. Put your note cards in order.

Step 4: Organize your presentation.

1. Begin your presentation by telling what the cycle is about.
2. Talk about one step at a time. Support each step with examples.
3. Summarize what the cycle is by using different words.

Step 5: Practice your presentation.

1. Practice your presentation with your partner. Take turns presenting the steps in the cycle.
2. Answer the questions on the Speaking Checklist. Your partner will do the same.
3. Make changes to your presentation if necessary.
4. Time your presentation so that you can finish in less than ten minutes.

Step 6: Give your presentation.

1. Stand in front of the room to give your presentation. Stand up straight.
2. Speak strongly to show that you understand what you are talking about.
3. Ask if there are any questions.
4. Ask your classmates to complete the Active Listening Checklist.

✓ **Speaking Checklist**

1. Did you speak too slowly, too quickly, or just right?

2. Did you speak loudly enough for the audience to hear you?

3. Was your voice too high, too low, or just right?

4. Did you look at your audience?

✓ **Active Listening Checklist**

1. I liked _____ because _____ .

2. I want to know more about _____ .

3. I thought the statements about the selection were interesting / not interesting.

4. The presentation did / did not stay on the topic.

Viewing Workshop

Interpret Events from Media

Use television and the Internet to learn about the cycle of weather.

1. View television and online weather reports for one week.
2. With a partner, create a form to record the information. Decide what information to record. Organize the form to make it easy to use.
3. Record the information. Include ideas and events from maps and charts.
4. Revise the form if necessary to include or delete information.
5. Interpret the information that you gathered. Answer questions such as:
   a. What weather events did you learn about?
   b. How are the weather events part of a cycle?

6. How were the television and online reports similar and different? Which do you think is better, and why?
7. How did each medium contribute to its message?
8. How did the television and online presentations influence you?
9. How did language and style of presentation help you understand?

Further Viewing

Watch the *Visions* CNN Video for Unit 4. Do the Video Worksheet.

CNN Video

Writer's Workshop

Compare and Contrast Ideas, Themes, and Issues

Writing Prompt

Compare and contrast the stories "Persephone and the Seasons" and "The Circuit."

Step 1: Gather information.

Answer these questions as you look for information from the two selections.

1. What is the theme of each story? How are they similar or different?
2. Describe the characters and their situations.
   a. Who are the main characters in each story?
   b. Who are other important characters in each story?
   c. How do the characters relate to each other?
   d. How do the characters feel about their situations? Can the characters change them?
3. What are the main ideas and events of each story? How are they the same and different?
4. What are the issues that each main character faces? Are they similar or different? How?
5. Summarize your ideas in a chart like the one shown.

Step 2: Write a first draft.

Review your notes and plan your paper. It should be five paragraphs long. Use a computer, if possible.

	"Persephone and the Seasons"	"The Circuit"
Theme	*Why we have different seasons*	
Main characters (who, and their traits)		
How they relate to other important characters		
Main ideas and events		
Issues		
How characters change		

1. Your first paragraph should be the introduction.
   a. Name the characters and the selections. Mention some of the other characters.
   b. Explain that you will compare the stories to show how they are similar and different.
2. The next three paragraphs of your paper should be the body.
   a. Write one paragraph about the themes and how they are the same and different.
   b. Write a paragraph describing the main events and ideas. Then tell how they are similar or different.

c. Write a paragraph to describe some of the issues faced by the characters. How are they similar or different?

3. The fifth paragraph should be the conclusion.

    a. Tell if the two stories are mostly the same or different.

    b. Tell how you feel about the two stories.

4. Select and use resource and reference materials to be sure you are using standard language, varied sentence structure, and appropriate word choice.

Step 3: Revise your draft.

1. Read your draft and ask yourself these questions:

    a. Do I compare stories clearly? Will readers see how they are similar and different?

    b. Have I supported my main ideas with examples from the text?

    c. Does each body paragraph answer one question about the two stories?

    d. Does the conclusion relate back to the introduction?

    e. Are my paragraphs organized and coherent? What should I add, delete, or combine? Do I need to elaborate anything? Should I rearrange sentences?

    f. Do I use effective transition words, such as *then, next, finally*?

2. Use revising reference and resource books such as your Student Handbook or a dictionary.

3. Share your draft with a partner. Ask each other for ideas about the strong and weak points of your drafts. Use the Peer Editing Checklist in your Student Handbook.

4. Talk about the ideas you and your partner have. Make any changes you feel are necessary. Use a computer and computer software, such as a CD-ROM dictionary or thesaurus, to help you revise.

Step 4: Edit and proofread your report.

1. Proofread your revised report. Check for correct punctuation, spelling, and grammar. If you are using a computer, use the spell check and grammar check.

2. Use the Editor's Checklist in your Student Handbook and other resources and references.

3. Type your paper on a computer or use your best handwriting.

Step 5: Publish your report.

1. Make a title page for your report with your name on it.

2. Make a drawing for the cover. If you can, use computer art.

3. Reread your finished report. Evaluate how well you think your writing achieved its purpose.

The Heinle Newbury House Dictionary

Student Handbook

Projects

These projects will help you apply what you learned about cycles. Work alone, with a partner, or with a group of classmates. If you need help, ask a teacher, a parent, or your school librarian.

Project 1: Explore Life Cycle Events

What are the basic events in the human life cycle? How are these events different for different people? What are some ways that people celebrate these events?

1. Gather information.
   a. Create questions to ask your parents and other adults you know. Take notes on what they think the main events in a person's life are. Ask how they have celebrated these events.
   b. Revise, add, or delete questions as necessary to get complete information.
   c. Make a timeline to summarize and organize events that you learned about.
2. Create a page for each life cycle event. Use a drawing or photograph to show each event. Write a few sentences to explain the event. If possible, present your information using presentation software.
3. Use capitalization and punctuation to clarify and enhance your presentation.

Project 2: Make a Poster About a Cycle

Think of other cycles you know about that were not presented in this unit. Research information about this cycle to make a poster. Your poster will show the steps of the cycle. Or show a different cycle you know about. Use the school library or the Internet.

1. Find pictures that show the different steps of a cycle. You can print pictures out from the Internet, copy them from a book, or cut them out of old magazines. Use the name of your cycle as a keyword for an Internet search. You can also draw the pictures.
2. Explain the steps of the cycle on a piece of posterboard.
3. Glue the pictures on the posterboard. Remember to put the pictures in the correct order in which the steps happen.
4. Write one to three sentences below each picture that explain the step.
5. Present your posters to the class.

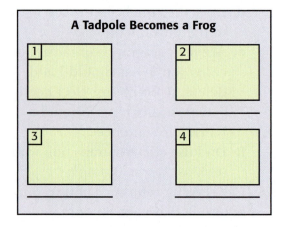

A Tadpole Becomes a Frog

Further Reading

The following is a list of books continuing the theme of cycles. Choose three of them to read. In your Reading Log, write answers to these questions.

1. What are the strengths of these books?
2. What are their weaknesses?
3. What goals can I set for myself as a writer based on my reading of these books?

The Circuit: Stories from the Life of a Migrant Child

by Francisco Jiménez, Houghton Mifflin Co., 1999. Francisco Jiménez immigrated with his family from Mexico to California as a child. He compiled many of his experiences as a migrant worker into short stories in this book.

Earth: The Incredible Recycling Machine

Paul Bennett (Contributor), Thomson Learning, 1993. This book explains how nature recycles Earth's resources through the process of the life cycle. Includes illustrations and projects about recycling.

Waste, Recycling, and Reuse: Our Impact on the Planet

by Rob Bowden, Raintree Publishers, 2002. This book examines how human development affects the planet. It discusses how pollution in one region of the world can affect a region on the other side of the world.

Life Cycles of a Dozen Diverse Creatures

by Paul Fleisher, Millbrook Press, 1998. This book compares and contrasts the lives of twelve different animals including bullfrogs, monarch butterflies, and jellyfish.

A Drop Around the World

by Barbara Shaw McKinney, Dawn Publications, 1998. This book follows the journey of a drop of rain around the world, on land, underground, in the sea, and in the sky.

El Niño and La Niña

by Sally Rose, Simon Spotlight, 1999. In 1997 and 1998, the phenomenon known as El Niño caused problems for North America's weather. This book explains how El Niño and La Niña affect weather cycles.

Yellowstone's Cycle of Fire

by Frank Staub, Carolrhoda Books, 1994. During the summer of 1988, Yellowstone National Park suffered from several forest fires. This book discusses the nature of the fires and the renewal of the land.

Companion Web site   Reading Log   Heinle Reading Library Black Beauty

Freedom

The Statue of Liberty, sculpture, Frédéric Auguste Bartholdi, 1871–1886.

View the Picture

1. How does this picture show freedom?
2. What are some other ways that a picture could show freedom?

In this unit, you will read a biography, a historical narrative, a speech, a novel, a poem, and an autobiography. You will also write some of these forms.

Rosa Parks

an excerpt from
a biography
by Andrea Davis Pinkney

Objectives

Reading Make inferences using text evidence as you read a biography.

Listening and Speaking Present reactions.

Grammar Recognize regular and irregular simple past tense verbs.

Writing Write a biography.

Content Social Studies: Learn about Constitutional amendments.

Use Prior Knowledge

Assess Fair and Unfair Situations

Read these definitions of *fair* and *unfair*.

fair /fɛr/ *adj.* **1** just; honest; treating all people or groups equally: *The judge's decision was fair to both sides.*
2 treating people in a way that they deserve: *It is fair that John got the lead in the play. He worked very hard for it.*

un•fair /ʌnˈfɛr/ *adj.* not fair, treating one person or group better than another: *He was unfair in giving higher raises to his favorite employees.*

1. With a partner, read the following statements.
2. Decide whether each is fair or unfair. Why do you think as you do?
   a. Ina's younger brother can stay up later than she can.
   b. I got a C on the test because I did not study for it.
   c. His mother bought ice cream for the whole family.
   d. Grace made a mess, and Tony has to clean it up.
3. Share your answers with the class.

Build Background

Segregation in the United States

For many years, African-Americans did not have the same rights (freedoms) as other Americans. They were segregated (separated) from other Americans in some states. For example, they had to go to different schools. Usually, African-American schools were much poorer than schools for other Americans. African-Americans also had separate restaurants and stores. In many places, they were not allowed to sit in the front of public (community) buses.

Starting in the 1950s, many states changed their segregation laws. Today, segregation is illegal (against the law) in the United States.

Content Connection

Until the mid-1800s, most African-Americans in the United States were slaves. They worked for no money and had no rights.

Build Vocabulary

Use Note Cards to Remember Meaning

To help you remember the meanings of new words, make note cards of them. Review the cards by yourself or with a partner.

1. Write each of these words on a separate note card.
   a. humiliation
   b. commitment
   c. plight
2. Use a dictionary to find the meaning of each word. Write the meaning on the back of each note card.
3. Work with a partner. Take turns testing each other on the meaning of each word. Continue until both of you remember the meaning of each word.
4. As you read the selection, make new note cards for words you want to remember.

The Heinle Newbury House Dictionary

Activity Book p. 153

Student CD-ROM

Text Structure

Biography

"Rosa Parks" is a **biography.** A biography tells the true story of a real person's life and experiences. Look for the features of a biography as you read the selection.

Pay attention to the important events in Rosa Parks's life. Write them in a timeline in your Reading Log.

Biography	
Events	special things the person did
Dates	when important events happened
People and Places	information about important people and places
Chronological Order	events usually written in the order that they happened

Reading Log   Student CD-ROM

Reading Strategy

Make Inferences Using Text Evidence

You can **make inferences** about people in a biography. An inference is a guess. You can use **text evidence** and your own experiences to guess what the people are like. Text evidence is information in a text. Read this text.

> Rosa Parks's mother sent her to a school in Montgomery, Alabama. During the school year, she lived with her aunt.

Text Evidence	Your Experience	Inference
Rosa lived with her aunt in Montgomery.	Children usually live with their parents.	Rosa's mother didn't live in Montgomery.

Student CD-ROM

ROSA PARKS

an excerpt from a biography
by Andrea Davis Pinkney

Prologue

Rosa Parks was born in 1913. She grew up in Pine Level, Alabama. Rosa's mother, Leona, was a teacher. Rosa's grandparents had been slaves. They taught her that all people should be treated the same. But Rosa and other African-Americans were not treated the same as other Americans. Rosa had to go to an African-American school in Pine Level. This school had no desks or windows. It was cold and had very few books. Leona worked hard to send Rosa to a better school.

> **Make Inferences Using Text Evidence**
>
> Do you think Leona thought going to a good school was important? Why do you think so?

1   Leona saved every penny she could, and when Rosa was eleven years old, her mother sent her to the Montgomery Industrial School for **Black** Girls, a **private school** in Montgomery, Alabama. During the school year, Rosa lived with her aunt Fannie. At her new school Rosa learned everything, from how to read world maps to how to mix **remedies** for sick and **ailing** souls. She even took cooking lessons.

2   But a private education couldn't **shield** Rosa from the public **humiliation** of **racism** that was common in the South in the 1920s. Rosa often rode streetcar **trolleys** to school—**segregated** streetcars in which she, along with every other black rider, was forced to sit in the back. . . .

3   In 1931 a neighbor introduced Rosa to Raymond Parks. . . . He was smart, smooth talking, **forthright,** and **persistent** . . . . Raymond was a barber who worked in downtown Montgomery. He took a quick liking to Rosa. But she was not immediately **impressed** with him. He came

---

black African-American

private school a school run by a private group, not by the government

remedies medicines, or things that make illnesses better

ailing sick

shield protect

humiliation a feeling of shame; a lowering of pride or self-respect

racism prejudice or unfairness against people of one race by those of another

trolleys a kind of bus that runs on rails in the streets

segregated separated according to race

forthright honest

persistent continuing to have a belief or to work for a goal

impressed admired someone

to Rosa's house several times to ask Rosa's mother if he could take Rosa for a drive in his car. It was clear to Leona that Raymond Parks was intelligent and **sincere.** She agreed to let him spend time with her daughter, but it was Rosa who kept turning down Raymond's offers.

4   Finally, when Rosa said yes to a short ride with Raymond, she saw that he was more than just a pretty boy with a **flashy** car. Like Rosa's grandfather, Raymond was a man of **conviction.** He was well-spoken and cared deeply about the plight of black people in the South. And he was an active member of the **National Association for the Advancement of Colored People (NAACP).**

5   The more Raymond told Rosa about his **commitment** to helping black people, the more Rosa's awareness grew. Her love for Raymond grew, too. In December 1932 Rosa McCauley and Raymond Parks were married, in Pine Level at the home of Rosa's mother. Rosa was nineteen years old. . . .

6   Rosa found work as a helper at Saint Margaret's Hospital in Montgomery. At night she worked as a **seamstress** at home, mending and tailoring clothes. Rosa was grateful for her job, but going to work drove home the sad reality of segregation. When Rosa took the city bus to work, she had to go through the same **degrading ritual** day after day. She would step on the bus at the front and buy a ticket from the driver. Then she'd have to leave the bus, walk around to the back, and enter the bus again through the rear door. All black passengers had to sit in the back. Only white people were allowed to ride at the front of the bus. This was the law. If you were black and the back of the bus was too

---

Make Inferences Using Text Evidence

Do you think Rosa enjoyed taking the bus? Use text evidence and what you know to answer.

---

sincere   honest in your thoughts and actions

flashy   showy

conviction   a strong belief

National Association for the Advancement of Colored People (NAACP)   a group that works to protect the rights of African-Americans

commitment   deep loyalty to a person or cause

seamstress   a woman whose job is sewing

degrading   causing shame

ritual   an act or actions that you repeat often

crowded, tough. You had to wait for the next bus, go through the same **drill,** and pray you would get to work on time.

> **Make Inferences Using Text Evidence**
>
> Do you think Rosa was brave? Use text evidence and what you know to answer.

7   Rosa was growing tired of this daily **disgrace.** Sometimes she would get onto the bus at the front and pay her **fare,** like always. Then before the driver had a chance to take full notice of her, Rosa would **breeze** through the front section of the bus to find her seat in the back.

8   Several drivers came to associate Rosa with her **defiance.** Once, in 1943, a driver kicked Rosa off his bus because she refused to enter the bus through the back door. . . .

9   As the wife of a **civil rights activist** (and the granddaughter of a civil rights believer), Rosa had learned three important things about changing the **unjust** treatment black people had suffered: Change takes time. Change takes strength. Change takes the help of others. Rosa Parks had all three.

10   She knew that one of the best ways to put these **advantages** to work would be to join the NAACP. But becoming an NAACP member wasn't as simple as it seemed. Rosa's husband didn't think it was a good idea. . . .

11   Raymond supported his wife's wish to stop segregation, but at the same time, he feared for her safety. . . . But . . . Rosa knew she had to join. . . . She attended the annual NAACP Montgomery meeting. This was the meeting to elect new officers. There were sixteen people at the meeting—fifteen men and Rosa Parks.

---

drill   an action or exercise that you repeat

disgrace   a cause of shame or dishonor

fare   the cost of a ride, such as on a bus, train, or boat

breeze   move quickly and easily

defiance   refusing to do something that someone in charge tells you to do

civil rights   the rights of each citizen promised by the U.S. Constitution

activist   a person who works to change things that he or she thinks are wrong

unjust   without justice, unfair

advantages   benefits, good features

12   When it came time to elect a **permanent** volunteer **secretary,** everybody looked to Rosa. They all figured secretarial work was women's work and she was the natural choice. Rosa accepted the job gladly. . . .

13   From that day on for the next twelve years, Rosa took her position as the NAACP Montgomery **chapter** secretary very seriously. . . .

14   Rosa organized branch meetings, kept the books, wrote and mailed letters and **press releases,** and at every turn, **drummed up** new members. When the office phone rang, Rosa answered it. When someone had a question about the workings of the branch, Rosa answered that, too.

Make Inferences Using Text Evidence

Rosa did many things as secretary of the NAACP. Make an inference about how Rosa felt about her job.

---

permanent lasting, or meant to last, forever or for a long time

secretary a person who works in an office and does jobs for a boss, such as writing letters and answering the phone

chapter a local office of a large group

press releases writings that tell the press (news) of an event that will happen

drummed up got or increased the amount of

15   As branch secretary . . . she recorded all the cases of **discrimination** and **violence** against black people in the state of Alabama. The cases seemed never ending. There were hundreds of them.

16   **Documenting** these cases showed Rosa that racism in Alabama was big. It was powerful. It gathered **momentum** with each mile it covered. It would take the force of one woman's **iron will** to stop it in its tracks.

17   Turns out, Rosa Parks was that woman.

18   December 1, 1955, started out like any other Thursday for Rosa. She went to her job at the Montgomery Fair department store, where she then worked as a seamstress. When the workday ended, Rosa gathered her purse and coat and walked to the Court Square bus stop. She waited patiently for the Cleveland Avenue bus—the bus she'd taken to and from work many times. When she stepped onto the bus and paid her dime to ride, she immediately spotted an empty seat on the aisle, one row behind the whites-only section of the bus. It was **rush hour.** Any seat on any bus at this time of day was a blessing. Rosa sat back and gave a quiet sigh of relief.

19   When the bus stopped to pick up passengers at the Empire Theater stop, six white people got on. They each paid the ten-cent fare, just as Rosa had done. All but one of them easily found seats at the front of the bus. The sixth passenger, a man, didn't mind standing. He curled his fingers around a holding pole and waited for the bus to pull away.

Make Inferences Using Text Evidence

What inference can you make about the sixth passenger?

---

discrimination   unfair treatment, especially because of race, gender, religion, and so forth

violence   injury or damage

documenting   providing written evidence

momentum   the speed at which something moves

iron will   strong determination (being set on doing something)

rush hour   a time when people are going to and from work

20   But according to the bus segregation laws for the state of Alabama, black people were **required** to give up a bus seat if a white person was left standing. And each bus driver in the state was allowed to **lay down the letter of the law** on his bus.

21   As it turned out, Rosa was sitting on the bus that was driven by the same driver who, twelve years before, had kicked Rosa off his bus because she would not enter through the back door. The driver remembered Rosa. And Rosa sure remembered him. He glared at Rosa through his rearview mirror. He ordered her up and out of her seat. But she wouldn't move. Instead, she answered him with a question. Why, she asked, should she have to **endure** his bossing her around?

22   Well, the driver didn't **take kindly to** Rosa **challenging** him. Next thing Rosa knew, he was standing over her, **insisting** that she give up her seat to the white man who needed a seat.

Make Inferences Using Text Evidence

Do you think the bus driver liked Rosa Parks? What text evidence helps you make this inference?

---

required   had to do something
lay down the letter of the law   make sure people follow the law
endure   bear, tolerate

take kindly to   like
challenging   questioning, arguing with
insisting   demanding

23   Rosa **clenched** her purse, which rested in her lap. When the driver asked Rosa to move a second time, Rosa put it to him plainly and firmly: No.

Make Inferences Using Text Evidence

How do you think E. D. Nixon felt about what Rosa did? What text evidence helps you make this inference?

24   He told Rosa he would call the police if she didn't move. Rosa didn't **flinch.** Maybe she was thinking about her grandpa Sylvester's solid belief in not allowing **mistreatment** from others. Or maybe she was just fed up with giving in to segregation's iron fist. Even the **threat** of police couldn't **rouse** Rosa. Once again her answer to the bus driver was simple: Do it. And he did—**lickety-split.** The police came right away. They **arrested** Rosa and took her to the city jail. Rosa called her husband and told him the whole story. News of Rosa's arrest had already begun to spread through Montgomery's black community. . . . E. D. Nixon from the NAACP was one of the first to hear about Rosa. . . . He told Rosa and Raymond that . . . the incident . . . had the power to **pound out** segregation. If Rosa was willing—and brave enough—to bring a case against Alabama's segregation laws, she could help end segregation in the state.

25   Rosa didn't have to think long about E. D. Nixon's **proposal.** Just a short time earlier, Rosa had been staring segregation in the face and saying *no.* Now she was looking the law in the eyes, and without blinking, she said *yes.* She agreed to attack the system that kept her and every black person in the United States of America from being treated equally. Years later, in reflecting on the events that led to her decision, Rosa said, "People always say that I [didn't give] up my seat because I was tired, but that isn't true. I was not tired **physically** . . . The only tired I was, was tired of giving in."

---

clenched   gripped tightly
flinch   move back suddenly without thinking
mistreatment   harmful behavior toward someone
threat   a danger, a menace
rouse   awaken and get up
lickety-split   slang for "very fast, quickly"

arrested   taken and held by the police, for breaking the law
pound out   eliminate, get rid of
proposal   something that is suggested as a possible plan
physically   relating to the body

Make Inferences Using Text Evidence

Make an inference about the effect that one person's actions can have. Use text evidence about Rosa Parks.

On December 5, 1955, Rosa and her attorney, Fred Gray, appeared before Judge John B. Scott in the city court of Montgomery, Alabama. Rosa was found guilty of breaking the Alabama State segregated bus law. She was fined ten dollars. Although Rosa was **convicted,** her act had **ignited** the Montgomery bus **boycott,** a civil rights movement that would change the face of segregation forever.

Epilogue

African-Americans in Montgomery showed their support for Rosa. They organized a bus boycott—they stopped riding the city's buses. The city lost a lot of money because of the boycott. In 1956, the United States Supreme Court said that segregated buses were illegal in Alabama. After this, Rosa continued to work for the rights of African-Americans.

---

convicted   found guilty of a crime in a court of law
ignited   set on fire (here, the author means "started")

boycott   when people refuse to buy certain products or services for political reasons

About the Author   Andrea Davis Pinkney

Andrea Davis Pinkney grew up in a family that worked hard for civil rights. Today, she writes about important African-Americans. She wants readers to know how much these people have given to their country. Pinkney has said, "I hope their lives reflect something in each of us—the courage to fight for what we believe is right. . . ."

► Why do you think Andrea Davis Pinkney wrote about Rosa Parks? To inform, to entertain, or to persuade?

Beyond the Reading

Reading Comprehension

Question-Answer Relationships (QAR)

"Right There" Questions

1. **Recall Facts** Where was Rosa's new school?
2. **Recall Facts** What is the NAACP? What job did Rosa Parks have in the NAACP?

"Think and Search" Questions

3. **Interpret Text Ideas** Act out the things that African-Americans in Montgomery had to do when they rode the bus.
4. **Analyze Cause and Effect** What was the cause and the effect of the Montgomery bus boycott?

"Author and You" Questions

5. **Support Your Opinion** How do you think Rosa Parks felt while she was arguing with the bus driver? Why do you think so?
6. **Understand Author's Perspective** How do you think the author wants you to feel about Rosa Parks?

7. **Speculate** Do you think that many African-Americans in Montgomery were angry about segregation? Why do you think so?

"On Your Own" Questions

8. **Evaluate** Do you think Rosa Parks was right for not giving up her seat? Why or why not?
9. **Connect Your Experiences** Do you think that people should work to change things that they think are wrong? Why or why not?
10. **Connect Issues Across Cultures** Think about "The Voyage of the Lucky Dragon" in Unit 3, Chapter 2. How do government decisions affect the people in that story and in "Rosa Parks"?

Activity Book
p. 154

Student
CD-ROM

Build Reading Fluency

Read Silently and Aloud

Reading silently for practice and reading aloud for expression are two important ways to become a fluent reader.

1. Listen to the audio recording of "Rosa Parks."

2. Follow along with the reading on page 288.
3. Read silently paragraphs 1–3 two times.
4. With a partner read aloud.
5. Your partner will time you reading aloud.

Listen, Speak, Interact

Present Reactions

Try this activity to understand better what segregation is like.

1. Hold up a pen or a piece of paper.
2. Students holding pens will sit on the floor in a small part of the classroom. Students holding paper will stay in their seats.
3. Your class is now segregated. Present your reactions by talking about these questions as a class:
   a. How does being segregated make you feel?
   b. Do you think it would be harder to learn sitting on the floor or at your desk? Why?
   c. Do you think this segregation is fair? Explain.
   d. Are your ideas about segregation the same as your classmates' ideas?
4. Segregation was a part of the culture of the United States at the time this story took place. Based on your reading of "Rosa Parks," compare and contrast characteristics of this culture to other cultures that you know about.

Elements of Literature

Recognize Style

Listen as your teacher reads these sentences. Their meanings are similar, but their **style** is different.

   a. If . . . the bus was too crowded, that was unfortunate for you.
   b. If . . . the bus was too crowded, tough.

Which sentence sounds more conversational? Which one sounds more like something from a textbook?

1. Which of the following statements describes the author's style?
   a. It sounds like she is telling the story to us aloud.
   b. It sounds like an article from an encyclopedia.
2. The author of "Rosa Parks" uses some words from the southern region of the United States. Read these sentences. Which words do you think reflect that region and culture?
   a. Rosa learned . . . how to mix remedies for sick . . . souls.
   b. The driver didn't take kindly to Rosa challenging him.

Reading Log   Activity Book   Student
p. 155   CD-ROM

Word Study

Recognize the Suffix *-ment*

Remember, a suffix is a group of letters added to a root word. The suffix *-ment* changes verbs into nouns.

1. Copy and complete the chart. Use a dictionary to help you.
2. Copy and complete the following sentences with a noun from the chart.
   a. They <u>treat</u> their dogs well. The dogs receive good ____ .
   b. Elena <u>committed</u> herself to helping people read. She has a ____ to these people.
   c. Li and Ken <u>agreed</u> to stop fighting. They reached an ____ .

Verb	Meaning	+ ment ⇒ Noun	Meaning
agree	have the same idea	agreement	a decision between two or more people
treat			
commit			

The Heinle Newbury House Dictionary

Activity Book *p. 156*

Student CD-ROM

Grammar Focus

Recognize Regular and Irregular Simple Past Tense Verbs

Simple past tense verbs describe an action that already happened.

Regular simple past tense verbs end in *-ed*. **Irregular simple past tense** verbs do not end in *-ed*. They are formed in different ways. Look at the chart.

1. Complete these sentences with the past tense of the verb in parentheses.
   a. Rosa's mother ____ her to school in Montgomery. (send)
   b. She ____ the bus to work. (take)
2. Write two sentences about what you did last weekend.

Base Verb	Past Tense
Regular	
walk	walked
answer	answered
call	called
Irregular	
send	sent
take	took
have	had

Activity Book *pp. 157–158*

Student Handbook

Student CD-ROM

From Reading to Writing

Write a Biography

Write a short biography of someone you know. Your biography will be three paragraphs long.

1. Interview the person and ask these questions. Summarize what the person says on note cards.
   a. What is your name?
   b. When and where were you born?
   c. What are two important events in your life? When did these events happen?
   d. What three things do you like to do?
2. Organize your note cards in chronological order.

3. Write an introduction. Tell who the person is.
4. Write the body of your biography. Describe two important events in the person's life.
5. Write a conclusion. Tell what the person likes to do.
6. Use regular and irregular simple past tense verbs to tell about past events.

Activity Book
p. 159

Student
Handbook

Across Content Areas

Learn About Constitutional Amendments

The U.S. Constitution promises certain rights (freedoms) to all Americans. People can add **amendments** (changes) to the U.S. Constitution. These amendments change old laws or add new laws. The U.S. Constitution has more than 20 amendments. Here are a few:

The First Amendment gives Americans the right to say and write what they want.

The Thirteenth Amendment ended slavery in the United States.

The Nineteenth Amendment gives women the right to vote.

Match each statement with the amendment it describes.

1. I am upset about that new law. I am going to write a letter to the newspaper about it.
2. When Rosa turns 18, she will vote for the President of the United States.
3. All people must be paid for the work they do.

Activity Book
p. 160

The Gettysburg Address

a historical narrative
by Kenneth Richards,

including a speech
by Abraham Lincoln

Into the Reading

Objectives

Reading Summarize and paraphrase as you read a historical narrative and a speech.

Listening and Speaking Give a speech.

Grammar Identify clauses with subject + verb + object + infinitive.

Writing Write a news article.

Content Math: Use vocabulary to answer math problems.

Use Prior Knowledge

Explore Your Knowledge of Civil Wars

What do you know about civil wars?

1. With a partner, copy the chart on a piece of paper.
2. Decide whether each of the following statements is true or false. Write the statement in the correct place on the chart.
   a. In a civil war, people in the same country fight against each other.
   b. The United States had a civil war in the 1800s.
   c. In a civil war, people in different countries fight against each other.
   d. After some civil wars, one country is divided into two countries.

True Statements	False Statements

Build Background

The U.S. Civil War

In a civil war, two or more groups from the same country fight against each other. There was a civil war in the United States from 1861 to 1865. The states were divided into two groups, the Confederacy and the Union. The Confederacy wanted to form its own country. One reason was that the Confederacy wanted to allow people to have slaves. The Union wanted all states to stay part of the United States. It also wanted to end slavery.

In July of 1863, the Union and the Confederacy fought a horrible three-day battle at Gettysburg, Pennsylvania. The Union army won. The Confederacy lost many men and supplies. This helped the Union win the war.

Content Connection

Abraham Lincoln was the president during the U.S. Civil War. He served from 1861 to 1865.

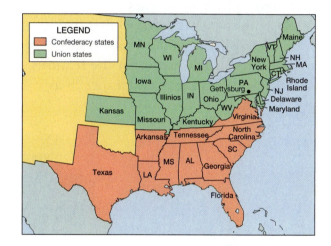

Build Vocabulary

Use Word Squares to Remember Meaning

Word squares can help you remember new words.

1. Find the definitions of these words. Use a dictionary.
   a. undivided **b.** orator
2. Make a word square for each word.
3. With a partner, ask each other the meanings of the words.
4. Make more word squares as you read "The Gettysburg Address."

Word	Symbol
address	
Meaning	**Sentence**
a speech	The president's address was very exciting.

The Heinle Newbury House Dictionary

Activity Book p. 161

Student CD-ROM

Text Structure

Historical Narrative and Speech

"The Gettysburg Address" is a **historical narrative.** It tells about an important speech in United States history. It also contains the words of a famous **speech.** In a speech, a person presents his or her ideas to an audience (people gathered to hear someone talk). People often write speeches down so that they remember what to say and so that others can read them later. Look for the features of a historical narrative and a speech as you read the selection.

Student CD-ROM

Historical Narrative	
Chronological Order	events usually given in the order in which they happened
Facts	true statements about people, places, and events
Primary Sources	documents, interviews, and other real information from the past
Interpretation	author's explanation of people and events

Speech	
Strong Message	tries to get readers to believe in or do something
Direct Address	uses the pronouns *we* and *us* to speak directly to the audience
Repeated Words	creates a rhythm (a beat, as in music) that may excite the audience

Reading Strategy

Summarize and Paraphrase

When you **summarize,** you tell the most important ideas of a text. You also use your own words.

When you **paraphrase,** you restate a text or a part of a text in your own words. You include all or most of the information in the text.

Summarize and paraphrase as you read "The Gettysburg Address." This will help you recall information.

Student CD-ROM

Text
The train arrived in the small town just as the sun was setting. A carriage drove Mr. Lincoln to the home of Mr. Wills, where he was to spend the night. . . . After dinner, the president went to his room to work on his speech.

Summary	Paraphrase
Lincoln arrived and went to the house where he would sleep. He worked on his speech.	Lincoln arrived in the small town by train in the early evening. He was going to spend the night at the home of Mr. Wills. He had dinner there, and then he spent some time on his speech.

The Gettysburg Address

a historical narrative by Kenneth Richards,
including a speech by Abraham Lincoln

Prologue

Many Union soldiers died in the Battle of Gettysburg. Union leaders built a **cemetery** in Gettysburg to bury these Union soldiers. This cemetery is called Soldiers' National Cemetery. This text begins right after the cemetery was built.

1   When the work was finished, the townspeople were very pleased. The brave men who had died now had an **honorable** resting place. "We must **dedicate** the cemetery," Mr. Wills said. "I will ask important people to speak at the ceremony."

2   A few days later, in Washington, D.C., President Lincoln received a letter from Mr. Wills. He asked the president to come to Gettysburg and make a few "**appropriate** remarks" at the dedication of the Soldiers' National Cemetery.

Summarize

Summarize this paragraph in one or two sentences.

Audio
CD 3, Tr. 2

President Lincoln was a very busy   3
man. The war was still going on and many matters needed his close personal attention. It was very difficult for him to get away from Washington, even for a little while. But he knew, perhaps more than anyone, how important the Battle of Gettysburg had been. He wrote Mr. Wills that somehow he would find the time to come to Gettysburg.

The night before he was to leave   4
Washington for the dedication, President Lincoln began working on his speech. He knew that the main speaker at the **ceremony** would be

---

cemetery   a graveyard, a place to bury the dead
honorable   respectable
dedicate   formally open in honor of someone

appropriate   correct, suitable
ceremony   a formal event usually with rituals (words and actions done many times before)

Edward Everett of Massachusetts, the most famous **orator** in America. He realized that Mr. Everett would talk for a long time and that there would be other speakers, so Lincoln decided to make his speech very short. Because he was aware that newspapers all over the country would print his speech, he wanted it to be perfect. He worked for hours, writing and rewriting the sentences. When he had finished the first draft, he went to bed.

5 Early the next morning, the president **boarded** the special train that was to carry him and other **dignitaries** to Gettysburg. As the countryside of Maryland and Pennsylvania rolled past his window, Lincoln thought of the war. He knew that peace would eventually come to the land and that the Union would remain strong and **undivided** because

of the efforts of brave men such as those buried at Gettysburg. "My speech does not express how deeply I feel about these men," he thought. "I must rewrite it. I want people everywhere to understand what freedom means to us and how much we owe to the brave soldiers who died at Gettysburg."

Summarize
Summarize this paragraph.

6 The train arrived in the small town just as the sun was setting. A carriage drove Mr. Lincoln to the home of Mr. Wills, where he was to spend the night. Mr. Everett was a guest in the house also. After dinner, the president went to his room to work on his speech.

not have died in vain— that this nation under God, shall have a new birth of freedom— and that government of the people, by the people, for the people, shall not perish from the earth.

Abraham Lincoln.

November 19, 1863.

---

orator   a person who is very good at giving speeches
boarded   got on a train, ship, or other vehicle

dignitaries   important people, especially high officials
undivided   complete, whole

7   During the evening, a group of people came to sing for the president beneath his window. Lincoln opened the window to wave, and then he spoke a few words to the crowd that had gathered. When they left, he returned to his work.

8   It was past midnight before the speech was finished. Lincoln had written it on two pieces of lined paper. There were only 269 words. "It is what I would call a short, short speech," he said. Then he went to bed.

> **Paraphrase**
>
> Paraphrase this paragraph. Put it in your own words.

9   At eleven o'clock the next morning, November 19, 1863, a parade to the cemetery began. **Congressmen,** generals, and governors were in the **procession,** as well as brass bands and **military units.** Mr. Lincoln rode on a handsome horse. He wore a black suit, white gloves, and his tall, black **stovepipe hat.**

10   Nearly every citizen of Gettysburg had come to see the parade and hear the speeches. The shops and the schools in the town were closed and thousands of people lined the streets to watch the procession pass.

11   The parade **wound** slowly out of the town and up the road leading to the cemetery. Most of the people had never seen the president before. They cheered as he passed, and he waved his hand or nodded his head. The crowd followed the procession to the **ridge.**

Congressmen   members of the U.S. Congress, a group that makes the nation's laws

procession   a parade

military units   groups of soldiers

stovepipe hat   a type of tall hat

wound   curved around

ridge   a long, narrow, high piece of land

12   At last the parade reached the cemetery. A **platform** decorated with red, white, and blue **bunting** had been built for the speakers. President Lincoln climbed the steps to the platform and took his seat in the front row. In the distance, he could see the great **battlefield.** The sounds of fighting were gone now and autumn leaves covered the ground. There was peace at Gettysburg.

Summarize

Would you include the colors of the bunting in a summary of this paragraph? Why or why not?

13   A band played to open the ceremony. When the music ended, the crowd grew silent as a minister said a prayer. Following the prayer, the United States Marine Band played and then, one after another, speakers rose from their seats to **address** the crowd. They told the people that the cemetery was a grand **achievement** and that the nation was very proud of the citizens of Gettysburg. Soon it was time for Mr. Everett to speak.

14   Mr. Everett had a powerful voice and even those farthest from the platform could hear his words. He spoke for nearly two hours. When he was finished, a choir sang a **hymn** that had been written especially for the occasion. At last, the president was introduced.

Edward Everett

---

platform   a flat, raised structure for making speeches
bunting   decorations made of cloth or paper
battlefield   a place where battles are fought

address   speak to
achievement   success
hymn   a song of praise

15   Lincoln rose slowly from his chair and put on his steel-rimmed glasses. He had a kindly, but **careworn,** face. When the crowd had grown silent, the president began to read from the two handwritten pages he held in his hand.

16   Four score and seven years ago our fathers brought forth on this continent, a new nation, **conceived** in **Liberty,** and dedicated to the **proposition** that all men are created equal.

Now we are **engaged** in a great civil war, testing whether that nation, or any nation so conceived and so dedicated, can long **endure.** We are met on a great battlefield of that war. We have come to dedicate a portion of that field, as a final resting place for those who here gave their lives that that nation might live. It is altogether **fitting** and proper that we should do this.   17

Paraphrase

Write the last sentence of this paragraph in your own words.

---

careworn showing signs of worry and tiredness
conceived thought of, created
liberty freedom
proposition plan, idea

engaged involved
endure survive, last
fitting suitable, right

18   But, in a larger sense, we can not dedicate—we can not **consecrate**—we can not **hallow**—this ground. The brave men, living and dead, who struggled here, have consecrated it, far above our poor power to add or **detract.** The world will little note, nor long remember what we say here, but it can never forget what they did here. It is for us the living, rather, to be dedicated here to the unfinished work which they who fought here have thus far so **nobly** advanced. It is rather for us to be here dedicated to the great task remaining before us—that from these honored dead we take increased **devotion** to that cause for which they gave the last full measure of devotion— that we here highly resolve that these dead shall not have died in **vain**—that this nation, under God, shall have a new birth of freedom—and that government of the people, by the people, for the people, shall not **perish** from the earth.

19   What did President Lincoln mean when he said "Four score and seven years ago"? The word *score* means twenty years, so "four score and seven years" would be eighty-seven years. In

1863, "eighty-seven years ago" would have been the year 1776. This was the year that the Declaration of Independence was written and the United States of America was born. When Lincoln spoke of "our fathers," he was referring to George Washington, Benjamin Franklin, Thomas Jefferson, and all the other political leaders who helped to **found** the new nation.

Paraphrase

Paraphrase the last sentence of this paragraph.

---

consecrate make something holy or sacred

hallow honor something as holy or sacred

detract take something good from; lower the value of something

nobly in a way that shows goodness

devotion dedication, loyalty

vain for nothing, without success

perish be killed in a sudden manner

found start and support something

20   What did Lincoln mean when he said the war was "testing our nation"? When the United States was born, the founding fathers created a new kind of government. It was founded on the belief that all men have an equal right to liberty and freedom. As Lincoln said, the citizens of the United States have a government of the people, by the people, and for the people. In other words, they **govern** themselves by free **elections.** Many people thought that this kind of government could not last very long. Lincoln was saying that the Union had to win the war in order to prove that a nation founded on this **principle** could last.

21   The president's speech **stressed** that it was not enough to just honor the soldiers who had fought at Gettysburg; but that we must not forget the reasons why they fought and died there. The soldiers gave their lives to save our government and our way of life. Lincoln was saying that Americans must work even harder now for the same cause; that unless the Union won the war and the nation was **preserved,** the soldiers would have died for nothing.

Summarize

Summarize this paragraph.

Plaque with Lincoln's Gettysburg Address

---

govern   rule a country, city, and so on
elections   events when people vote for or against
   someone or something

principle   a basic belief
stressed   emphasized, put importance on
preserved   maintained, kept in good condition

22   The people **applauded** when the president's speech was finished. Then everyone joined in singing a hymn. A final prayer was said, and the ceremony ended. Mr. Lincoln **mounted** his horse, and he and the other dignitaries rode down the hill to the town.

> ### Paraphrase
> Paraphrase this paragraph.

Epilogue

The Union won the Civil War. The country was reunited, and slavery was ended. Abraham Lincoln was shot and killed in 1865, a few days after the Civil War ended.

---

applauded   clapped their hands in approval

mounted   climbed on

About the Author   Kenneth Richards (born 1926)

Kenneth Richards has been interested in the U.S. Civil War since he was a boy. Members of his family fought for the Union at the Battle of Gettysburg. Richards has written many books and articles about the Civil War.

► Why do you think Kenneth Richards wrote "The Gettysburg Address"? To inform, to entertain, or to persuade? What strategies do you think he used to gather the information to write this selection?

Beyond the Reading

Reading Comprehension

Question-Answer Relationships (QAR)

"Right There" Questions

1. **Recall Facts** Why did President Lincoln go to Gettysburg?
2. **Recall Facts** When did the speech take place?

"Think and Search" Questions

3. **Identify Steps in a Process** What steps did President Lincoln take to write his speech?
4. **Identify Cause and Effect** Why did President Lincoln feel that his speech had to be very special?
5. **Identify Main Ideas** Based on his speech, why did Lincoln want the Union to win the war? (Hint: Look at paragraph 20.)

"Author and You" Questions

6. **Understand Genre Features** Why do you think Kenneth Richards includes the actual words of Lincoln's speech?

7. **Make Inferences** President Lincoln spoke after many other people. Even though people had been standing a long time, they cheered after Lincoln's speech. How do you think they felt about the speech?

"On Your Own" Questions

8. **Make Judgments** Why do you think people today still think Lincoln's speech was so great?
9. **Connect Your Experiences** Have you heard a speech on the radio or TV recently that had a strong effect on you? What was it about? What made it have a strong effect on you?
10. **Evaluate Oral Language** Read "The Gettysburg Address" aloud to a partner. Show that you understand. How does the speech engage the listener?

Activity Book
p. 162

Student
CD-ROM

Build Reading Fluency

Adjust Your Reading Rate to Memorize

When you memorize you must adjust your reading rate to read slowly.

1. Reread paragraph 16.
2. Read each line slowly.
3. Practice memorizing the paragraph.
4. In small groups, present the entire speech.

Listen, Speak, Interact

Give a Speech

Your school is going to dedicate the school flagpole to someone who has contributed a lot to the school. Write and give the dedication speech.

1. Decide who should be honored, for example, a teacher, the principal, or a graduate of your school who is now famous.
2. Write your speech.
   a. Start with a sentence that will get the audience's attention. Use the beginning of Lincoln's "Gettysburg Address" as a model.
   b. Tell why the person should be honored.
   c. Remember that the occasion is formal, the audience is the entire school, and your purpose is to talk about an important person.
   d. Prepare a visual that shows the person's contributions.
3. Give your speech to the class.
   a. Practice your speech before giving it. Ask a partner to evaluate your speech.
   b. Pay attention to your voice. Use the right pitch and tone to make your speech credible (believable).

Elements of Literature

Analyze and Evaluate the Delivery of a Speech

A speech is read aloud before an audience. The words and the presentation of the words—how the speaker uses his or her voice—contribute to the message.

1. Listen to the audio recording of "The Gettysburg Address."
2. Analyze the effect of the speech.
   a. What feelings do you have as you listen to the speech? Why?
   b. How does the speaker's delivery affect your feelings?
   c. What ideas do you get from the speech? How do you react to the ideas? Why?
3. Analyze the speech for the beauty of the language and the writer's skill.
   a. Why does Lincoln say "Four score and seven years ago" instead of "Eighty-seven years ago"?
   b. Why does Lincoln say ". . . we can not dedicate—we can not consecrate—we can not hallow—this ground" instead of ". . . we can not dedicate, consecrate, or hallow this ground"?

Activity Book
p. 163

Student
CD-ROM

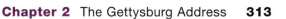

Word Study

Use the Suffix -or

The suffix -or can change verbs into nouns. The suffix means "someone who does something."

Verb		Noun
act	+ -or →	act**or** (someone who acts)

For Verbs Ending in e

Drop the final e before adding the suffix -or.

creat~~e~~ + -or → creat**or** (someone who creates)

Verb +	Suffix ⇒	Noun	Noun Meaning
orate +	-or ⇒		
+	-or ⇒	governor	

1. Copy this chart in your Personal Dictionary.
2. Fill in the correct verb and noun. Then write the meanings of each noun. Use a dictionary if needed.

Personal Dictionary   The Heinle Newbury House Dictionary   Activity Book p. 164   Student CD-ROM

Grammar Focus

Identify Clauses with Subject + Verb + Object + Infinitive

A **clause** is a group of words that contains a subject and a verb. Some clauses contain a verb, a subject, an object, and an infinitive.

A **subject** is a noun that does the action. A **verb** is a word that describes an action. An **object** is a word that takes the action of the verb. An **infinitive** contains the word *to* plus a simple verb.

I want you to go home.

I is the subject. *Want* is the verb. *You* is the object. *To go* is the infinitive.

1. Write the following sentences on a piece of paper. Underline the subject once. Underline the verb twice. Circle the object. Draw a box around the infinitive.
   a. He asked the president to come.
   b. He wanted it to be perfect.
2. Write two of your own sentences using these parts of speech.

Activity Book pp. 165–166   Student Handbook   Student CD-ROM

From Reading to Writing

Write a News Article

Imagine that you and a partner are newspaper reporters in Gettysburg in 1863. Write a news article about Lincoln's visit and the speech.

1. Organize your ideas.
   a. Review the summaries and paraphrases that you wrote about Lincoln's visit. Review your analyses of the Gettysburg Address on page 313.
   b. Put your ideas in the order in which you want to present them.
2. Compose your news article. Use a computer.
   a. Tell who, what, when, and where it happened. Tell why it was important.
   b. Tell about the speech and its effect on the audience.
3. Use the computer to revise, edit, and publish your article.
4. Evaluate how well your news article informs and influences the reader.
5. How does the purpose of your news article compare with Kenneth Richards's historical narrative of the event? Evaluate how the two forms of writing influence and inform.

Activity Book
p. 167

Student
Handbook

Across Content Areas

MATH

Use Vocabulary to Answer Math Problems

In "The Gettysburg Address," you learned that **score** can mean "20 years." Look at these other words for numbers of years. Use the words to figure out the math problems below.

decade 10 years

century 100 years

millennium 1,000 years

1. Two decades is ＿＿ years.
2. Two score and one century is ＿＿ years.
3. Half a millennium is ＿＿ years.
4. One score minus one decade is ＿＿ years.
5. Which is larger, eight centuries or one millennium?

Activity Book
p. 168

So Far from the Bamboo Grove

an excerpt from a novel based on a true story by Yoko Kawashima Watkins

Objectives

Reading Predict as you read an excerpt from a novel.

Listening and Speaking Present an experience with danger.

Grammar Use the conjunction *so that* to connect ideas.

Writing Write a historical fiction story.

Content Language Arts: Use punctuation and intonation.

Use Prior Knowledge

Describe Getting Help

People help each other all the time. Describe a time when someone helped you do something.

1. Think of how someone has helped you. Did someone help you with your homework? Help you clean the house? Help you carry something heavy?
2. Draw a picture of this person helping you.
3. Label the people and things in the picture.
4. Describe your picture to a partner.
5. Listen carefully as your partner describes his or her picture.

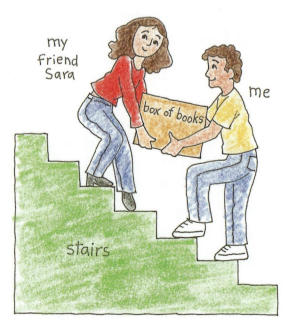

my friend Sara

me

box of books

stairs

Build Background

World War II in Korea

World War II was mostly fought in Europe and Asia. It started in 1939 and ended in 1945. Before World War II, Japan took over Korea. Most Koreans did not like this. In 1945, Japan seemed to be losing the war. Many Japanese people living in Korea tried to return to Japan. This was difficult and dangerous because some Koreans felt that the Japanese were enemies.

Content Connection

In 1948, Korea was divided into two countries, North Korea and South Korea.

Build Vocabulary

Use Text Features to Understand

The selection you will read includes Korean words. The Korean words are in *italic* type. The English meanings of the Korean words are in **parentheses** (. . .). You can use these text features to learn new words.

Korean word   **English word**
"Komapsŭmnida (Thank you)," whispered Hideyo.

Read these sentences. Use the text features to help you understand.

1. The woman said, "*Ŭnhe rŭl ichi an gesŭmnida* (I will not forget your kindness)."
2. He whispered, "*Chosim haesŏ kaseyo* (Go carefully)."
3. "*Chigŭm kaseyo* (Go now)!"

Activity Book
p. 169

Student
CD-ROM

Text Structure

Fiction Based on a True Story

The selection "So Far from the Bamboo Grove" is from a novel. A novel is fiction. It is a story that fills a book. Most novels are made up, but this novel is based on a true story. The story takes place in Korea near the end of World War II. Look for the features of fiction based on a true story as you read the selection.

Fiction Based on a True Story	
Setting	a real time and place in history
Characters	real people
Plot	the main events
Problems	events that happen because of the setting of the story
Problem Resolution	how problems are solved

Student
CD-ROM

Reading Strategy

Predict

When you **predict** you guess what will happen next. You use text clues and your experience to predict what will happen in a story. Read this paragraph:

> Sue yawns and looks at her watch. She says, "It's late and I'm tired." Then she stands up.

Look at the chart. Using the clues and your experience, you can predict that Sue will go to sleep.

As you read the selection, predict what will happen next. Share your ideas with the class.

Text Clues	Your Experience	You Predict
Sue yawns. Sue is tired. It is late.	People go to sleep when they are tired.	Sue will go to sleep.

Student
CD-ROM

So Far from the Bamboo Grove

an excerpt from a novel based on a true story

by Yoko Kawashima Watkins

Predict

What kind of trip do you think Hideyo is taking? Do you think he will be coming back?

1   But he must go, Hideyo said. As soon as the spring work was finished and when the moon was dark, so that he would not be **spotted.**

2   When the last supper with the **generous** Korean family was finished, he gathered his few belongings. His student's **uniform,** underwear, pants, and socks were washed and folded by Mrs. Kim. Hideyo put the fur coat in the bottom of the **rucksack,** then the family **album** and savings book, then his clothes.

3   Mrs. Kim packed large rice balls in a **bamboo** box and Mr. Kim handed Hideyo a little money. Hideyo tried to refuse the money, for Mr. Kim was a poor farmer who had to give almost all his earnings to the **government,** but Mr. Kim insisted that he carry some Korean money.

spotted   seen

generous   very giving

uniform   a special kind of clothing worn by people belonging to certain groups

rucksack   a bag carried on the back

album   a book with blank pages for saving photographs and other things

bamboo   tall plant of the grass family, used in houses and furniture

government   the people who rule a place or country

4   He wanted to tell Mrs. Kim many things to express his **gratitude,** but the tears came and his chest tightened. Mrs. Kim held his hands and cried, *"Aigo!"* an **expression** of sadness. He shook hands with Mr. Kim, and the hand, rough from years of hard work in the fields, seemed gentle and soft. Mr. Kim, in tears, bit his **chapped** lips and nodded his wrinkled face, as if to say, "Don't say anything. I understand."

Predict

What might happen to Hideyo if he looks Japanese?

5   Then, because a rucksack would give away the fact that he was Japanese, Mrs. Kim put the rucksack in a **burlap** bag tied with a long rope and told him to carry it around his hips like a Korean.

---

gratitude   thankfulness, appreciation
expression   a word or group of words
chapped   dried, cracking

burlap   a rough cloth used to make bags for holding coffee beans, onions, and so on

6   Hee Cho went with Hideyo as far as the river. Imjŏon, the fourth-largest river in Korea, crosses the **thirty-eighth parallel.** American soldiers controlled southern Korea, and Hideyo knew he would be safer once he crossed this **boundary.** The river was four miles from the Kims' house. As they left the house the sun was about to set. Hideyo kept looking back, waving to Mr. and Mrs. Kim and Hee Wang. Just before they **vanished** into the deep forest he waved a towel three times for a final **farewell.** At their doorway the Kims waved back.

Predict

What do you think will happen to Hideyo when he tries to cross the river?

7   The river was well guarded by the **Communists.** From a **watchtower** nearby, a **searchlight** swept over the area, throwing its strong **beam** on the river surface. Hideyo untied his burlap bag and took off all his clothes, even his rubber-soled tabi. He shoved them all into the bag, put the bag on his head, and fastened it to him with the rope. That way, if the bag fell off his head it would still be tied to him.

---

thirty-eighth parallel   a line that marks the border between North and South Korea

boundary   a line dividing two places

vanished   disappeared

farewell   good-bye for a long time or forever

Communists   people who are part of a group in which all businesses and land are owned by the government

watchtower   a tower from which something is guarded

searchlight   a strong, movable lamp used for seeing at a distance in the dark

beam   a ray of light

Predict

Do you think that Hideyo will try to swim across the water?

8   He **cast his eyes** onto the dark, wide river and wondered if he could swim across. The thought flashed through his mind that if he was spotted and killed, this running water would be **crimsoned** by his blood.

9   The boys looked at each other. They shook hands.

10   Hee Cho whispered, "*Chosim haesŏ kaseyo* (Go carefully)."

11   "*Komapsŭmnida* (Thank you)," whispered Hideyo.

12   "*Chaphi jianko kaseyo* (Travel so that you do not get caught)."

13   "*Ŭnhe rŭ ichi an gesŭmnida* (I will not forget your kindness)."

14   "*Chigŭm kaseyo* (Go now)!"

---

cast his eyes looked   **crimsoned** made red in color

15   When the searchlight had passed over them, Hideyo slipped into the river. It was much colder than he had expected and the **current** was very strong. He swam. Each time a light came toward him he dove under, so that only his bag showed, half **submerged** and looking, he hoped, like a floating log. Again and again he had to dive.

16   Gunfire burst in the air, **echoing** in a thousand directions. Hideyo did not know whether it was aimed at him, at some other **escapees,** or at wild animals. The light swept over him again and he submerged deeper. He could see the shore not far from him, but the current kept pushing him downstream and so many **submergings** slowed him.

Predict

Now do you think Hideyo will be seen? What clues from the story make you think this?

current   a flow of water

submerged   under the surface of the water

echoing   repeating of a sound caused by bouncing off a hard surface

escapees   people who try to get away

submergings   times gone under the surface of the water

17   Again gunfire. A bullet hit the bag on Hideyo's head and dropped to the surface. He could hear the bullets piercing the waters all around him. He dove deeper and let the current carry him. Then he swam again. When he finally reached the south side he lay as dead when the light shone his way, then crawled toward the bushes, **exhausted.**

18   He had escaped across the dangerous thirty-eighth parallel. He took a deep breath of freedom. He thanked God for the Kim family and hoped that they would see in a dream that he had made it to the other side.

Predict

What do you think will happen to Hideyo now? Will his life get better? Why?

---

exhausted   extremely tired

About the Author

Yoko Kawashima Watkins (born 1933)

"So Far from the Bamboo Grove" is about Yoko Kawashima Watkins's childhood. Watkins is Japanese. She spent her early years in North Korea. Near the end of World War II, her family escaped from North Korea. Her family had many problems on their way back to Japan. Later, Watkins married an American soldier and moved to the United States.

►What strategies do you think Yoko Kawashima Watkins used to write her novel? What challenges did she face?

Beyond the Reading

Reading Comprehension

Question-Answer Relationships (QAR)

"Right There" Questions

1. **Recall Facts** Who is Hideyo?
2. **Recall Facts** What is Hideyo trying to do in the story?

"Think and Search" Questions

3. **Recognize Plot** What is the plot of this story?
4. **Make Inferences** Why would carrying a rucksack tell others that Hideyo is Japanese?
5. **Identify Cause and Effect** Why does Hideyo want to cross the thirty-eighth parallel?
6. **Give Reasons** Why does Hideyo swim underwater? Why does he leave his bag on the surface?

"Author and You" Questions

7. **Connect Your Experiences** How do you think Hideyo feels when he says good-bye to the Kims? How do you feel when saying good-bye to people you care about?

8. **Analyze Problem Resolution** What is the resolution of the story?
9. **Analyze Characteristics of Cultures** What differences between Korean and Japanese culture did you notice in the story? What are the common characteristics? How does your family's culture compare or contrast?

"On Your Own" Questions

10. **Speculate** Hideyo would probably travel more quickly if he carried nothing. Why do you think Hideyo brings his things with him?
11. **Identify Themes** How does Hideyo feel when he gets across the river?
12. **Analyze Plot** Is the plot exciting to you? Why or why not?

Activity Book
p. 170

Student
CD-ROM

Build Reading Fluency

Repeated Reading

Repeated reading helps increase your reading rate and builds confidence. Each time you reread, you improve your reading fluency.

1. Turn to page 320.
2. Your teacher or partner will time you for six minutes.
3. With a partner, take turns reading each paragraph aloud.
4. Stop after six minutes.

Listen, Speak, Interact

Present an Experience with Danger

Think about a time when you or someone you know has been in danger. Write notes on a piece of paper.

1. Interview your partner about his or her dangerous experience.
   a. Ask questions with who, what, when, where, why, and how.
   b. Add and revise questions.
   c. Take notes on note cards.
2. Tell your partner's story to the class.
   a. Use your voice and gestures to make the story interesting.
   b. Use your voice to make people believe you.

3. After presenting the story, ask your classmates if they believed you.
4. Listen to another classmate's presentation. Did you understand your classmate's verbal and nonverbal messages? If not, ask for clarification.

Elements of Literature

Analyze Character Motivation

Motivation is the reason why someone does something. For example, you may work after school to earn money for college. Your motivation is to go to college.

"So Far from the Bamboo Grove" describes people who do dangerous things. What is their motivation for doing these things?

1. Work with a small group. Answer these questions.
   a. Why does Hideyo swim through the cold river at night? What is his motivation?
   b. Why do you think the Kims help Hideyo? What is their motivation?
2. Identify other things that the characters do. What is the motivation for each one?
3. Present one of your ideas to the class.

Activity Book
p. 171

Student
CD-ROM

Word Study

Identify the Latin Root Word *Grat*

Root words are words from which other words are made. The root word *grat* comes from the Latin word *gratus*. It means "pleasing." You can use *grat* with several suffixes to make new words.

In "So Far from the Bamboo Grove," Hideyo feels *gratitude* (thankfulness) toward Mrs. Kim. *Gratitude* has the root *grat*.

1. Copy the chart in your Personal Dictionary.
2. Look at the words and their definitions. Read the sentences.
3. Write your own sentences using words with *grat*.

Notice that you add an *e* to *grat* before adding *ful*.

Use the Root Word *Grat*

gratify give satisfaction or pleasure: It will <u>gratify</u> me to see you learn English.

My Sentence It will gratify me to show you around my classroom.

grateful thankful, appreciative: I am <u>grateful</u> for all your help.

My Sentence

congratulate praise for something well done or important: I <u>congratulate</u> you for winning the prize.

My Sentence

Personal Dictionary

The Heinle Newbury House Dictionary

Activity Book p. 172

Student CD-ROM

Grammar Focus

Use the Conjunction *So That* to Connect Ideas

A **conjunction** is a word that joins two clauses. A clause is a part of a sentence that has a subject and a verb. *So that* is a conjunction. The clause with *so that* usually gives a reason.

I put on my swimsuit <u>so that</u> I could swim.

1. Copy the chart on a piece of paper.
2. Read paragraphs 1, 12, and 15 from the selection.
3. In your chart write the sentence from each paragraph that uses the conjunction *so that*.

Use the Conjunction *So That*

Paragraph	Sentence
1	
12	
15	

4. On a piece of paper, write two sentences with *so that*.

Activity Book pp. 173–174

Student Handbook

Student CD-ROM

From Reading to Writing

Write a Historical Fiction Story

Hideyo faces many problems while trying to escape from northern Korea. Write your own story about someone trying to escape from a place. Your story will be five paragraphs long. Use the Narrative Draft form in your Student Handbook as a guide.

1. Choose a real time and place in history for your story. Use textbooks or library resources to help you.
2. Write what happens as your character tries to escape. Remember to answer: Who? What? When? Where? Why? How?
3. Tell your character's motivation.
4. Think of a title for your story.
5. Revise and edit your writing using the Editor's Checklist in your Student Handbook. Use a computer, if possible.
6. When you are finished, exchange papers with a partner. Peer edit each other's work.
7. How well did you and your partner achieve your purpose for writing?

Activity Book
p. 175

Student
Handbook

Across Content Areas

LANGUAGE ARTS

Use Punctuation and Intonation

In "So Far from the Bamboo Grove," Mrs. Kim says, "Aigo!" Notice the **exclamation point (!)** after *aigo*. An exclamation point shows forceful speech, as when you are angry, surprised, or frustrated.

A **question mark (?)** comes at the end of a question. You can make informal questions with just a single word. You do this by raising your voice at the end of the word.

Listen as your teacher pronounces this exclamation and question. Can you hear the difference in intonation?

No! No?

1. Read the following sentences and respond in writing with *no*. To clarify your answer, punctuate *no* with an exclamation point or a question mark.
   a. I can't come now.
   b. Would you write my science report for me?
2. Read the sentences and the "no" responses with a partner. Use the correct intonation.

Activity Book
p. 176

Into the Reading

Alone

a poem
by Samantha Abeel

Samantha's Story

an autobiography
by Samantha Abeel

Objectives

Reading Compare and contrast as you read a poem and an autobiography.

Listening and Speaking Respond to literature.

Grammar Use superlative adjectives.

Writing Write a poem.

Content Language Arts: Identify genres.

Use Prior Knowledge

Talk About Strengths and Weaknesses

Everybody has strengths—things they are good at. Everybody has weaknesses—things they are not good at. Your strengths are part of who you are. An example might be that you can make people laugh. An example of a weakness might be that you can't run really fast.

1. Copy the chart shown on a piece of paper.
2. Write a few of your strengths and weaknesses.
3. Talk about your list with a partner. How are your lists the same and different?

4. Summarize each other's strengths and weaknesses.

Strengths	Weaknesses
can make people laugh	can't run very fast

Build Background

Learning Disabilities

Some people have trouble learning. Their trouble can be caused by a learning disability—something that gets in the way of learning. People with learning disabilities can be very smart. With the help of technology, medicine, and other people, people with disabilities can do many great things.

Content Connection

About 10 to 15 percent of children in the United States have learning disabilities. Many receive special teaching in school to help them succeed.

Build Vocabulary

Spell Frequently Misspelled Words

Some words sound the same but have different spellings and meanings. One example is *to, two,* and *too.* When you write, be sure you choose the correct spelling.

Read the following sentences. Look at the definitions for each pair of words. Choose the correct word to complete each sentence. Write the words and their definitions in your Personal Dictionary.

1. There is a place where the (sun / son) and its flowers bow in shadow.
   a. **son** a male child
   b. **sun** the star that gives heat and light to the earth

2. Yet one (hour / our) of my day was a refuge.
   a. **hour** a time period of 60 minutes
   b. **our** belonging to us

3. I could (rays / raise) my hand in class.
   a. **rays** thin lines of light or energy
   b. **raise** lift up

Personal Dictionary

Activity Book
p. 177

Student CD-ROM

Text Structure

Poem and Autobiography

In this chapter you will read a poem and an autobiography. Look at the charts. They show features of some poems and autobiographies. Look for these features as you read.

Autobiography	
First Person Narration	The author tells the story using the pronouns *I, me, we, us.*
Main Character	The main character is the author.
Events	The autobiography tells the story of the author's life.
Setting	The autobiography is set in a real time and place.

Poem	
Images	The poem includes descriptions that help readers create mental images (pictures in their minds).
Repetition	The poem repeats some words and phrases.

Student
CD-ROM

Reading Strategy

Compare and Contrast Texts

When you **compare,** you see how things are similar. When you **contrast,** you see how things are different. Look at the example. It shows how you can compare and contrast a lemon and a banana.

Compare Both are yellow and are fruit.

Contrast A banana is sweet. A lemon is not.

1. Compare and contrast "Alone" and "Samantha's Story" as you read.
2. Think about how the descriptions in each selection are similar and different.

3. Copy a diagram like this in your Reading Log. As you read, write your comparisons and contrasts on it.

Reading Log   Student CD-ROM

Alone

a poem by Samantha Abeel

Samantha's Story

an autobiography by Samantha Abeel

Alone

a poem by Samantha Abeel

Compare and Contrast

Look at the poem. How do you think it will be different from Samantha's autobiography?

There is a place where we all go
when we must sit alone:
A place where the birds are free to fly,
A place where the sun and its flowers bow in shadow,
A place where the fog is like a **veil**
and everything is protected,
A place where our souls are set free
and we are allowed to play our own song.

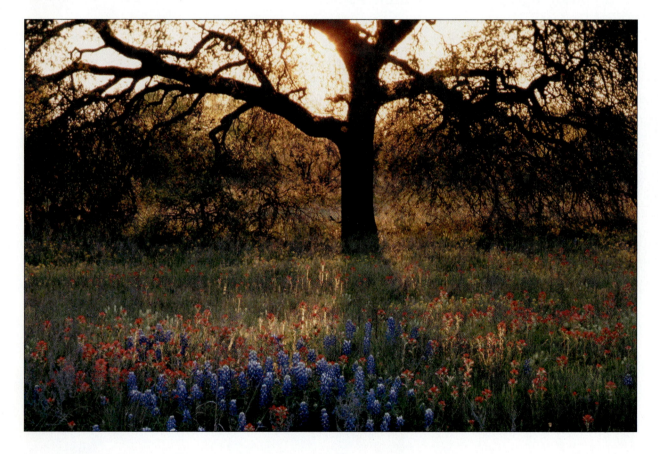

---

veil a light cloth worn over the face

Audio
CD 3, Tr. 5

Samantha's Story
an autobiography by Samantha Abeel

Compare and Contrast

What is the first difference you see between this selection and "Alone"?

1   A TREE that stands in the moonlight reflects the light, yet also casts a shadow. People are the same. They have gifts that let them shine, yet they also have **disabilities,** shadows that **obscure** the light. When I started this project in seventh grade, I had trouble telling time, counting money, remembering even the simplest of addition and subtraction problems. Yet no matter how hard it was to stay **afloat** in this ocean of troubles, there was something inside of me, something that became my **life preserver**—and that was writing.

2   SEVENTH GRADE was a horrible year. I hated school. . . . Yet one hour of my day was a **refuge.** Here, there weren't any concepts with numbers, measurements, algebra, or failure. It was my seventh-grade writing class. I had begun to **experiment** with creative writing in sixth grade, but in seventh grade I discovered how much writing was a part of me and I was a part of it.

3   TO BUILD on this, my mother asked Mrs. Williams, who was my English teacher, if she would work with me by giving me writing assignments and **critiquing** them as a way of focusing on what was right with me and not on what was wrong. . . . I discovered that by crawling inside and becoming what I wrote, it made my writing and ideas more powerful.

---

disabilities   things that take away a normal ability

obscure   hard to see or understand

afloat   on or above the water; not in bad trouble, surviving

life preserver   equipment used to keep a person above water

refuge   a place of safety

experiment   test, try something

critiquing   evaluating, especially someone's written work

Compare and Contrast

How do Samantha's feelings in this paragraph compare to her feelings in the poem?

4 IN EIGHTH GRADE I was finally recognized as **learning disabled.** I was taken from my seventh grade algebra class, where I was totally lost, and placed in a **special education resource** classroom. Special education changed my life. It was the best thing that ever happened to me. I could raise my hand in that class, even when being taught the most **elementary concepts,** and say, "I don't get it." It was the most wonderful feeling in the world. Eighth grade was my best year at the junior high. It is an **illusion** that students in special education have no abilities. Special education just means that you learn differently. I am so thankful for **specially** trained teachers who have been able to help me and many other kids like me.

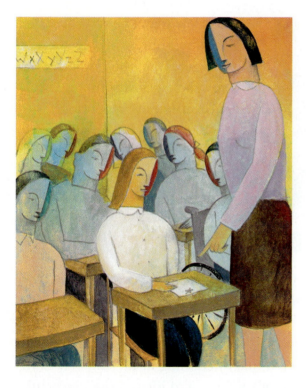

5 IF YOU STRUGGLE with a disability, the first thing you need to do is find something that you are good at, whether it's singing or skate boarding, an interest in science or acting, even just being good with people. Then do something with that. If you are good with people, then **volunteer** at a nursing home or at a day care center; if you love skate boarding, work toward a **competition.** If it's singing, join a school choir. Even if you can't read music (like me) or read a script, you can find ways of **coping** and **compensating.** . . .

---

learning disabled   someone who has problems learning things

special education resource   materials for teaching students who need extra help

elementary concepts   simple ideas

illusion   a mistaken idea

specially   carefully, with more attention than usual

volunteer   do something without being forced or paid

competition   an organized event in which people try to do something better than everyone else

coping   facing problems and trying to overcome them

compensating   fighting against a weakness with a strength

6

REMEMBER that if you have trouble in school, it might not be because you don't fit the school, it might be because the school doesn't fit you. Be an **advocate** for yourself. Keep trying. You may not fit in now, but whether you're seven or seventy, one day you will find a place where you **excel.**

Compare and Contrast

Think about what Samantha says in her poem and autobiography. How is what she says the same? How is it different?

---

advocate   a worker for a cause; a supporter   **excel**   do very well

About the Author

Samantha Abeel (born 1978)

Samantha Abeel grew up and went to school in Traverse City, Michigan. She got help with her learning disabilities from special education teachers in her school. She then went to college. She studied English and art history. Samantha Abeel likes to write. She is working on her second book.

► What question would you like to ask Samantha Abeel? What challenges did she overcome?

Beyond the Reading

Reading Comprehension

Question-Answer Relationships (QAR)

"Right There" Questions

1. **Recall Facts** In "Alone," what are birds free to do?
2. **Recall Facts** In "Samantha's Story," what help does Samantha get to make schoolwork easier?

"Think and Search" Questions

3. **Describe Setting** In "Alone," how is the place described?
4. **Recognize Cause and Effect** In "Samantha's Story," why did Samantha hate school in the seventh grade?

"Author and You" Questions

5. **Recognize Mood** In "Alone," what feelings do you get about the place in the poem? A warm feeling? A cold feeling?
6. **Connect Your Experiences** Why is Samantha thankful for her teachers? How does her school experience compare with yours?

7. **Recognize Tone** What tone does Samantha Abeel use in the autobiography? How does it add to the effect of the text?

"On Your Own" Questions

8. **Compare and Contrast Themes Across Texts** How do the poem and the autobiography connect with the theme of freedom? Compare and contrast them with other readings in the unit.
9. **Speculate** What might have happened to Samantha without special education?
10. **Connect Issues Across Texts** What connections do you see between Samantha's school experiences and those of the boy in "The Circuit" (Unit 4, Chapter 3)? Compare and contrast.

Activity Book
p. 178

Student
CD-ROM

Build Reading Fluency

Read Aloud to Engage Listeners

Reading aloud helps increase your fluency and expression. Learning to read with expression makes others want to listen to you.

1. Listen to the audio recording of "Alone."
2. Turn to page 334 and follow along.
3. Listen to the phrasing and expression.
4. With a partner, practice reading aloud.
5. Read the poem aloud with expression in front of the class.

Listen, Speak, Interact

Respond to Literature

How did you respond to "Alone" and to "Samantha's Story"?

1. Work with a small group to review "Alone" and "Samantha's Story."
2. Talk about what you liked and did not like about the selections.
3. Write what you liked on one note card. Write what you did not like on another note card.
4. Choose one person in the group to present the review to the class.
5. Practice reading the poem "Alone" aloud. Memorize it if you can. Present it to your group. Use correct pronunciation and intonation.

Elements of Literature

Recognize Figurative Language

Figurative language helps readers see mental images—pictures in their minds. A **metaphor** is a type of figurative language. It describes something by presenting it as something else.

Anna's beautiful blue eyes were two sparkling jewels.

This metaphor describes Anna's eyes as jewels. We know that her eyes are not really jewels, but the metaphor helps us picture her eyes.

1. Find the metaphors in the following sentences from "Samantha's Story." In your Reading Log, write the real things and the things that are presented as real.

   a. A tree that stands in the moonlight reflects the light, yet also casts a shadow. People are the same. They have gifts that let them shine, yet they also have disabilities, shadows that obscure the light.
   b. Yet no matter how hard it was to stay afloat in this ocean of troubles, there was something inside of me, something that became my life preserver—and that was writing.

2. Write two sentences of your own containing metaphors.

Reading Log   Activity Book   Student
                    p. 179   CD-ROM

Word Study

Learn Related Words

Some English words have the Latin form **able** or **ible.** *Able* and *ible* mean having the skill and power to do something.

1. Copy the chart in your Personal Dictionary.
2. From the list below, write the correct definitions of the underlined words.
   a. things that people can do
   b. things that people cannot do
   c. having the power to do something well
3. Use a dictionary to help you.

Sentence	Meaning
She was a talented and <u>capable</u> person.	
They have <u>disabilities</u>, shadows that obscure the light.	
People in special education still have <u>abilities</u>.	

Personal Dictionary

The Heinle Newbury House Dictionary

Activity Book *p. 180*

Student CD-ROM

Grammar Focus

Use Superlative Adjectives

Adjectives are words that describe nouns (people, places, or things). **Superlative adjectives** compare three or more nouns. They make writing more vivid or precise.

Juan is the tall**est** person in the class.

This sentence compares Juan to all the other students in the class.

Superlative adjectives are formed by adding *-est* to short adjectives. They can also be formed by putting the word *most* or *least* in front of long adjectives.

Superlative adjectives usually have the article *the* in front of them: *the* tallest person.

1. Find superlative adjectives in paragraphs 1 and 4 of "Samantha's Story."
2. Write the sentences on a piece of paper. Underline the superlative adjectives.
3. Write two sentences of your own.

Activity Book *pp. 181–182*

Student Handbook

Student CD-ROM

From Reading to Writing

Write a Poem

Samantha Abeel writes a poem to tell about a place where she is free to be herself. Write a poem about a place where you are free to be yourself. As you plan your writing, and as you write, think about what you discover about yourself in your place.

1. Describe the place in your poem. Use figurative language, such as metaphors, to tell how this place looks, sounds, smells, and feels.
2. Use superlative adjectives in your description.
3. Draw a picture of your place.

4. Choose print or cursive handwriting, and copy your poem onto your picture.
5. Read your poem and share your picture with the class.
6. Make a collection of your class's poems. Create a cover and table of contents. Share the collection with another class or place it in the library.

Activity Book
p. 183

Student
Handbook

Across Content Areas

LANGUAGE ARTS

Identify Genres

When authors write, they choose the **genre**—a type of literature—that helps them express their message best.

1. Look at page 282 of this book.
   a. The first selection, "Rosa Parks," has the words *a biography* under the title. The genre is biography.
   b. What is the genre of "So Far from the Bamboo Grove"?
2. With a partner, identify the genres of "Alone" and "Samantha's Story." Why do you think Abeel chose to write about her special place in a poem?

3. Discuss the following writing topics. Which genre would you choose? Both answers are possible, but you have to explain your choice.
   a. Why the Seasons Change (Informational text or poem?)
   b. A Trip in Time (Myth or science fiction?)

Activity Book
p. 184

Apply and Expand

Listening and Speaking Workshop

Present an Autobiographical Narrative

Topic

Think of an important time in your life. An example might be when something exciting happened. Another example might be a time when a big event occurred and changed your life. Tell what happened. Tell how you felt during this time.

Step 1: Use a Sunshine Organizer to organize your narrative.

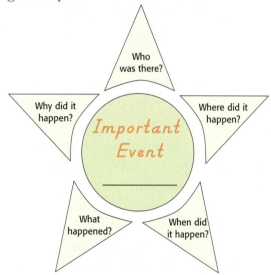

Step 2: Plan your narrative.

1. Use your organizer to think about the details of this important time in your life.
2. Decide which senses—sight, sound, smell, touch, taste—you will use to describe this time. Use figurative language.

3. Think of things you can compare with the event. Create similes or metaphors to make your story interesting.

Step 3: Prepare your narrative.

1. Write each main idea of your narrative on a note card.
2. Present the details in chronological order.
3. Think of a way to get your audience's attention. For example, you can ask them to think about an important time in their lives.
4. Include music to help set the mood for your audience.
5. Prepare visuals to give information and make your presentation interesting.

Step 4: Practice your narrative with a partner.

1. Use your note cards. Make sure they are in order.
2. Practice speaking slowly and clearly.
3. Listen to your partner's narrative.
4. Complete the checklists. Exchange checklists with your partner.
5. Revise your narrative using the checklists.

Step 5: Present your narrative.

Present your revised narrative to a friend, family member, or your class. Record your presentation if possible.

✔ **Active Listening Checklist**

1. I liked ____ because ____ .

2. I want to know more about ____ .

3. I thought your narrative was interesting / not interesting.

4. Your presentation did / did not stay on the topic.

✔ **Speaking Checklist**

1. Did you speak too slowly, too quickly, or just right?

2. Did you speak loudly enough for the audience to hear you?

3. Did you include descriptions using senses?

Step 6: Listen actively and purposely.

1. Listen to your classmates' presentations. Listen for main ideas and details.

2. Determine ways to evaluate your presentation and those of your classmates.

3. Create your own evaluation form.

Student Handbook

Viewing Workshop

View and Think

Compare and Contrast Visual Media with a Written Story

1. View pictures and videos about Korea during World War II. Use the Internet and library resources.

2. Find and interview someone who participated in World War II or who has studied it extensively.

3. Compare and contrast the pictures and videos you find to "So Far from the Bamboo Grove."

4. Answer the following questions:
   a. What new information did you learn?
   b. What information is the same or different from the selection?
   c. Which purposes and effects are the same or different? Do the pictures and videos explain, persuade, or inform? Are the purposes and effects the same in "So Far from the Bamboo Grove"?

Further Viewing

Watch the *Visions* CNN Video for Unit 5. Do the Video Worksheet.

CNN Video

Writer's Workshop

Response to Literature: Write a Biographical Narrative

Writing Prompt

Research a person that you respect. Write a biography of a part of that person's life.

Step 1: Research the person.

1. Ask yourself questions about what you want to know about the person.
2. Gather facts from library reference and resource books and the Internet. Use the person's name as the keyword for an Internet search. If the person is someone you know, interview the person and people who know the person to get facts.
3. Use tables of contents and text headings to locate and organize your information. Also use information in photos, illustrations, and charts.
4. Organize the events in a timeline. Write the dates the events happened in time order.

(Name of Person I Respect)

Dates:

Events:

5. Evaluate your research. Is it accurate? Is it complete? Did you overlook any important sources of information? Do you need to revise your questions? Are there any new questions that you need to ask yourself?

Step 2: Write a first draft.

1. Use a computer, if possible, to create your draft.
2. Outline your narrative. It should be five paragraphs long.
3. Use chronology to tell the events. Use transition words like *first, next, then,* and *finally.*
4. Cite the sources of your information using the format in your Student Handbook.
5. Use headings to organize your biography. Also use graphic features such as boldface and italics for important words or information.

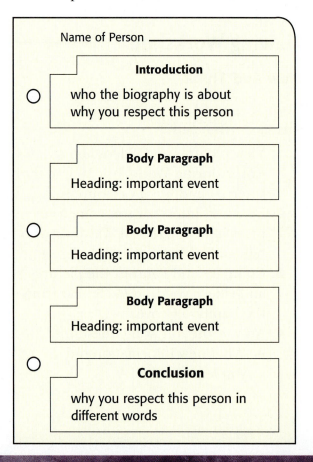

Step 3: Revise.

1. Reread your draft. Answer the following questions:
   a. Do readers know why I chose to write about this person?
   b. Did I describe the person and events clearly?
   c. Did I put the events in chronological order?
   d. Did I use reference materials and other resources, such as computer software, to revise my writing?
   e. Did I use chronological time words like *first, next,* and *then* to blend paragraphs together?
   f. Do I need to add or delete text to make my meaning clearer?
   g. How well does my writing achieve its purpose of informing the reader?
2. Share your narrative with a partner.
3. Listen to your partner's comments. Revise your narrative. Use a computer, if possible.
4. Review your partner's narrative. Give comments that will help your partner revise his or her narrative.

Step 4: Edit and proofread.

1. Proofread your revised narrative. Make sure you used standard punctuation, spelling, and grammar. Choose references and resources such as computer software, your Student Handbook, a dictionary, or an expert such as your teacher.
2. Make sure you vary your sentence structure using simple, compound, and complex sentences.

3. Proofread a classmate's writing and give helpful suggestions.

Step 5: Publish.

Prepare a class biography collection for your school library.

1. Collect everyone's work in a binder.
2. If the narratives were prepared electronically, use the software's spell check and grammar check.
3. Make a table of contents to organize the biographies.
4. Choose a title for the binder. Write your teacher's name and the school year. Draw a picture for the cover of the binder.
5. If possible put your collection of biographies on a web site.

Step 6: Evaluate.

1. Review the collection of biographies. Write answers to these questions.
   a. What are the strengths of this collection?
   b. What are its weaknesses?
   c. How can I use this collection to become a better writer?
2. Discuss your answers with your class.

The Heinle Newbury House Dictionary   Student Handbook

Projects

These projects will help you expand your ideas about freedom. Work with a partner or a small group.

Project 1: Investigate Service Learning

Reread "Samantha's Story" on page 335 with the purpose of taking action.

Abeel tells us to do something with our strengths. What action could you take to improve the lives of other people?

One way to take action is to volunteer your time to help others. This is often called service learning.

1. Brainstorm some places where you could serve and list them in a chart.

Place	Service
Senior Citizen Center	Play cards or board games
	Entertain with music
Library	Organize magazines

2. With the help of your teacher, guidance counselor, or parents, choose a place where you can help others.
3. Find out when and how you can volunteer.
4. After you finish your service, write a summary of your experience.
   a. Tell where you worked.
   b. Tell what you did.
   c. What did you learn about your strengths and weaknesses? What other things did you learn?
5. Give a presentation about your experience. Use visuals and presentation software.

Project 2: Start a Freedom Magazine

Think about the different kinds of freedom discussed in this unit. Use that information to create a freedom magazine.

1. Work with a small group.
2. Use multiple sources to find pictures that show freedom. Look in books for words people have used to describe freedom.
3. Search the Internet for times in history when people struggled for freedom. Use the keywords "freedom" and "history."
4. Ask your social studies teacher about famous people who have fought for freedom.
5. Use magazines and newspapers to locate information about people seeking freedom today.
6. Summarize your information in an outline. Use your outline to write short news articles about people seeking freedom.
7. Organize your articles and pictures in the form of a magazine. Create a table of contents. Look at published magazines as models.
8. Use a computer to publish your magazine.

Further Reading

The following books discuss the theme of freedom. Choose one or more of them. Write your thoughts and feelings about what you read in your Reading Log. Take notes about your answers to these questions:

1. What is your definition of freedom?
2. How have the characters you read about changed the world around them?

The Gettysburg Address
by Kenneth Richards, Children's Press, 1994. This book discusses the Battle of Gettysburg and President Lincoln's famous speech.

So Far from the Bamboo Grove
by Yoko Kawashima Watkins, Beech Tree Books, 1994. This is a novel based on a true story of a boy who escapes from Korea after World War II.

Reach for the Moon
by Samantha Abeel, Scholastic, Inc., 2001. Samantha Abeel has overcome her learning disorder to create this book of poetry and prose.

Amistad Rising: The Story of Freedom
by Veronica Chambers, Harcourt, 1998. This is a work of historical fiction about a revolt aboard a ship, the *Amistad,* in 1839.

Walking the Road to Freedom: A Story About Sojourner Truth
by Jeri Ferris, Carolrhoda Books, 1989. This biography is about the life of the African-American speaker who spoke out against slavery.

Let It Shine: Stories of Black Women Freedom Fighters
by Andrea Davis Pinkney, Gulliver Books, 2000. This book is a collection of biographies about women who fought against racism. Included are stories about Rosa Parks, Biddy Mason, and Harriet Tubman.

Riding Freedom
by Pam Muñoz Ryan, Scholastic, Inc., 1999. This book is based on the true story of Charlotte "Charley" Darkey Parkhurst. At the age of 12, Charlotte realizes that she does not have the same opportunities as boys. She cuts her hair and disguises herself as a boy.

Companion Web site   Reading Log

Heinle Reading Library Little Women

UNIT 6

Visions

Le Faux Miroir (The False Mirror), René Magritte, oil on canvas, 1928.

View the Picture

1. What is the artist trying to show by choosing this medium, this style, and these elements?
2. How do color, shape, and line influence the artist's message?
3. How does the art represent the meaning of "visions"? Did the artist do a good job?

In this unit, you will read a play, excerpts from two novels, and an article from the World Wide Web. You will practice writing these forms.

Into the Reading

Mr. Scrooge Finds Christmas

an excerpt from a play
by Aileen Fisher

adapted from
A Christmas Carol
by Charles Dickens

Objectives

Reading Use chronology to locate and recall information as you read an excerpt from a play.

Listening and Speaking Present a scene from the play.

Grammar Use the present perfect tense.

Writing Write a persuasive letter.

Content Math: Answer math questions about currency.

Use Prior Knowledge

Talk About the Past, Present, and Future

Time is divided into three parts: past, present, and future. The past has already happened. The present is happening right now. The future will happen later.

1. Make a chart like the one below on a piece of paper.
2. List something you did in the past. Use the past tense or the past perfect tense.
3. List something you are doing in the present. Use the present tense or the present progressive tense.
4. List something you will do in the future. Use the future tense.
5. Share your answers with a small group. Listen carefully as your classmates share their answers.

Past	Present	Future
Last year I learned to swim.	Now I live in Newtown.	Next year, I will study biology.

Build Background

Scrooge

"Mr. Scrooge Finds Christmas" is based on the novel "A Christmas Carol" by Charles Dickens. The setting of the story is London, England, in the mid-1800s. At that time, many people in England did not have jobs, and most people had very little money. Some of the people who did have money were greedy. They wanted more money than they already had.

The main character in the story is named Ebenezer Scrooge. Scrooge is a rich, greedy man. He is also a selfish man who does not care about helping others.

Many English words have their origins in fiction. "A Christmas Carol" is a very popular story. Mr. Scrooge and his traits are so well known that his name has become a noun in the English language. Someone who is a *scrooge* is a person who has money but is very selfish.

Content Connection

Charles Dickens (1812–1870) is considered to be one of the greatest British authors. He wrote 16 novels including *David Copperfield* and *A Tale of Two Cities.*

Build Vocabulary

Distinguish Denotative and Connotative Meanings

Denotative meanings of words are the definitions you find in a dictionary. Connotative meanings refer to the feelings that we attach to the word.

The denotative definition of *Christmas* is "the Christian holiday celebrating the birth of Jesus Christ." But for many people, *Christmas* suggests many other things, such as gift-giving and special food. These are some of the connotative meanings of *Christmas.*

As you read the selection, look for these other words and phrases that have connotative meanings. Check the dictionary for the denotative meanings. Ask your teacher about their connotations. Remember that connotative meanings can be negative or positive.

a. idiot　　**b.** idle people　　**c.** charity

The Heinle
Newbury House
Dictionary

Activity Book
p. 185

Student
CD-ROM

Text Structure

Play

"Mr. Scrooge Finds Christmas" is a **play.** In a play, actors act out a story. The actors speak lines in front of an audience. They pretend to be characters in the play. Look for the features of a play as you read the selection.

Usually, actors act on a **stage**—a raised floor. This stage is usually decorated to show the setting.

As you read, think about the play's setting. What do you think the stage looks like?

Play	
Scenes	different parts of the story
Names of Characters	names before each line of dialogue to tell you which character is speaking
Setting	where and when the story happens
Stage Directions	actions that the characters do
Dialogue	what the characters say to each other

Student
CD-ROM

Reading Strategy

Use Chronology to Locate and Recall Information

Chronology is the order in which events happen. You can use chronology to **locate** information in a text. Chronology can also help you **recall** (remember) what you read.

Copy the following sentences on a piece of paper. In what order do you think the events happen? Number the events in chronological order. Use *1* for the first event, *2* for the second event, and so on.

_____ **a.** He went to work.

_____ **b.** He went home.

_/_ **c.** Bob got up early.

_____ **d.** He went to bed.

_____ **e.** He had dinner with his family.

_____ **f.** He worked all day.

Student
CD-ROM

MR. SCROOGE FINDS CHRISTMAS

an excerpt from a play by Aileen Fisher

adapted from *A Christmas Carol* by Charles Dickens

Characters	
EBENEZER SCROOGE	BOB CRATCHIT, *his* **clerk**
FRED, *Scrooge's nephew*	MARLEY'S **GHOST**
A **SOLICITOR**	BOY **CAROLERS**
GHOST OF CHRISTMAS PAST	}
GHOST OF CHRISTMAS PRESENT	} *three spirits*
GHOST OF CHRISTMAS YET TO COME	}

Scene 2

1 **Setting:** *The office of Scrooge and Marley.*

At Rise: *On a stool, hunched over a high bookkeeper's desk, sits* BOB CRATCHIT. *He has a long white muffler around his neck.* SCROOGE *sits at his desk at the other side of the room. There is a meager fire in the grate on each side of the room.* BOB *shivers, rubs his hands. Then, with a* **furtive** *glance at* SCROOGE, *gets off his stool, takes the* **coal** *shovel and carefully approaches the coal-box.*

Use Chronology to Locate and Recall Information

What did Bob Cratchit do before he got up to put more coal in the fire?

2 **Scrooge** *(Looking up, angrily):* At three o'clock in the afternoon, Cratchit? Wasting coal, so close to closing time?

3 **Bob:** It's cold and foggy, sir. Penetrating . . .

4 **Scrooge:** Cold, nonsense! Haven't you a candle there on your desk?

5 **Bob:** Yes, sir. But the figures suffer when my hand shakes.

6 **Scrooge:** Warm your hands over the candle, then. How many times do I have to tell you? If you persist in being so **extravagant** with the coal, we shall have to part company, you and I. I can get another clerk, you know. More easily than you can get another position, I **warrant.**

---

solicitor   a salesperson
clerk   a person who keeps records in an office
ghost   the spirit of a dead person
carolers   people who sing Christmas songs

furtive   sneaky
coal   a mineral that people burn for heat
extravagant   using too much
warrant   guarantee

7 **Bob** *(Going back to stool):* Yes, sir. *(Rubs hands over candle. Huddles in muffler. After a moment of silence,* FRED *bursts into the room.)*

8 **Fred** *(Cheerfully):* A Merry Christmas, uncle! God save you!

9 **Scrooge** *(Without looking up):* Bah! **Humbug!**

10 **Fred:** Christmas is a humbug, uncle? You don't mean that, I am sure!

11 **Scrooge:** I do. Merry Christmas! What reason have you to be merry? You're poor enough.

12 **Fred:** Come, then, what reason have you to be dismal? You're rich enough.

13 **Scrooge** *(Banging down ruler):* Bah! Humbug!

14 **Fred:** Don't be **cross,** uncle.

15 **Scrooge:** What else can I be when I live in such a world of fools as this? What's a Christmas-time to you but a time for paying bills without money; a time for finding yourself a year older, and not an hour richer? If I could work my will, every idiot who goes about with "Merry Christmas" on his lips should be boiled with his own **pudding,** and buried with a **stake** of holly through his heart.

16 **Fred:** Uncle!

17 **Scrooge:** Keep Christmas in your own way, and let me keep it in mine. Much good it has ever done you.

18 **Fred:** I have always thought of Christmas-time as a good time . . . a kind, forgiving, **charitable,** pleasant time; the only time I know of when men and women seem by one consent to open their shut-up hearts freely . . . I say, God bless it! *(BOB claps his hands, then, embarrassed at his impulse, huddles over his work.)*

Use Chronology to Locate and Recall Information

What does Scrooge say after Fred wishes him Merry Christmas?

---

humbug an expression meaning "nonsense!"

cross angry

pudding a smooth, sweet dessert made with eggs and milk

stake a narrow, pointed piece of wood

charitable giving help or money to those who need it

19 **Scrooge** (*To* BOB)*:* Let me hear another sound from *you*, and you'll keep your Christmas by losing your position.

20 **Fred:** Don't be angry, uncle. Come, **dine** with us tomorrow.

21 **Scrooge:** Good afternoon!

22 **Fred:** I want nothing from you. I ask nothing of you. Why cannot we be friends?

23 **Scrooge:** Good afternoon!

24 **Fred** (*Shrugging, cheerfully*)*:* Well, Merry Christmas, uncle! And a happy New Year!

25 **Scrooge:** Good *afternoon!* (FRED *stops at* BOB'S *desk, and they exchange smiles and greetings.* BOB *goes with him to the door. As* FRED *exits, a* SOLICITOR *comes in with books and papers.* BOB **gestures** *him toward* SCROOGE *then goes back to his work.*)

Use Chronology to Locate and Recall Information

What is the last thing that Fred says to Scrooge?

26 **Solicitor:** Scrooge and Marley's, I believe? Have I the pleasure of addressing Mr. Scrooge or Mr. Marley?

27 **Scrooge:** Mr. Marley has been dead these seven years.

28 **Solicitor** (*Presenting credentials*)*:* At this **festive** season of the year, Mr. Scrooge, it is more than usually desirable that we should make some slight **provision** for the poor and **destitute** . . .

29 **Scrooge:** Are there no prisons? No workhouses?

30 **Solicitor:** There are. But, under the impression that they scarcely **furnish** Christian cheer, a few of us are **endeavoring** to raise a fund to buy the poor some meat and drink, and means of warmth. What shall I put you down for?

31 **Scrooge:** Nothing!

---

dine   eat a meal
gestures   makes a movement with the head or hand to show something
festive   joyful

provision   preparation
destitute   without any money or hope of having any
furnish   provide, give something
endeavoring   trying

32 **Solicitor:** You wish to be anonymous—is that it?

33 **Scrooge:** I wish to be left alone. I don't make merry myself at Christmas, and I can't afford to make idle people merry. Good afternoon, sir.

34 **Solicitor:** *Good afternoon!* (SOLICITOR *goes out, shaking his head.* BOB *opens door for him, then hurries back to his stool.*)

35 **Scrooge** *(Glaring at* BOB*):* You'll want all day tomorrow, I suppose?

36 **Bob:** If quite **convenient,** sir.

37 **Scrooge:** It's not convenient, and it's not fair.

38 **Bob:** It's only once a year, sir.

39 **Scrooge** *(Bangs down ruler):* A poor excuse for picking a man's pocket every twenty-fifth of December!

Use Chronology to Locate and Recall Information

What day is "tomorrow"? Use what you have read so far.

Curtain

Scene 3

40 **Before Rise:** MARLEY'S GHOST *and* THREE SPIRITS *appear in spotlight on darkened stage (or enter before curtain).*

41 **Marley:** There!

42 **1st Spirit:** I see what you mean, Mr. Marley. Ebenezer Scrooge is a bad case.

43 **2nd Spirit:** No wonder you need help, if you want to try to **reform** *him.*

44 **3rd Spirit:** He's been this way so long, I'm afraid it's a bad habit.

45 **Marley:** Surely we must try to save him, my friends. We can at least warn him, at least give him a chance to escape my **fate.** (*Clanks chain*) Poor man, he has no idea what lies ahead of him if he doesn't change his ways.

46 **1st Spirit:** What is your plan? How can we warn him? When?

---

convenient acceptable and suitable to one's time or needs

reform improve

fate the force that is thought to determine events

47 **Marley:** This very night of **Christmas Eve!** After closing the office, he will take his dinner in the usual tavern, read the papers, go over his accounts, and then home to bed. I know his lodgings well. Fact is, they used to belong to me. He will be quite alone in the house. I will appear before him as he gets drowsy.

48 **2nd Spirit:** Won't it be rather a **shock** to him—to see you?

49 **Marley:** He needs a shock to open his eyes, poor fellow.

50 **3rd Spirit:** And what about us? Where do we come in?

51 **Marley:** You wait in the shadows until I call you. First I must lay the groundwork. When I stand before Ebenezer in my usual waistcoat, tights, and boots, I will clank this **infernal** chain about my middle—this chain made of cash-boxes, keys, padlocks, **ledgers,** deeds, and heavy purses wrought in steel!

52 **1st Spirit:** He will be scared out of his wits!

53 **Marley:** He needs to be. I will tell him that he is forging a chain just like mine, that I have no rest, no peace, because in life my spirit never roved beyond the narrow limits of our **countinghouse.** It is no way to live.

54 **2nd Spirit:** Can a man of business understand such talk, Mr. Marley?

55 **Marley:** We must make him understand, my friends. We must get him to see that **mankind,** not money, is his business. That common welfare is his business. **Charity,** mercy, forbearance, and **benevolence** are all his business! And you are to impress it upon him.

56 **Spirits:** How?

Use Chronology to Locate and Recall Information

What is Mr. Marley going to do before he calls the spirits?

Christmas Eve the night before Christmas, December 24
shock surprise in a bad way
infernal terrible
ledgers journals in which numbers are recorded, especially for businesses

countinghouse a business office
mankind people
charity giving to the needy
benevolence kindness

Use Chronology to Locate and Recall Information

List in chronological order the events that the spirits will show Mr. Scrooge.

57 **Marley:** I will warn Ebenezer that he will be **haunted** by three Spirits in his sleep tonight. *(Points to* 1ST SPIRIT*)* As Ghost of Christmas Past, you will take him back to his life as a schoolboy and as an **apprentice,** and show him that Christmas meant something to him then. That he shouted "Merry Christmas" with the rest of them, in good spirit. *(Points to* 2ND SPIRIT*)* As Ghost of Christmas Present, you will show him how joyously his clerk Bob Cratchit will celebrate Christmas with his family tomorrow, for all Bob's **meager salary.** *(Points to* 3RD SPIRIT*)* And you, as Ghost of Christmas Yet to Come, will show him what will happen if he dies as he is—if he does not change.

58 **1st Spirit:** And all this to be done tonight?

59 **Marley:** Tonight, while Ebenezer Scrooge lies **abed.** Otherwise, we shall be too late for Christmas tomorrow.

60 **Spirits:** Lead on! We're with you! *(In a moment* BOY CAROLERS *come singing "God Rest You Merry, Gentlemen." After a stanza or two, they move on. A brief pause . . . then* SCROOGE *and* GHOST OF CHRISTMAS PAST *enter before curtain.)*

---

haunted   visited by ghosts
apprentice   a person who is learning a skill from an expert

meager   very little
salary   payment received for work
abed   an old way of saying "in bed"

About the Author Charles Dickens (1812–1870)

Charles Dickens grew up in London, England. At the age of 12, Dickens worked in a factory to help his family. Later, he wrote for a newspaper. In 1836, Dickens published his first book. Shortly after, he became very famous as a writer.

► Why do you think Charles Dickens wrote "A Christmas Carol"? To entertain or to give his opinion about greed?

Beyond the Reading

Reading Comprehension

Question-Answer Relationships (QAR)

"Right There" Questions

1. **Recall Facts** What is Bob Cratchit's job?
2. **Recall Facts** Who is Fred's uncle?
3. **Recall Facts** What is Mr. Scrooge's first name?

"Think and Search" Questions

4. **Identify** What is Marley's chain made of?
5. **Paraphrase** What does Marley want Mr. Scrooge to understand?
6. **Make Inferences** What does Marley think will happen to Mr. Scrooge if Scrooge does not change?

"Author and You" Questions

7. **Make Inferences** Do you think Marley was a nice person while he was alive? Why or why not?
8. **Analyze Characters** Why doesn't Mr. Scrooge want Bob Cratchit to use coal in the office?

9. **Analyze Characters** Why do you think Bob Cratchit continues to work for Mr. Scrooge?
10. **Analyze Conflict** What is the conflict between Scrooge and his nephew, Fred?

"On Your Own" Questions

11. **Predict** Do you think Mr. Scrooge will change after the three spirits visit him? Why or why not?
12. **Understand Setting** Why do you think this play is set during Christmas?
13. **Compare Communication** Read the same passage in Dickens's novel or view these scenes in the film version. How are these versions the same or different? What did you learn from the other version?

Activity Book
p. 186

Student
CD-ROM

Build Reading Fluency

Audio CD Reading Practice

Listening to the Audio CD of "Mr. Scrooge Finds Christmas" is good reading practice. It helps you to learn to read with expression.

1. Listen to Scene 2 on the Audio CD.
2. Follow along in your student book on page 354.
3. Listen to the phrases, pauses, and expression of the reader.

Listen, Speak, Interact

Present a Scene from the Play

Work with a group to present a scene from "Mr. Scrooge Finds Christmas."

1. Meet with three other students. You will present Scene 2 or Scene 3 of the selection.
2. Each student should play a character.
3. With your group, read the scene aloud. Practice it a few times. Use gestures, tone of voice, and pitch to show what your character is feeling and to engage your listeners.
4. Present your scene to your class. If you can, memorize your part.
5. Evaluate each other's presentations for content, credibility, and delivery.

Elements of Literature

Recognize Dialogue and Stage Directions

In a play, **stage directions** tell what the characters are supposed to do. Stage directions are often in parentheses (. . .). Sometimes, they are also in *italic* type.

> **Scrooge:** *(Banging down ruler)* Bah! Humbug!

1. With a partner, read these lines from the selection.

> **Solicitor:** Good afternoon! *(SOLICITOR goes out, shaking his head. BOB opens door for him, then hurries back to his stool.)*
>
> **Scrooge** *(Glaring at BOB):* You'll want all day tomorrow, I suppose?

2. Use the stage directions and act out these lines. Speak slowly, clearly, and loudly. Use a tone that helps the listener understand your mood. Use nonverbal language such as gestures.
3. Listen to your partner's interpretation of these lines. Interpret the use of verbal and nonverbal language. Is your partner credible (believable)? Are you persuaded that your partner is expressing true feelings?

Activity Book
p. 187

Student
CD-ROM

Word Study

Analyze Contractions

You form **contractions** by joining two words together. You also drop some letters from the second word. In their place, put an apostrophe (').

do + not ➡ don't

1. Copy this chart.
2. In the chart, list the contractions.
3. Write the two words that form each contraction.

Sentences	Contractions	Words in Contractions
You're rich enough!	you're	you are
You'll be happy.		
It's not convenient.		

Note: Don't confuse *it's* (it is) with *its* (the possessive): The dog wagged <u>its</u> tail.

Activity Book p. 188   Student CD-ROM

Grammar Focus

Use the Present Perfect Tense

The **present perfect tense** is used to show that something started in the past and continues up to the present.

Mr. Marley has been dead these seven years.

Study the chart to learn how to form the present perfect tense.

Copy and complete these sentences. Use the present perfect tense of the verbs in parentheses.

1. We _____ in Houston for two years. (live)
2. My mother _____ at the bank for a long time. (work)
3. I _____ soccer for six years. (play)

Present Perfect Tense			
Subject	**Auxiliary Verb**	**Past Participle**	**Rest of Sentence**
I You We They	have	lived	here for one year.
He She It	has		

Activity Book pp. 189–190   Student Handbook   Student CD-ROM

From Reading to Writing

Write a Persuasive Letter

When you persuade, you cause a person to believe or do something.

With a partner, write a persuasive letter to Mr. Scrooge. Try to persuade him to give money to needy people.

1. Organize your letter.
   a. List two reasons why he should give money to needy people.
   b. List one reason why he might not want to give money to needy people. Give your opinion of this reason.
2. Compose your persuasive letter.
3. Reread your letter to evaluate if it achieves its purpose.

> (Date)
>
> Dear Mr. Scrooge,
>
> I think that you should give money to needy people. One reason is that _____ .
>
> Another reason is that _____ . I know that you do not want to do this. You think that _____ . But I think that _____ .
>
> I hope this letter has persuaded you.
>
> Yours truly,
>
> _____

Activity Book
p. 191

Student Handbook

Across Content Areas

MATH

Answer Math Questions About Currency

Currency is money. In the United States, the currency is made up of **coins** and paper **dollars.**

1. Look at the chart. It tells you how much the currency is worth.
2. Work with a partner to solve this math problem.

Nick has 5 quarters, 3 dimes, and 2 nickels. Dean has 4 quarters, 5 dimes, 3 nickels, and 6 pennies. How much money does each boy have? Who has more money?

Currency	Worth	
penny	1 cent	$ .01
nickel	5 cents	$ .05
dime	10 cents	$ .10
quarter	25 cents	$ .25
dollar	100 cents	$1.00

Activity Book
p. 192

The House on Mango Street

an excerpt from a novel
by Sandra Cisneros

Objectives

Reading Paraphrase to recall information as you read an excerpt from a novel.

Listening and Speaking Talk about mental images.

Grammar Spell frequently misspelled words.

Writing Write a description.

Content Science: Learn about animal habitats.

Use Prior Knowledge

Talk About the Meanings of *Home*

The place where you live is your home. This is the **denotative** definition of *home*—the definition that you find in a dictionary.

Home also has many **connotative** meanings—feelings and attitudes that the word *home* makes you think of. For example, when you hear the word *home*, you may think of a warm, safe place.

1. Work with a partner. Talk about the denotative and connotative meanings of the word *home*.
2. Write your ideas in a Cluster Map like this one.

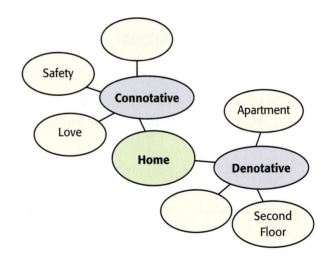

3. With your classmates, talk about the connotative meanings that are most important to you.

Build Background

Chicago

The selection you will read takes place in Chicago, Illinois. Chicago is the third largest city in the United States, with a population of about three million. It is located on Lake Michigan. People from many different cultures live in Chicago. The city has many different ethnic neighborhoods—areas where people of the same culture live.

SOCIAL STUDIES

Content Connection

Chicago became a city in 1837. Chicago is a major center for business and industry.

Build Vocabulary

Identify Antonyms

Antonyms are words that have opposite meanings. For example, the antonym of *large* is *small*. Using antonyms can help you make your writing more precise.

1. Read each of the following sentences. Choose the correct antonym for each underlined word. Use a dictionary or ask your teacher.
2. Choose two antonyms. Use them in a sentence. Write the sentences in your Personal Dictionary.

a. There is no <u>front</u> yard, only four little elms by the curb. (back/side)

b. There are stairs in our house, but they are <u>straight</u> hallway stairs. (plain/crooked)

c. "For the time being," says Mama. "<u>Temporary</u>," says Papa. (permanent/changing)

Personal Dictionary   The Heinle Newbury House Dictionary   Activity Book *p. 193*   Student CD-ROM

Text Structure

Fiction

Fiction is a type of story that includes characters and events imagined by the author. Look for the features of fiction as you read "The House on Mango Street."

The events that happen in the story make up the **plot.** When you read fiction, the author wants you to follow the plot to find out how the story ends.

Fiction	
Characters	The people in the story are made up.
Events	The things that happen in the story are made up.
Setting	The events happen in a certain time and place.

Student
CD-ROM

Reading Strategy

Paraphrase to Recall Information

When you **paraphrase,** you state what the author says, but you use your own words. Paraphrasing can help you remember information that you read.

1. To paraphrase, follow these steps.
   a. Read the part of the text that you are going to paraphrase several times, until you are sure you know what it means.
   b. Close your book. Write or say the meaning of the text in your own words.
   c. Open your book and check your paraphrase against the text. Did you include all or most of the information? Did you use your own words?

2. Paraphrase this part of the text.

   The house on Mango Street is ours, we don't have to pay rent to anybody. . .

3. As you read the selection, paraphrase parts of it that you want to remember.

Student
CD-ROM

The House
on Mango Street

an excerpt from a novel
by Sandra Cisneros

Audio
CD 3, Tr. 7

1   We didn't always live on Mango Street. Before that we lived on Loomis on the third floor, and before that we lived on Keeler. Before Keeler it was Paulina, and before that I can't remember. But what I remember most is moving a lot. Each time it seemed there'd be one more of us. By the time we got to Mango Street we were six—Mama, Papa, Carlos, Kiki, my sister Nenny and me.

2   The house on Mango Street is ours, we don't have to pay **rent** to anybody, or share the yard with the people downstairs, or be careful not to make too much noise, and there isn't a **landlord** banging on the ceiling with a broom. But even so, it's not the house we'd thought we'd get.

3   We had to leave the **flat** on Loomis quick. The water pipes broke and the landlord wouldn't fix them because the house was too old. We had to leave fast. We were using the **washroom** next door and carrying water over in empty milk gallons. That's why Mama and Papa looked for a house, and that's why we moved into the house on Mango Street, far away, on the other side of town.

> **Paraphrase to Recall Information**
>
> Paraphrase the first sentence of this paragraph.

---

rent   the amount of money paid to live somewhere

landlord   a person who owns land that he or she rents to others

flat   an apartment

washroom   a bathroom

4   They always told us that one day we would move into a house, a real house that would be ours for always so we wouldn't have to move each year. And our house would have running water and **pipes** that worked. And inside it would have real stairs, not hallway stairs, but stairs inside like the houses on T.V. And we'd have a basement and at least three washrooms so when we took a bath we wouldn't have to tell everybody. Our house would be white with trees around it, a great big yard and grass growing without a fence. This was the house Papa talked about when he held a **lottery** ticket and this was the house Mama dreamed up in the stories she told us before we went to bed.

Paraphrase to Recall Information

Paraphrase the first two sentences in this paragraph.

5   But the house on Mango Street is not the way they told it at all. It's small and red with tight steps in front and windows so small you'd think they were holding their breath. Bricks are **crumbling** in places, and the front door is so **swollen** you have to push hard to get in. There is no front yard, only four little elms the city planted by the curb. Out back is a small garage for the car we don't own yet and a small yard that looks smaller between the two buildings on either side. There are stairs in our house, but they're **ordinary** hallway stairs, and the house has only one washroom. Everybody has to share a bedroom—Mama and Papa, Carlos and Kiki, me and Nenny.

---

pipes   tubes through which liquids pass
lottery   a game in which people buy tickets with numbers

crumbling   falling into pieces
swollen   increased in size
ordinary   normal, regular

Paraphrase to Recall Information

Paraphrase the first sentence of this paragraph.

6   Once when we were living on Loomis, a **nun** from my school passed by and saw me playing out front. The **laundromat** downstairs had been boarded up because it had been **robbed** two days before and the owner had painted on the wood YES WE'RE OPEN so as not to lose business.

7   Where do you live? she asked.

8   There, I said pointing up to the third floor.

9   You live *there*?

10   *There.* I had to look to where she pointed—the third floor, the paint peeling, wooden bars Papa had nailed on the windows so we wouldn't fall out. You live *there*? The way she said it made me feel like nothing. *There.* I lived *there.* I nodded.

---

nun   a woman in a religious group
laundromat   a place to clean clothes

robbed   stole something from someone

Paraphrase to Recall Information

Paraphrase this paragraph.

11   I knew then I had to have a house. A real house. One I could point to. But this isn't it. The house on Mango Street isn't it. **For the time being,** Mama says. **Temporary,** says Papa. But I know how those things go.

---

for the time being   for a brief time   **temporary**   for the time being

About the Author

Sandra Cisneros (born 1954)

Sandra Cisneros was born in Chicago, Illinois. As a child, Cisneros lived in a Spanish-speaking neighborhood like the one in "The House on Mango Street." After college, she worked as a teacher. In 1984, she published "The House on Mango Street." Cisneros has also written many novels, several books of poetry, and a book of short stories. She writes in English and in Spanish.

► Why do you think Cisneros wrote about the neighborhood she chose? What challenges do you think she faced in becoming a successful writer?

Beyond the Reading

Reading Comprehension

Question-Answer Relationships (QAR)

"Right There" Questions

1. **Recall Facts** How many people are in the family?
2. **Recall Facts** How many times can the author remember moving?

"Think and Search" Questions

3. **Explain** Why did the family move out of the apartment on Loomis?
4. **Describe** Describe the house that Papa talked about and Mama dreamed up in stories.
5. **Describe** Describe the house on Mango Street.

"Author and You" Question

6. **Identify the Narrator** Who do you think is telling the story? How old do you think the narrator is? What makes you think this?

"On Your Own" Questions

7. **Analyze Characters** Do you think the narrator is happy with the house on Mango Street? Why do you think this?
8. **Appreciate Writer's Craft** Why do you think the author is famous for her writing?
9. **Monitor Comprehension** When you had difficulty understanding the reading, what did you do? Did you reread the sentences? Did you look for clues? Did you read more slowly?
10. **Discover Models** How can you use this selection as a model for your writing?

Activity Book
p. 194

Student
CD-ROM

Build Reading Fluency

Read Aloud to Engage Listeners

Reading aloud helps increase your fluency and expression. Learning to read with expression makes others want to listen to you.

1. Listen to the audio recording of "The House on Mango Street."
2. Turn to page 368 and follow along.
3. Pay attention to phrasing and expression.
4. With a partner, read aloud paragraphs 1–2 three times.
5. Select your favorite paragraph.
6. Read in front of the class with expression.

Listen, Speak, Interact

Talk About Mental Images

With your classmates, talk about your mental images of the house on Mango Street. Images are the pictures you make in your mind.

1. Listen to the audio recording of paragraphs 4 and 5 of the selection.
2. Close your eyes as you listen. Pay attention to the pictures you make in your mind.
3. Draw pictures of your images of how the real house and the imaginary house look.
4. Describe your pictures to a small group.
5. Listen to the entire recording. What effect does the author's choice of language have on you? What is the author's perspective?

Elements of Literature

Recognize First-Person Narratives

A narrative is often the telling of a story. Sometimes a character in the narrative tells the story. The character uses the pronouns *I, me, we,* and *us* to tell the story. This is called a **first-person narrative.**

1. Using the chart, find three sentences in "The House on Mango Street" that show first-person narrative. Look in paragraphs 4, 10, and 11.
2. Write the sentences in your Reading Log. Underline the pronouns *I, we, me,* and *us.*
3. Write a first-person narrative that is one paragraph long.
4. Share your narrative with a partner.

First-Person Narrative		
Who?	**How?**	**Example**
A character in the narrative tells the story.	The character uses the pronouns *I, me, we,* and *us.*	We didn't always live on Mango Street.

Reading Log   Activity Book *p. 195*   Student CD-ROM

Word Study

Learn English Words from Other Languages

Many words in English come from other languages. Knowing about word origins helps you understand historical influences of other languages and cultures on English. People from many countries live in English-speaking countries. They bring their languages and cultures with them. English speakers borrow or adapt some of their words. Here are some examples.

mango (Tamil)   *lottery* (Dutch)

magazine (Arabic)   *kindergarten* (German)

ranch (Spanish)

Complete these sentences with one of the examples. Use a dictionary for words you don't know.

1. My sister is not in first grade yet. She is still in _____ .
2. I had nothing to do, so I decided to read a _____ .
3. This _____ is delicious!
4. We keep sheep on our _____ .

Personal Dictionary	The Heinle Newbury House Dictionary	Activity Book p. 196	Student CD-ROM

Grammar Focus

Spell Frequently Misspelled Words

Some words are pronounced the same, but they have different spellings and meanings.

The words *their, there,* and *they're* all sound the same. However, they are different parts of speech and have different meanings.

1. Read paragraphs 2, 5, and 9 of "The House on Mango Street."
2. Find sentences with *there* and *they're*.
3. Write three sentences of your own using each of these words. Be sure to use the correct part of speech in your sentence.

There, They're, and *Their*		
Word	**Meaning**	**Sentence**
there	Meaning 1: at or to a specific place	The play starts at seven, and I must be *there* by six.
	Meaning 2: to indicate a place	That chair over *there* is broken.
	Meaning 3: to begin a statement	*There* is still time before school starts.
they're	the contraction of *they are*	*They're* going to the movies.
their	possessive form of *they*	*Their* house was on Mango Street.

Activity Book pp. 197–198	Student Handbook	Student CD-ROM

From Reading to Writing

Write a Description

Write a five-paragraph description of a place where you have lived or want to live.

1. Choose a genre such as a letter, science fiction, or realistic fiction.
2. Decide on your purpose. For example, do you want to entertain the reader or to discover your own thoughts and feelings?
3. Use technology to create, revise, and edit your work.
4. As you write, answer these questions:
   a. Where is the place?
   b. How do you know about it?
   c. What is it like?
   d. Why do you want to live there?
5. Revise your draft.
   a. Blend your paragraphs by using transitional words.
   b. Use conjunctions and dependent clauses to combine some of your short sentences into longer ones.
   c. Rearrange some of your sentences if necessary.
   d. Use vivid adjectives and adverbs and prepositional phrases to describe the place.
6. Write a final draft. Include a visual. Present your work to the class.

Activity Book
p. 199

Student
Handbook

Across Content Areas

SCIENCE

Learn About Animal Habitats

Habitats are places where animals live. There are different habitats for different animals.

cave a hole in the ground, usually with an opening in the side of a hill

desert a place with little or no rain and large areas of sand and rock

jungle a hot, rainy place with many trees and plants

tundra a very cold area with no trees near the Arctic

What do you think is the habitat of each of these animals? Use references and resources to help you.

monitor lizard	cave
bat	desert
chimpanzee	jungle
polar bear	tundra

Activity Book
p. 200

The Pearl

an excerpt from a novel
by John Steinbeck

Reading Make inferences using text evidence as you read an excerpt from a novel.

Listening and Speaking Listen to and present the story.

Grammar Use conjunctions to form compound sentences.

Writing Write a fiction story.

Content Social Studies: Learn about bodies of water.

Use Prior Knowledge

Talk About the Ocean

The ocean is very important to people. We get food from it, we travel on it, and we have fun in it.

1. Copy the Cluster Map on a piece of paper.
2. With a partner, add your ideas to the Cluster Map.
3. Discuss the ideas with your partner.
4. Choose one idea cluster. Present your ideas to the class.

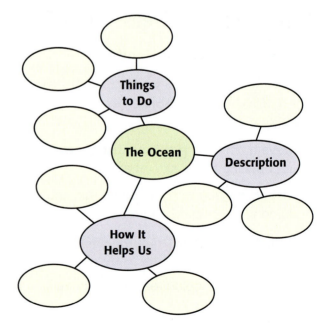

Build Background

Oysters

Oysters are types of shellfish (water animals with outer shells). They mainly live in large bodies of water along the coast (the part of water near land). Many people like to eat oysters. Some oysters have pearls in their shells. Pearls are white, round jewels. People have used pearls to make jewelry for thousands of years.

SOCIAL STUDIES

Content Connection

The largest pearl ever discovered was found in the Philippines in 1934. It weighed more than 14 pounds.

Build Vocabulary

Locate Pronunciations and Derivations

When you look up the meaning of a new word in a dictionary, you can also find its pronunciation and its derivation (origin).

1. Read these dictionary entries for words from "The Pearl."
   a. What is the definition?
   b. Find the pronunciation. Your teacher will show you how to use the symbols.
   c. What is the derivation of the word? Which language does it come from originally?
2. For each word, write a sentence in your Personal Dictionary.

stern /stɜrn/ *n* the rear section of a ship [Middle English *sterne*]

coordination /koʊˌɔrdn'eɪʃən/ *n* the act of making arrangements for a purpose [Latin *ōrdinātiō*, arrangement]

decorate /'dɛkəˌreɪt/ *v* to beautify, make festive [Latin *decorāre*, to beautify]

Personal Dictionary

The Heinle Newbury House Dictionary

Activity Book *p. 201*

Student CD-ROM

Text Structure

Realistic Fiction

"The Pearl" is **realistic fiction.** This type of story includes made-up characters and events that could be real. Take notes in your Reading Log as you read the selection. Think about the following points.

1. Analyze the characters' traits, motivations, and relationships.
2. What problems do the characters have? How do the characters change?
3. What is the story setting? Analyze it. How does it contribute to the effect of the story?
4. Summarize the story plot. How do you think the characters' problems will be resolved?

Realistic Fiction	
Characters	The people in the story act like real people. They have traits, motivations, problems, and relationships.
Setting	The story happens in a real place.
Plot	The story has a beginning, a middle, and an end. The events of the story could happen in real life.

Reading Log   Student CD-ROM

Reading Strategy

Make Inferences Using Text Evidence

You learned that you can **make inferences** as you read. When you make inferences, you use **text evidence.** Remember that text evidence is the information in a selection. You also use your knowledge and experience.

Read these sentences. What inference can you make?

> John got off his bike. Sweat was dripping from his brow and he was breathing heavily.

You may know that you sweat and breathe heavily after a long bike ride. You can make an inference that John just finished a bike ride.

Make inferences based on text evidence, your knowledge, and experiences as you read "The Pearl."

Student CD-ROM

The Pearl

an excerpt from a novel
by John Steinbeck

Prologue

The main character of this story is Kino, a poor Native American man living in Mexico. Kino is a pearl diver (a person who looks for pearls in the sea). He lives in a small Indian village in Mexico with his wife, Juana, and his baby son, Coyotito. Coyotito becomes sick after he is stung by a scorpion. (A scorpion is a type of spider with poison in its long, pointed tail.) Kino and Juana do not have money to pay a doctor to take care of Coyotito. When the reading begins, the family goes out to sea in their small boat. Kino hopes that he will find a pearl that he can sell for money.

1   Now Kino and Juana slid the canoe down the beach to the water, and when the bow floated, Juana climbed in, while Kino pushed the stern in and waded beside it until it floated lightly and trembled on the little breaking waves. Then in coordination Juana and Kino drove their double-bladed paddles into the sea, and the canoe creased the water and hissed with speed. The other **pearlers** were gone out long since. In a few moments Kino could see them clustered in the **haze,** riding over the oyster bed.

2   Light **filtered** down through the water to the bed where the **frilly** pearl oysters lay fastened to the rubbly bottom, a bottom **strewn** with shells of broken, opened oysters. This was the bed that had raised the King of Spain to be a great power in Europe in past years, had helped to pay for his wars, and had decorated the churches for his soul's sake. The gray oysters with ruffles like skirts on the shells, the **barnacle**-crusted oysters with little bits of weed **clinging** to

Make Inferences Using Text Evidence

What inference can you make about oysters in this paragraph? What text evidence tells you this?

---

pearlers   people who look for pearls
haze   a condition in the air similar to light fog
filtered   passed through
frilly   decorated like a lace border

strewn   scattered
barnacle   a small shellfish that grows on rocks and the bottoms of ships
clinging   holding closely or tightly

the skirts and small crabs climbing over them. An accident could happen to these oysters, a **grain** of sand could lie in the folds of muscle and **irritate** the flesh until in self-protection the flesh coated the grain with a layer of smooth **cement.** But once started, the flesh continued to coat the foreign body until it fell free in some **tidal flurry** or until the oyster was destroyed. For centuries men had dived down and torn the oysters from the beds and ripped them open, looking for the coated grains of sand. **Swarms** of fish lived near the bed to live near the oysters thrown back by the searching men and to **nibble** at the shining inner shells. But the pearls were accidents, and the finding of one was luck, a little pat on the back by God or the gods or both.

3   Kino had two ropes, one tied to a heavy stone and one to a basket. He stripped off his shirt and trousers and laid his hat in the bottom of the canoe. The water was oily smooth. He took his rock in one hand and his basket in the other, and he slipped feet first over the side and the rock carried him to the bottom. The bubbles rose behind him until the water cleared and he could see. Above, the surface of the water was an **undulating** mirror of brightness, and he could see the bottoms of the canoes sticking through it.

Make Inferences Using Text Evidence

Why does Kino have one rope tied to a heavy stone? What experience tells you this?

---

grain   a very small, hard piece of something
irritate   annoy, bother
cement   a substance that holds things together
tidal   referring to the rise and fall of the ocean's surface

flurry   a rush of activity
swarms   large groups of people or animals
nibble   take small bites
undulating   moving in a waving motion

4   Kino moved **cautiously** so that the water would not be **obscured** with mud or sand. He hooked his foot in the loop on his rock and his hands worked quickly, tearing the oysters loose, some singly, others in clusters. He laid them in his basket. In some places the oysters clung to one another so that they came free in lumps.

5   Now, Kino's people had sung of everything that happened or existed. They had made songs to the fishes, to the sea in anger and to the sea in calm, to the light and the dark and the sun and the moon, and the songs were all in Kino and in his people—every song that had ever been made, even the ones forgotten. And as he filled his basket the song was in Kino, and the beat of the song was his pounding heart as it ate the **oxygen** from his held breath, and the **melody** of the song was the gray-green water and the little **scuttling** animals and the clouds of fish that flitted by and were gone. But in the song there was a secret little inner song, hardly **perceptible,** but always there, sweet and

Make Inferences Using Text Evidence

What inference can you make about Kino? What text evidence tells you this?

cautiously   carefully
obscured   hidden from view
oxygen   a gas in the air that living things need

melody   a song
scuttling   moving quickly
perceptible   capable of being seen

secret and clinging, almost hiding in the counter-melody, and this was the Song of the Pearl That Might Be, for every shell thrown in the basket might contain a pearl. Chance was against it, but luck and the gods might be for it. And in the canoe above him Kino knew that Juana was making the magic of prayer, her face set **rigid** and her muscles hard to force the luck, to tear the luck out of the gods' hands, for she needed the luck for the **swollen** shoulder of Coyotito. And because the need was great and the desire was great, the little secret melody of the pearl that might be was stronger this morning. Whole phrases of it came clearly and softly into the Song of the Undersea.

6   Kino, in his pride and youth and strength, could remain down over two minutes without strain, so that he worked **deliberately,** selecting the largest shells. Because they were disturbed, the oyster shells were tightly closed. A little to his right a **hummock** of rubbly rock stuck up, covered with young oysters not ready to take. Kino moved next to the hummock, and then, beside it, under a little overhang, he saw a very large oyster lying by itself, not covered with its clinging brothers. The shell was partly open, for the overhang protected this ancient oyster, and in the lip-like muscle Kino saw a ghostly **gleam,** and then the shell closed down. His heart beat out a heavy rhythm and the melody of the maybe pearl **shrilled** in his ears.

Make Inferences Using Text Evidence

Why does Kino work "deliberately"? What text evidence tells you this?

---

rigid stiff
swollen enlarged in size
deliberately slowly, carefully

hummock a small mound or hill
gleam a bright light
shrilled made a high-pitched sound

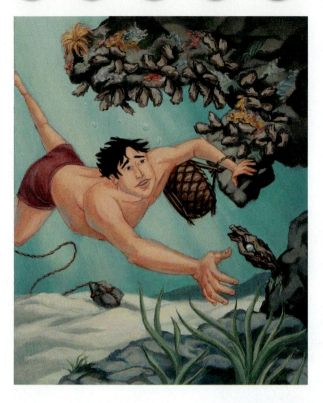

Slowly he forced the oyster loose and held it tightly against his breast. He kicked his foot free from the rock loop, and his body rose to the surface and his black hair gleamed in the sunlight. He reached over the side of the canoe and laid the oyster in the bottom.

7   Then Juana **steadied** the boat while he climbed in. His eyes were shining with excitement, but in **decency** he pulled up his rock, and then he pulled up his basket of oysters and lifted them in. Juana sensed his excitement, and she pretended to look away. It is not good to want a thing too much. It sometimes drives the luck away. You must want it just enough, and you must be very **tactful** with God or the gods. But Juana stopped breathing.

Make Inferences Using Text Evidence

Why does Juana steady the boat? What experience or knowledge tells you?

---

steadied   made firm

decency   respectful concern for doing the right thing

tactful   careful in dealing with

Very deliberately Kino opened his short strong knife. He looked **speculatively** at the basket. Perhaps it would be better to open *the* oyster last. He took a small oyster from the basket, cut the muscle, searched the folds of flesh, and threw it in the water. Then he seemed to see the great oyster for the first time. He squatted in the bottom of the canoe, picked up the shell and examined it. The **flutes** were shining black to brown, and only a few small barnacles **adhered** to the shell. Now Kino was **reluctant** to open it. What he had seen, he knew, might be a reflection, a piece of flat shell accidentally drifted in or a complete **illusion.** In this Gulf of uncertain light there were more illusions than realities.

8   But Juana's eyes were on him and she could not wait. She put her hand on Coyotito's covered head. "Open it," she said softly.

Make Inferences Using Text Evidence

How do you think Juana is feeling as Kino looks at the oysters? What experience tells you this?

---

speculatively in an uncertain way
flutes long, round holes
adhered attached to

reluctant not wanting to do something
illusion an idea that is not real

9   Kino **deftly** slipped his knife into the edge of the shell. Through the knife he could feel the muscle tighten hard. He worked the blade lever-wise and the closing muscle parted and the shell fell apart. The lip-like flesh **writhed** up and then **subsided.** Kino lifted the flesh, and there it lay, the great pearl, perfect as the moon. It captured the light and **refined** it and gave it back in silver **incandescence.** It was as large as a sea-gull's egg. It was the greatest pearl in the world.

10   Juana caught her breath and moaned a little. And to Kino the secret melody of the maybe pearl broke clear and beautiful, rich and warm and lovely, glowing and **gloating** and **triumphant.** In the surface of the great pearl he could see dream forms. He picked the pearl from the dying flesh and held it in his palm, and he turned it over and saw that its curve was perfect. Juana came near to stare at it in his hand, and it was the hand he had smashed against the doctor's gate, and the torn flesh of the knuckles was turned grayish white by the sea water.

Make Inferences Using Text Evidence

What do you think Kino was thinking as he looked at the pearl? What experience tells you this?

---

deftly   skillfully
writhed   twisted and turned in pain
subsided   became less strong
refined   made finer; improved

incandescence   a bright shining light
gloating   showing great pleasure, bragging
triumphant   successful

11   **Instinctively** Juana went to Coyotito where he lay on his father's blanket. She lifted the **poultice** of seaweed and looked at the shoulder. "Kino," she cried shrilly.

12   He looked past his pearl, and he saw that the swelling was going out of the baby's shoulder, the **poison** was **receding** from its body. Then Kino's fist closed over the pearl and his emotion broke over him. He put back his head and **howled.** His eyes rolled up and he screamed and his body was rigid. The men in the other canoes looked up, startled, and then they dug their paddles into the sea and raced toward Kino's canoe.

Make Inferences Using Text Evidence

Why do you think emotion broke over Kino? What text evidence tells you this?

---

instinctively in a way that is done from feeling instead of knowledge

poultice a mixture of herbs placed on the body as medicine

poison a substance that may hurt or kill people, animals, and plants

receding lessening

howled cried loudly

About the Author   John Steinbeck (1902–1968)

John Steinbeck was born in Salinas, California. By the age of 15, he was writing short stories and sending them to publishing companies. He went to Stanford University. He then worked as a writer. John Steinbeck wrote many books and became famous. Some of his best known works are *Of Mice and Men, The Grapes of Wrath,* and *East of Eden.* Steinbeck received awards for his writing, including the Pulitzer Prize and the Nobel Prize. He also spent time studying sea life. John Steinbeck is remembered as one of the greatest writers of the 20th century.

► How do you think John Steinbeck got the information and background knowledge he needed to write *The Pearl?* What strategies did he use? What questions would you ask him?

Beyond the Reading

Reading Comprehension

Question-Answer Relationships (QAR)

"Right There" Questions

1. **Recall Facts** What is the name of Kino and Juana's baby?
2. **Recall Facts** Kino uses two ropes when he dives. What are they tied to? Why?

"Think and Search" Question

3. **Explain** How do the pearlers find pearls?

"Author and You" Questions

4. **Analyze Characters** Why do you think Kino dives for oysters?
5. **Recognize Symbolism** What does the pearl symbolize (represent) to Kino and Juana?
6. **Analyze Organization** How does the author organize and present the story? Is it chronological? How does he tell the reader about past events?

"On Your Own" Questions

7. **Recognize Character Traits** How do you think Kino feels after finding the pearl? How do you think Kino feels after seeing the swelling go down in Coyotito's shoulder?
8. **Predict** What do you think Kino will do with the pearl?
9. **Raise Questions** Based on what you read and on your own knowledge, what additional questions would you ask about this story?

Activity Book
p. 202

Student
CD-ROM

Build Reading Fluency

Repeated Reading

Repeated reading helps increase your reading rate and builds confidence. Each time you reread, you improve your reading fluency.

1. Turn to page 380.
2. Your teacher or partner will time you for six minutes.
3. With a partner, take turns reading each paragraph aloud.
4. Stop after six minutes.

Listen, Speak, Interact

Listen to and Present the Story

Understand and enjoy the story by listening to it and then acting it out.

1. With your class, listen to the audio recording of the story.
   a. What effect does the telling of the story have on you?
   b. Take notes on the main ideas.
   c. Monitor your understanding and ask for clarification if you don't understand something.

2. With a partner, act out a part of the story for your classmates.
   a. Write out dialogue and stage directions.
   b. Use gestures and nonverbal language.

3. Watch and listen to your classmates' presentations. Evaluate their performances. Were they believable? Did they tell the story accurately?

Elements of Literature

Analyze Plot and Problem Resolution

The **plot** is the main events that make up a story. A story's plot usually has a beginning, a middle, and an end. The chart shows what happens in each part.

Decide if each sentence below: (a) introduces the problem; (b) shows how the character tries to solve the problem; or (c) shows how the problem is resolved.

1. Then Kino's fist closed over the pearl and his emotion broke over him.
2. But the pearls were accidents, and the finding of one was luck.
3. Slowly he forced the oyster loose and held it tightly against his breast.

The Plot of a Story

Beginning
Characters and setting are introduced. A problem is introduced.

Middle
The characters try to solve the problem.

End
The characters solve the problem.

Activity Book
p. 203

Student
CD-ROM

Word Study

Learn Words from Latin

The spelling of many English words has been influenced by other languages and cultures. The word *pretended* is used in "The Pearl." This word comes from the Latin word *tendere* meaning *to stretch*.

The words listed in the box also come from *tendere*.

attend be present at

extend make longer in space and time; stretch out

intend plan to do something

intense strong in feeling or emotion; concentrated

Complete each sentence with the correct word from the box.

1. The store is going to _____ its business hours.
2. Will you _____ the party?
3. She showed _____ happiness at her wedding.
4. I _____ to finish my homework.

Personal Dictionary

The Heinle Newbury House Dictionary

Activity Book *p. 204*

Student CD-ROM

Grammar Focus

Use Conjunctions to Form Compound Sentences

You have learned that a clause is a part of a sentence. It has a subject and a verb. A **conjunction** is a word that connects two clauses in a sentence to make a compound sentence. Some words that can be used as conjunctions are *and, but, or,* and *because.*

In the sentence below, the conjunction is circled. The subject of each clause is underlined once. The verb is underlined twice.

Then Kino's <u>fist</u> <u>closed</u> over the pearl (and) his <u>emotion</u> <u>broke</u> over him.

1. Copy these sentences on a piece of paper.
   a. Because they were disturbed, the oyster shells were tightly closed.
   b. He never found a pearl before, but today he was lucky.
   c. Juana sensed his excitement, and she pretended to look away.
2. Circle the conjunction in each sentence. Underline the subject of each clause once and the verb twice.

Activity Book *pp. 205–206*

Student Handbook

Student CD-ROM

From Reading to Writing

Write a Fiction Story

Make up a story about someone who solves a problem.

1. Your story should have a beginning, a middle, and an end.
2. Use conjunctions to make compound sentences in your story.
3. Combine other sentences into complex sentences using words like *when, while, if,* and *that.*
4. Be sure your clauses have a subject and a verb, and that the subjects and verbs agree.
5. Select reference materials, such as your Student Handbook, for revising and for editing final drafts.
6. As you revise and edit, decide if you need to elaborate—say more about—any of your ideas.

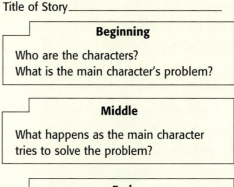

Title of Story_____

Beginning

Who are the characters?
What is the main character's problem?

Middle

What happens as the main character tries to solve the problem?

End

What happens when the main character solves the problem?

Student Handbook

The Heinle Newbury House Dictionary

Activity Book *p. 207*

Student CD-ROM

Across Content Areas

  SOCIAL STUDIES

Learn About Bodies of Water

More than 70% of the earth's surface is covered with water. Water is found in oceans, seas, lakes, rivers, and waterfalls. Look at the chart. It shows information about some bodies of water. Use a globe or world map to locate each place.

Activity Book *p. 208*

Largest Ocean	Pacific Ocean	area: 64,186,000 square miles (166,241,000 sq. km.)
Largest Sea	South China Sea	area: 1,149,000 square miles (2,974,600 sq. km.)
Largest Lake	Caspian Sea, Europe-Asia	area: 143,245 square miles (371,000 sq. km.)
Largest River	Nile River, Africa	length: 4,241 miles (6,825 km.)
Largest Waterfall	Angel Falls, Venezuela	height: 3,281 feet (979 meters)

CHAPTER 4

What Will Our Towns Look Like?

an article on the World Wide Web by Martha Pickerill

Objectives

Reading Summarize text to recall ideas as you read an article on the World Wide Web.

Listening and Speaking Give a persuasive speech.

Grammar Use *will* to predict future events.

Writing Create a form, interview, and summarize.

Content Science: Learn about acid rain.

Use Prior Knowledge

Test Your Knowledge of Natural Resources

In this chapter, you will read about natural resources. Natural resources are things from nature that people use.

1. Test what you already know about natural resources. Decide if each of these statements is true or false.
   a. We can use as many natural resources as we want. The earth will make more.
   b. We can help conserve natural resources by recycling things.
   c. It is better to travel by car than by bicycle.
   d. There is very little we can do to save natural resources.

2. Now make a **Know/Want to Know/ Learned** Chart. Complete the first two columns now. Complete the third column at the end of the chapter.

Topic: Natural Resources		
Know	**Want to Know**	**Learned**
What do I already know about the topic?	What do I want to know about the topic?	What did I learn about the topic?

Build Background

Fossil Fuels

Fossil fuels are natural resources that are used to make energy. We get them from the earth's crust (outside layer of the earth). Some fossil fuels are oil, gas, and coal.

Fossil fuels took thousands of years to form. They come from plants and animals that lived many years ago. The amount of fossil fuels we have is limited. We cannot replace them.

Content Connection

Fossil fuels make energy when they are burned. They can be used to heat homes and to make gas for cars.

Oil well

Build Vocabulary

Put Words into Groups

The reading selection includes words that relate to nature. It also includes words that relate to things made by people.

1. Read the list of words and their definitions.
2. Write the words in the correct columns of a chart.

Nature	Made by People

innovation a new thing made with creativity

organic without chemicals

factory a place where things are manufactured

marsh a wet area of land with many plants and birds

grain a single seed of a plant

The Heinle Newbury House Dictionary

Activity Book p. 209

Student CD-ROM

Text Structure

Informational Text

You have learned that an **informational text** explains facts about a topic. In this selection, the author explains how people can take care of things in nature.

The chart lists some features of an informational text. Look for these features in "What Will Our Towns Look Like?"

As you read, identify the author's purpose. Is it just to inform, or does the author have another purpose as well?

Informational Text	
Problem	The author explains a problem.
Examples	Examples are details that show how something is true.
Solutions	The author explains ways to solve the problem.
Headings	Headings are titles used within a text to organize it. They help the reader locate information.

Student
CD-ROM

Reading Strategy

Summarize Text to Recall Ideas

When you **summarize** part of a reading, you say or write the most important information in the reading. Summarizing helps you remember what you read. How would you summarize this paragraph?

> Casey and her family care about protecting natural resources. They always turn the lights out when they leave a room. They recycle newspapers, bottles, cardboard boxes, and soda cans. They never leave the water running. They even pick up garbage in the neighborhood park.

You can summarize the paragraph in one sentence:

> Casey and her family do many things to protect natural resources.

As you read the selection, stop to summarize parts of it that you want to recall.

Reading Log

Student
CD-ROM

What Will Our Towns Look Like?

an article on the World Wide Web
by Martha Pickerill

Audio
CD 3, Tr. 9

Visions: What Will Our Towns Look Like? (if we take care of our planet) New inventions will help us build cleaner, greener places to live.

Heat and light burn up limited coal and oil.

Gas-powered cars pollute our air.

1   Fantastic **inventions** made daily life easier in the past century but often at the expense of our natural resources. Gas-powered cars got us everywhere in a flash, but they **polluted** our air. Electric heat and light made our homes warm and welcoming but also burned up limited coal and oil. Factories **revolutionized** the way we worked, but **industrial** waste trashed rivers, streams and oceans.

Summarize Text to Recall Ideas

How would you summarize what the author says about inventions?

Lifestyle changes on the **horizon** for the next 100 years may actually improve our planet's health. We can use cleaner energy and fewer chemicals while working, playing and bringing up families in the towns of tomorrow. This is not an impossible dream. Most of the **innovations** shown here already exist or are being developed. If we put our minds to it, our towns can **preserve** Earth's natural riches and still be lovely places to call home. Here's how things might be—if we make the **environment** a top concern. 2

---

inventions   new things created from an idea
polluted   made dirty
revolutionized   caused a new way of doing something
industrial   related to making and selling products
horizon   the place in one's view where Earth and sky meet; the near future

innovations   new things made with creativity
preserve   protect from harm or change
environment   the air, land, water, and surroundings that people, plants, and animals live in

3 **Work/Transportation**

More grownups will work in their homes and keep in touch with **co-workers** through computers. Others will make a short trip to a nearby office park. A few will ride swift electric trains to the nearest city. Cars and trucks will run on clean, hydrogen-powered fuel cells. Most entertainment and stores will be close by, so we'll often travel on old-fashioned, earth-friendly bicycles.

> **Summarize Text to Recall Ideas**
>
> Summarize how changes in transportation will affect the environment.

Food 4

We'll grow fruits, **grains** and vegetables close to home, either in our gardens or on nearby **organic farms.** Since the farms will use natural forms of pest control, such as **predatory insects,** there will be far fewer chemicals in the food supply.

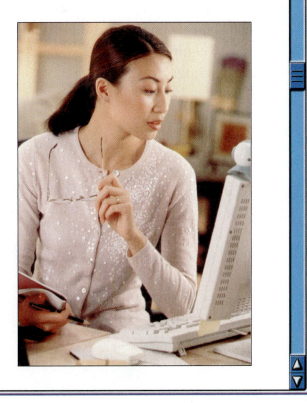

---

co-workers people with whom one works
grains single seeds of plants

organic farms farms that do not use chemicals to grow food
predatory insects insects that eat other insects

Shopping

5

Even if online stores are here to stay, there will be a **mall.** But it will be small, with sidewalks and bike racks instead of a giant parking lot. An airy place in which a flood of natural light will cut down on energy use, the mall will be one big **recycling** operation; when you're through using any product you buy there, the store will be required to take it back for recycling.

Energy

6

Our power will come from sources cleaner than coal, oil and gas. Some energy will flow from windmills, but much of it will be generated in our own homes. Rooftop **solar panels** will supply electricity to our **appliances** and to a basement fuel cell, which will produce **hydrogen.** When the sun is not shining, the cell will use the hydrogen to make electricity.

> **Summarize Text to Recall Ideas**
>
> Summarize this paragraph.

---

mall   a building or group of buildings with shops, theaters, restaurants, and so on

recycling   related to the collection, processing, and reuse of waste materials, such as used bottles and newspapers

solar panels   panels that take in sunlight to make energy

appliances   machines used for a certain purpose

hydrogen   the lightest element that is a gas

7 **Waste**

Plumbing lines will empty into enclosed **marshes,** where special plants, fish, snails and **bacteria** will naturally **purify** wastewater. Clean water will flow back into streams and **reservoirs.**

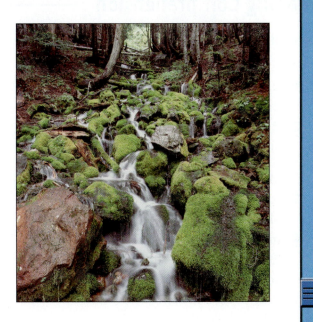

> **Summarize Text to Recall Ideas**
>
> How would you summarize the entire selection in one to three sentences?

---

marshes   wet areas of land with many plants
bacteria   tiny living things

purify   make clean
reservoirs   bodies of water saved for use

About the Author   Martha Pickerill (born 1964)

Martha Pickerill was born in Ames, Iowa. She knew she wanted to be a writer when she was in sixth grade. She studied journalism in college. After college she worked as a newspaper reporter in Ames. Her job helped her become a better writer. She says, "To be a reporter in Ames, Iowa, you REALLY have to be able to dig. It's not like there's a million fascinating stories just waiting to be told."

➤ What type of research do you think Martha Pickerill had to do to write this article?

Beyond the Reading

Reading Comprehension

Question-Answer Relationships (QAR)

"Right There" Questions

1. **Recall Facts** What prediction does the author make about cars?
2. **Recall Facts** What two resources are electric heat and light burning up?

"Think and Search" Questions

3. **Identify Theme** What is the theme of the selection?
4. **Identify Supporting Details** Does the author think that using cleaner energy and fewer chemicals is an "impossible dream"? Why not?

"Author and You" Questions

5. **Analyze Cause and Effect** What have gas-powered cars done to the environment?

6. **Make Inferences** Why does the author write that there will always be malls?
7. **Connect to Theme** What is the author's vision of the future?
8. **Use Text Features** How do the headings help you locate information?

"On Your Own" Questions

9. **Compare Your Experiences** What can you do to help the environment?
10. **Ask Questions** What questions did you think of after reading the selection?

Activity Book
p. 210

Student
CD-ROM

Build Reading Fluency

Adjust Your Reading Rate to Scan

Remember that when you scan for information you need to adjust your reading rate to read quickly. Work with a partner. Read aloud key words in the reading selection as you scan for the answers. Write your answers on a piece of paper.

1. Where will people work from in the future?
2. How will trucks and cars run?
3. Will we use more or fewer chemicals to grow food?
4. Will we still have malls?
5. What types of energy will we use?

Listen, Speak, Interact

Give a Persuasive Speech

Give a speech to persuade people to take care of the environment.

1. Use multiple sources to research environmental issues.
   a. Use the headings in the selection to locate and organize your information.
   b. Use the Table of Contents of this book to find other selections about the environment.
   c. Use other library resources such as newspapers, magazines, or the Internet.
2. Summarize and organize your information from these resources by outlining your ideas.
3. Look at your research and choose a topic you want to make a speech about.

Ways to Persuade	
Appeal to Logic	Give facts to support your opinion. Tell about real problems.
Appeal to Emotion	Say things so that listeners respond with their feelings.
Appeal to Ethics	Explain why taking care of the environment is the right thing to do.

4. Use different ways to persuade. Look at the chart for ideas.
5. Put some of your research findings in a chart. Use this visual with your audience.
6. Present your persuasive speech to a small group.
7. Listen to your classmates' speeches. What is each person's purpose?
8. Analyze your classmates' speeches. Who gave the most persuasive speech?

Elements of Literature

Identify Author's Purpose

The **author's purpose** is the reason why the author writes a text.

Purposes for Writing	
to inform	to give information about a topic
to persuade	to try to get the reader to agree with an opinion
to entertain	to give the reader enjoyment

1. When Martha Pickerill wrote "What Will Our Towns Look Like?" what was her purpose? Note that an author may have more than one purpose for writing.
2. What features of the text support your ideas of the author's purpose?
3. Did she succeed in her purpose?

Activity Book
p. 211

Student
CD-ROM

Word Study

Study the Latin Prefix *co-*

You have learned that a prefix is a group of letters added to the beginning of a word. A prefix may change the meaning of a word.

The word *co-workers* is used in the selection. This word has the prefix *co-*. This prefix is from Latin and means "together or with." *Co-workers* means "people who work together."

1. Copy and complete the chart in your Personal Dictionary.
2. Guess the meaning of each word that has the prefix *co-*. Use the meaning of each root word to help you.
3. Write a sentence for each word.

Root Word	Word	Meaning
exist (to be present)	coexist	
author (a person who writes a work)	coauthor	
star (an actor with an important part)	costar	

Personal Dictionary

The Heinle Newbury House Dictionary

Activity Book p. 212

Student CD-ROM

Grammar Focus

Use *Will* to Predict Future Events

When you predict, you tell what is going to happen in the future. The word *will* + a simple verb is often used to predict a future event. A simple verb is a verb form with no endings or other changes. *Climb* is a simple verb. *Climbed* is not a simple verb.

Tony <u>will win</u> the race.

It <u>will rain</u> tomorrow.

1. Look at paragraphs 3 through 7 of the Web article. Find three sentences that use *will*.
2. Write the sentences on a piece of paper. Underline the simple verb.
3. Write three sentences with *will* to predict what will happen to you in the future.

Activity Book pp. 213–214   Student Handbook   Student CD-ROM

From Reading to Writing

Create a Form, Interview, and Summarize

Work with a partner to find out what other people think about the ideas in "What Will Our Towns Look Like?" Interview people and create a chart to record your findings.

1. Reread the selection. Develop some questions you want to ask.
2. Go over your questions carefully to revise them. Are your questions clear? Are they too long?
3. Create, organize, and revise a form that you will use to conduct your interviews. Make a place for the following information.

a. The interviewer's name
b. The interviewee's name
c. The questions
d. The answers

4. Conduct your interviews. You and your partner should interview at least five people each.
5. Evaluate your interview forms. Make a chart to record what people think about the ideas. Organize and revise the chart as necessary.
6. Share your summaries in class.
7. Send a summary of your findings to your town government. Use a letter or an e-mail.

Activity Book
p. 215

Student
Handbook

Across Content Areas

Learn About Acid Rain

When fossil fuels burn, they create harmful chemicals. For example, an automobile creates gases when it burns gasoline. These gases can make the air dirty. We call this **pollution.** Pollution may come back to the ground as **precipitation**—rain, sleet, and snow.

Some scientists say that this precipitation, which is called acid rain, can hurt farm crops, forests, and water. They also think that acid rain can **damage** the **surfaces** of some buildings.

Match each word with its definition:

1. **pollution**
2. **precipitation**
3. **damage**
4. **surfaces**

a. hurt
b. outside layer of things
c. the dirtying of air, water, and earth
d. the release of moisture in the air

Activity Book
p. 216

Listening and Speaking Workshop

Write and Present a Persuasive Role Play

Topic

In "Mr. Scrooge Finds Christmas," you met Mr. Scrooge and the Solicitor. These men have different ideas about helping others. Present a role play. The Solicitor will try to persuade Mr. Scrooge to give money to the needy.

Step 1: Analyze the characters.

1. Work with a partner. One of you will be Mr. Scrooge. The other will be the Solicitor.
2. Answer the following questions. Use information from the selection and your own experiences.
   a. What does each man care about?
   b. Why do you think each man thinks this way?
   c. Who is a happier person?
3. Write your answers and other ideas in a Cluster Map.

Step 2: Identify reasons.

1. On a note card, list two reasons why the Solicitor thinks Mr. Scrooge should give money to the needy.
2. List two reasons why Mr. Scrooge does not want to give money to the needy. Write these reasons on a note card.

Step 3: Write dialogue.

1. Write what the characters will say. The dialogue should be a conversation. Use quotation marks around the words people say.
2. How will you start the dialogue? Will it begin when the Solicitor enters Mr. Scrooge's office?
3. Use the reasons you listed in Step 2.
4. How will your dialogue end? Will the Solicitor persuade Mr. Scrooge to give money to the needy?

Step 4: Organize your role play.

1. Add stage directions. How do the characters move?
2. Write the stage directions next to the dialogue on each note card.

Step 5: Practice.

1. Practice your role play in front of another pair of students.
2. Ask them to complete the Active Listening Checklist.
3. Use the checklist to revise your role play.
4. Listen carefully to your classmates' role play.

Active Listening Checklist

1. Did each character give reasons for his opinion?
2. Did they speak slowly and clearly?
3. Were they believable?

Step 6: Present your role play.

1. Use tone of voice to show how your character feels.
2. If possible, videotape your role play.
3. Review what you liked about your role play. Talk about how you could improve.

Student
Handbook

Viewing Workshop

View and Think

Compare and Contrast a Play and a Movie

1. Ask your librarian or an adult to help you find a movie version of "A Christmas Carol."
2. Compare and contrast "Mr. Scrooge Finds Christmas" with the movie. Do the characters in the movie look as you imagined them? Does the setting?
3. You read only part of "Mr. Scrooge Finds Christmas." The movie shows the rest of the story. Were you surprised by what happened in the movie? Explain.

4. What is the purpose of the movie? Does it entertain, inform, or persuade? Is the purpose of the play the same or different?
5. Does the filmmaker do a good job of presenting the story? Why or why not?
6. How does using film help present Dickens's message?

Further Viewing

Watch the *Visions* CNN Video for Unit 6. Do the Video Worksheet.

CNN Video

Writer's Workshop

Response to Literature: Collaborate to Write a Persuasive Letter

Writing Prompt

With a partner, think about the city or town where you live. Is there a problem to be solved? Does the city need to recycle more? Does it need more public transportation?

Write a five-paragraph letter to the mayor (or person in charge) of your city or town. Try to persuade the mayor to solve the problem.

Step 1: Brainstorm.

1. Think of solutions for the mayor to consider.
2. Choose two of these solutions.
3. Write each solution on a separate note card.

Step 2: Find facts to support your solutions.

1. Use note cards to summarize information you find.
   a. Use the name of the problem as the keyword for an Internet search.
   b. Talk to adults who know about the topic.
   c. Use and interpret maps, graphs, or tables you find to help support your position.
2. Organize your information, outlining the main idea and supporting details.

Step 3: Write a draft of your letter.

1. Use business letter format.
2. Organize your ideas in coherent paragraphs. Follow the model.
3. Remember to indent each paragraph.
4. Be sure to use capital letters for the names of people, places, and organizations.

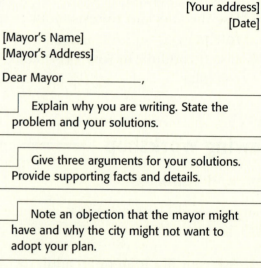

[Your address]
[Date]

[Mayor's Name]
[Mayor's Address]

Dear Mayor _____,

Explain why you are writing. State the problem and your solutions.

Give three arguments for your solutions. Provide supporting facts and details.

Note an objection that the mayor might have and why the city might not want to adopt your plan.

Give a response to the objection. Use your research to explain.

Restate the problem and your solutions in different words. Thank the mayor.

Yours truly,
_____ [Your signature]

Step 4: Revise, edit, and proofread.

1. Exchange letters with another pair of students. Ask them to answer the questions in the Writing Checklist.

2. As you revise, check your facts. Do you need more facts to support your argument? If so, use resource materials such as reading selections in this book or experts to revise your letter.

3. As you edit, make sure that your facts are accurate. Check resource materials such as Internet sites or primary sources.

4. Talk about your classmates' answers. Make any necessary changes.

5. Proofread your revised letter. Look for punctuation, spelling, and grammar mistakes.

6. Use the Editor's Checklist in your Student Handbook.

Step 5: Write your final draft.

If you are writing your letter by hand, use your best handwriting. Use manuscript or cursive. If you are using a computer, check for typing mistakes.

✔ Writing Checklist

1. Is my reason for writing this letter clear?

2. Do I say what problem needs to be resolved?

3. Do I say why a change is needed?

4. Do I give possible solutions?

Step 6: Mail or e-mail your letter.

Send your letter to the mayor. Ask your teacher for the address.

Step 7: Post copies of your letters.

Post copies of all the letters on a bulletin board. Review the letters and ask yourself these questions.

1. What are the strengths of these letters?

2. What are their weaknesses?

3. How can these letters help me set goals to become a better writer?

The Heinle Newbury House Dictionary

Student Handbook

Projects

These projects will help you develop your ideas about visions.

Project 1: Interpret Text Ideas in a Video

Think about the visions that are expressed in this unit. With a small group, choose one reading selection and create a video presentation about the visions in it.

1. Decide which selection to use.
2. List two or three ideas about visions from the text that you want to interpret (express in your own way).
3. Write the script—the words—for your video. It can be a drama (a play) or a documentary (informational). Remember: You are writing your interpretation of the ideas.
4. Write the stage directions and plan the visuals for your video.
5. Practice your script several times. Then record it on videotape.
6. Show your video to your class. Take it home to share with your family. If you can't make a video recording, perform your work for your class.

Project 2: Present "Vision for My Future"

Think about your visions for your life.

1. Think about where you would like to be and what you would like to be doing 10 years from now.
2. What steps do you need to take to make these goals happen?
3. Create a storyboard on poster board to describe the steps. Use words and illustrations to show what will happen.
4. Use capitalization and punctuation to enhance meaning.
5. Present your "Vision for My Future" to your class. Display your poster.

1 **Graduate from High School!**

2 **Graduate from College, Degree in Biology**

3 **Work at a Major Hospital?**

4 **Get Married, Have Children**

Further Reading

These books explore the theme of visions. Read one or more of them. Write your thoughts about what you read in your Reading Log. Then answer these questions:

1. Compare and contrast an artist's vision of the future with a scientist's.
2. What are your visions for the future?
3. As you review your readings, set goals for yourself as a writer. Who do you want to write like?

A Christmas Carol

by Charles Dickens, Bantam Classics, 1999. This is the famous story of Ebenezer Scrooge. Scrooge, a man who loves money more than people, has strange visitors on Christmas Eve.

The House on Mango Street

by Sandra Cisneros, Vintage Books, 1991. This is the story of a Hispanic girl growing up in Chicago, Illinois, in the 1980s.

The Pearl

by John Steinbeck, Penguin USA, 2000. This is a classic story about Kino, a poor Mexican pearl diver who finds a very valuable pearl. Kino thinks that finding the pearl will solve most of his problems. However, owning the pearl changes the life of Kino and his family in ways that he never imagined.

Future World: A Beginner's Guide to Life on Earth in the 21st Century

by Sarah Angliss and Colin Uttley, Copper Beech Books, 1998. This book predicts what the future will be like. It talks about possible sources of power and future jobs. It also discusses the effects of population growth on the planet.

Eye on the Wild: A Story About Ansel Adams

by Julie Dunlap, Carolrhoda Books, 1995. Ansel Adams saw beauty in the landscape of the American West. This biography tells about his life as a photographer.

Visions: Stories About Women Artists

by Leslie Sills, Albert Whitman, 1993. This book discusses the lives and works of famous women artists such as Mary Cassatt and Leonora Carrington.

How the Future Began: Communications

by Anthony Wilson, Kingfisher Publications, 1999. This book talks about communications with a focus on telecommunications and computers. It also considers communications in the future.

Companion Web site   Reading Log

Heinle Reading Library A Christmas Carol

Reading

Comprehension

■ Writing

Connections

Forms

Inquiry and Research

Purpose

Viewing and Representing

Credits

Text

Unit 1

Pp. 5–9, THE LOCH NESS MONSTER. From BEASTLY TALES: YETI, BIGFOOT AND THE LOCH NESS MONSTER by Malcolm Yorke. Published in the United States by DK Publishing, Inc. Copyright © 1998 Dorling Kindersley Limited, London. Reproduced by permission of Dorling Kindersley Ltd.

Pp. 17–21, MYSTERY OF THE CLIFF DWELLERS. From *National Geographic World,* February 1998. Copyright © 1998 by National Geographic Society. Reprinted by permission.

Pp. 29–33, YAWNING, by Haleh V. Samiei. From MUSE magazine, December 2000, Vol. 4, No. 10 by Haleh V. Samiei. Copyright © 2000 by Haleh V. Samiei. Reprinted by permission of the author.

Pp. 41–45, THE SNEAK THIEF. Adapted with permission of Sterling Publishing Co., Inc., NY, NY 10016 from GREAT BOOK OF WHODUNIT PUZZLES by Falcon Travis. Text © 1982 by Falcon Travis. Illustrations © 1982 by Hodder & Stoughton, Ltd.

Pp. 53–59, THE LEGEND OF SLEEPY HOLLOW. From *The Legend of Sleepy Hollow and Rip Van Winkle* by Washington Irving. Text copyright © 1995 by Playmore Publishers and Waldman Publishing Corporation. Reprinted by permission of Waldman Publishing.

Unit 2

Pp. 75–81, HOW I SURVIVED MY SUMMER VACATION. Reprinted by permission of Carus Publishing Company, excerpted from How I Survived My Summer Vacation; and Lived to Write the Story by Robin Friedman, 2000 by Robin Friedman. All rights reserved.

Pp. 89–97, THE VOYAGE OF THE *FROG.* From THE VOYAGE OF THE *FROG* by Gary Paulsen. Published by Orchard Books, an imprint of Scholastic Inc. Copyright © 1989 by Gary Paulsen. Reprinted by permission.

Pp. 105–111, TO RISK OR NOT TO RISK. From MUSE magazine, January 2002, Vol. 6, No. 1. Copyright © 2001 by David Ropeik. Reprinted by permission of the author.

Pp. 119–125, ISLAND OF THE BLUE DOLPHINS. From ISLAND OF THE BLUE DOLPHINS by Scott O'Dell. Copyright © 1960, renewed 1988 by Scott O'Dell. Reprinted by permission of Houghton Mifflin Company. All rights reserved. Audio rights: copyright © 1960, renewed 1988 by Scott O'Dell. From the book ISLAND OF THE BLUE DOLPHINS published by Houghton Mifflin Co. Reprinted by permission of McIntosh and Otis, Inc.

Pp. 133–139, THE NEXT GREAT DYING. From *Endangered Species* by Karin Vergoth and Christopher Lampton. Copyright © 1988, 1999 Karin Vergoth and Christopher Lampton. Reprinted by permission of Franklin Watts, a division of Grolier Publishing. All rights reserved.

Unit 3

Pp. 155–157, I HAVE NO ADDRESS. From *The Space Between Our Footsteps* selected by Naomi Shihab Nye. Copyright © 1998 by Hamza El Din. Reprinted by permission of the author.

Pp. 165–173, THE VOYAGE OF THE LUCKY DRAGON. From *The Voyage of the Lucky Dragon* by Jack Bennett. Copyright © 1981 by Jack Bennett. Used by permission of HarperCollins Publishers.

Pp. 181–185, THE TIME BIKE. Text copyright © 2000 by Jane Langton. Used by permission of HarperCollins Publishers. Audio rights: text copyright © 2000 by Jane Langton. Used by permission of the author.

Pp. 193–199, WHY WE CAN'T GET THERE FROM HERE, by Neil de Grasse Tyson. Reprinted from *Natural History* September 1998; copyright © *Natural History* Magazine, Inc., 1998.

Pp. 208–209, THE CALIFORNIA GOLD RUSH. From *The California Gold Rush* by Pam Zollman. Copyright © 2003 by Steck-Vaughn Company. Reprinted by permission.

Pp. 210–213, DAME SHIRLEY AND THE GOLD RUSH. From *Dame Shirley and the Gold Rush* by Jim Rawls. Copyright © 1993 Dialogue Systems. Published by Metropolitan Teaching and Learning Company, Inc. Reprinted by permission of Metropolitan Teaching and Learning Company, Inc.

Unit 4

Pp. 229–233, WATER DANCE. Entire text and five illustrations from WATER DANCE, copyright © 1997 by Thomas Locker. Back matter text copyright © 1997 by Candace Christiansen, reprinted and recorded by permission of Harcourt, Inc. This material may not be reproduced in any form or by any means without the prior written permission of the publisher.

Pp. 241–245, PERSEPHONE AND THE SEASONS, by Heather Amery. Reproduced from *Greek Myths for Young Children* by permission of Usborne Publishing Ltd, 83-85 Saffron Hill, London EC1N 8RT, England. Copyright ©1999 Usborne Publishing Ltd.

Pp. 253–259, THE CIRCUIT. From *The Circuit: Stories from the Life of a Migrant Child* by Francisco Jiménez. Copyright © 1997 by Francisco Jiménez. Reprinted by permission of University of New Mexico Press.

Pp. 267–271, THE ELEMENTS OF LIFE. From *Earth: The Incredible Recycling Machine* by Paul Bennett. Copyright © 1993 by Hodder and Stoughton Limited. Reproduced by permission of Hodder and Stoughton Limited.

Unit 5

Pp. 287–295, ROSA PARKS. Excerpts from LET IT SHINE: STORIES OF BLACK WOMEN FREEDOM FIGHTERS, copyright © 2000 by Andrea Davis Pinkney, reprinted by permission of Harcourt, Inc. Illustrations from "Rosa Parks" in LET IT SHINE: STORIES OF BLACK WOMEN FREEDOM FIGHTERS by Andrea Davis Pinkney, illustrations copyright © 2000 by Stephen Alcorn, reproduced by permission of Harcourt, Inc. Audio rights: excerpt adapted from LET IT SHINE: STORIES OF BLACK WOMEN FREEDOM FIGHTERS text copyright © 2000 by Andrea Davis Pinkney. Published by Harcourt, Inc. All rights reserved. Used with permission.

Pp. 303–311, THE GETTYSBURG ADDRESS. From *The Gettysburg Address* by Kenneth Richards. Copyright 1992, 1969 by Childrens Press®, Inc. Reprinted by permission. All rights reserved.

Pp. 319–325, SO FAR FROM THE BAMBOO GROVE. Copyright © 1986 by Yoko Kwashima Watkins. Used by permission of HarperCollins Publishers.

Pp. 334, ALONE. From REACH FOR THE MOON by Samantha Abeel. Text copyright © 1994 by Samantha Abeel. Reprinted by permission of Scholastic Inc.

Pp. 335–337, SAMANTHA'S STORY. From REACH FOR THE MOON by Samantha Abeel. Text copyright © 1994 by Samantha Abeel. Reprinted by permission of Scholastic Inc.

Unit 6

Pp. 353–359, A CHRISTMAS CAROL, by Charles Dickens. From *Christmas Play Favorites for Young People* edited by Sylvia E. Kamerman. Copyright © 1982 by Sylvia E. Kamerman. Reprinted by permission of Kalmbach Publishing Co.

Pp. 367–371, THE HOUSE ON MANGO STREET. From THE HOUSE ON MANGO STREET. Copyright © 1984 by Sandra Cisneros. Published by Vintage Books, a division of Random House, Inc., and in hardcover by Alfred A. Knopf in 1994. Reprinted by permission of Susan Bergholz Literary Services, New York. All rights reserved.

Pp. 379–387, THE PEARL. From THE PEARL by John Steinbeck, copyright 1945 by John Steinbeck, © renewed 1973 by Elaine Steinbeck, Thom

Steinbeck and John Steinbeck IV. Used by permission of Viking Penguin, a division of Penguin Putnam Inc.

Pp. 395–399, WHAT WILL OUR TOWNS LOOK LIKE?, by Martha Pickerill. Used with permission from *TIME for Kids* magazine, © 2002.

Illustrators

Barry Ablett: pp. 155–157 (© Barry Ablett/Irmeli Holmberg); **Matthew Archambault:** pp. 54–58 (© Matthew Archambault/Scott Hull Associates); **Shelly Bartek:** pp. 254–259 (© Shelly Bartek/Munro Campagna); **Ralph Canaday:** pp. 75–80 (© Ralph Canaday/Wilkinson Studios, LLC); **Viviana Diaz:** pp. 380–386 (© Viviana Diaz/Irmeli Holmberg); **James Edwards:** pp. 90–91, 93–96 (© James Edwards/The Beranbaum Group); **Bill Ersland:** pp. 181–186 (© Bill Ersland/Irmeli Holmberg); **Tom Foty:** pp. 41–45 (© Tom Foty/Munro Campagna); **Gershom Griffith:** pp. 18, 20 (© Gershom Griffith/Craven Design Studios, Inc.); **Clint Hansen:** pp. 354–358 (© Clint Hansen/Scott Hull Associates); **Greg Harris:** p. 134 (© Greg Harris/Cornell and McCarthy, LLC); **Kveta Jelinek:** p. 395 (© Kveta Jelinek/Three In a Box, Inc.); **Rosanne Kaloustian:** pp. 120–124 (© Rosanne Kaloustian/Irmeli Holmberg); **Cheryl Kirk Noll:** pp. 319–325 (© Cheryl Kirk Noll/Christina A. Tugeau); **Mapping Specialists, Ltd.:** pp. 7, 15, 25, 51, 68, 73, 92, 117, 163, 177, 191, 205, 301, 317, 365; **Julie Perterson:** pp. 367–371 (© Julie Peterson/Square Moon); **Andy Powell:** pp. 333, 335–337 (© Andy Powell/Scott Hull Associates); **Precision Graphics:** pp. 3, 30, 32, 193, 198, 227, 239, 270, 396; **Rex Schneider:** p. 153 (© Rex Schneider/Blue Mouse Studios); **Richard Stergulz:** p. 308 (© Richard Stergulz/Wilkinson Studios, LLC); **Carol Stutz:** pp. 275, 316, 408 (© Carol Stutz); **Carlotta Tormey:** pp. 210–212 (© Carlotta Tormey/Wilkinson Studios, LLC); **Raoul Vitale:** pp. 242–244 (© Raoul Vitale/Scott Hull Associates); **Suling Wang:** pp. 166–172 (© Suling Wang/Kolea Baker)

Author Photos

p. 33 (Haleh V. Samiei); p. 45 (Falcon Travis); p. 59 (Washington Irving, © Bettmann/CORBIS); p. 81 (Robin Friedman); p. 97 (Gary Paulsen); p. 111 (David Ropeik); p. 125 (Scott O'Dell, reprinted by permission of Houghton Mifflin Children's Books); p. 139 (Karin Vergoth); p. 157 (Hamza El Din, © Kim Harwood); p. 187 (Jane Langton, © Janet Boynton); p. 199 (Neil de Grasse Tyson, © Jared Pava); p. 209 (Pam Zollman, © Sue Erb); p. 213 (Jim Rawls); p. 233 (Thomas Locker); p. 259 (Francisco Jiménez); p. 295 (Andrea Davis Pinkney); p. 337 (Samantha Abeel); p. 359 (Charles Dickens, © Bettmann/CORBIS); p. 371 (Sandra Cisneros, © 2002, all rights reserved Armando Rascón); p. 387 (John Steinbeck, © Hulton Archive/Getty Images); p. 399 (Martha Pickerill)

Photos

American Museum of Natural History: p. 12 (© Negative no. 35604, courtesy of the Library, American Museum of Natural History)

Art Resource: (All © Art Resource, NY) p. 53 (*The Headless Horseman Pursuing Ichabod Crane, 1858* by John Quidor © Smithsonian American Art Museum, Washington, D.C./Art Resource, NY); p. 89 (*Sea-piece by Moonlight,* oil on canvas by Erich Lessing © Erich Lessing/Art Resource, NY); p. 241 (*Proserpine, 1874* by Dante Gabriel Rossetti, oil on canvas © Tate Gallery, London/Art Resource, NY); p. 251 (© Morton Beebe/CORBIS); p. 253 (© Joseph Sohm; ChromoSohm Inc./CORBIS); pp. 348–349 (*Le Faux Miroir (The False Mirror), 1935,* by Rene Magritte © Phototheque R. Magritte–ADAGP/Art Resource, NY)

CORBIS: (All © Corbis) pp. xii–1 (© Stapleton Collection/CORBIS); pp. 5–6 (© Vo Trung Dung/CORBIS); p. 21 (© Jan Butchofsky-Houser/CORBIS); p. 26 (© Chuck Savage/CORBIS); p. 29 (© Royalty-Free/CORBIS); pp. 70–71 (© Sanford/Agliolo/CORBIS); p. 87 (© Randy Lincks/CORBIS); p. 105 (© Duomo/CORBIS); p. 106 (© Joe McDonald/CORBIS); p. 107

(© Japack Company/CORBIS); p. 119 (© Nik Wheeler/CORBIS); p. 131 (© Tom Brakefield/CORBIS); p. 135 (© Wolfgang Kaehler/CORBIS); p. 136 (© Michael DeYoung/CORBIS); p. 137 (© Ed Kashi/CORBIS); p. 138 (© Chris Hellier/CORBIS); p. 138 (© Academy of Natural Sciences of Philadelphia/CORBIS); p. 138 (© Bettmann/CORBIS); pp. 150–151 (© Franklin McMahon/CORBIS); p. 165 (© Nik Wheeler/CORBIS); p. 179 (© Carl & Ann Purcell/CORBIS); p. 195 (© Roger Ressmeyer/CORBIS); p. 196 (© AFP/CORBIS); p. 207 (© Bettmann/CORBIS); p. 208 (© CORBIS); p. 209 (© Steve Starr/CORBIS); pp. 224–225 (© Ralph A. Clevenger/CORBIS); p. 265 (© Chris Collins/CORBIS); p. 267 (© Richard Hamilton Smith/CORBIS); p. 268 (© David Lees/CORBIS); p. 268 (© CORBIS); p. 269 (© Peter Johnson/CORBIS); pp. 282–283 (© Kevin Fleming/CORBIS); p. 287 (© Raymond Gehman/CORBIS); p. 303 (© Bettmann/CORBIS); p. 304 (© CORBIS); p. 305 (© Todd Gipstein/CORBIS); p. 306 (© Medford Historical Society Collection/CORBIS); p. 307 (© Bettmann/CORBIS); p. 309 (© CORBIS); p. 311 (© Lester Lefkowitz/CORBIS); p. 353 (© Robbie Jack/CORBIS); p. 377 (© Stephen Frink/CORBIS); p. 397 (© Jon Feingersh/CORBIS); p. 398 (© Chinch Gryniewicz; Ecoscene/CORBIS); p. 399 (© Michael T. Sedam/CORBIS)

Fortean Picture Library: p. 9 (© Fortean Picture Library)

Getty Images: (All © Getty Images) p. 17 (© C. McIntyre/PhotoLink/Getty Images); p. 19 (© Getty Images); p. 108 (© Joe McBride/Getty Images); p. 109 (© Paul Chesley/National Geographic/Getty Images); p. 133 (© Stephen Wilkes/Getty Images); p. 268 (© Marco Prozzo/Getty Images); p. 334 (© Darrell Gulin/Getty Images); p. 393 (© Getty Images)

Index Stock Imagery: (All © Index Stock Imagery) p. 31 (© Omni Photo Communications, Inc./Index Stock Imagery); p. 310 (© Jeff Greenberg/Index Stock Imagery); p. 379 (© Eric Kamp/Index Stock Imagery)

Photo Edit: (All © Photo Edit) p. 110 (© Michael Newman/Photo Edit)

Robert Rines/Academy of Applied Science: p. 11 (© Robert Rines/Academy of Applied Science)

Texas Parks & Wildlife: p. 133 (Photo courtesy of Texas Parks & Wildlife © 2002, Phil A. Dotson)

PE1128 .M32548 2004
McCloskey, Mary Lou.
Visions : language,
literature, content

SIMMONS COLLEGE LIBRARY

DATE DUE

Demco, Inc. 38-293